THE
PATIENT
DOCTOR

THE
PATIENT
DOCTOR

Dr Ben Bravery

Published in Australia and New Zealand in 2022
by Hachette Australia
(an imprint of Hachette Australia Pty Limited)
Gadigal Country, Level 17, 207 Kent Street, Sydney, NSW 2000
www.hachette.com.au

Hachette Australia acknowledges and pays our respects to the past, present and future Traditional Owners and Custodians of Country throughout Australia and recognises the continuation of cultural, spiritual and educational practices of Aboriginal and Torres Strait Islander peoples. Our head office is located on the lands of the Gadigal people of the Eora Nation.

 A catalogue record for this book is available from the National Library of Australia

ISBN: 978 0 7336 4744 4 (paperback)

Cover design by Christabella Designs
Cover photographs courtesy of Alamy
Author photographs courtesy of J Bradley
Typeset in 12.1/18 pt Minion Pro by Bookhouse, Sydney
Printed and bound in Australia by McPherson's Printing Group

 The paper this book is printed on is certified against the Forest Stewardship Council® Standards. McPherson's Printing Group holds FSC® chain of custody certification SA-COC-005379. FSC® promotes environmentally responsible, socially beneficial and economically viable management of the world's forests.

FOR THOSE WHO SAVED, SUPPORTED AND TAUGHT ME -
YOU KNOW WHO YOU ARE.

AND FOR EVREN,
I'M SORRY IF YOUR COLON ENDS UP DODGY LIKE MINE.

CONTENTS

AUTHOR'S NOTE

The names of people in my personal life have not been changed; the names of my treatment team, patients and colleagues have been. Patients discussed in detail have been disguised where possible or combined with the details of other patients to protect their confidentiality and privacy. The essence of a patient's experience was not altered as a result of this process. Medical place names have been omitted.

Small portions of this work previously appeared, in different form, as articles for Radio National, ABC Science, ABC Life, BMJ Blogs, *Medical Observer* and *The Medical Journal of Australia*.

INTRODUCTION

This is not your typical cancer memoir. There are plenty of those already, written by people with worse cancers who overcame greater tragedies than me. Don't get me wrong, there is a lot about cancer in this book, but what I really want to share with you is what happened *after* I got cancer.

When I got cancer, I was a zoologist living in China, working for scientists. Now, I live in Australia and practise medicine as a doctor. The leap from zoologist to cancer patient was not my choice, but the leap from cancer patient to doctor was. That decision – what it's like on both sides of the hospital curtain, and how medicine can be made better for patients *and* doctors – is the point of this book.

I was twenty-eight years old when I noticed blood in the toilet bowl. Blood leaking from anywhere is scary, but it takes on special horror when it's from your backside and mixed with everything else usually found in a toilet bowl. I didn't tell anyone.

This early stage of my disease was private, a secret between me and my illness. It took time to process the repeated internet searches, panic and denial. I learnt that for people in their twenties, blood in the toilet bowl is nearly always the result of haemorrhoids. *That's what I must have*, I thought, *haemorrhoids*.

I clung on to this idea, even as I developed crippling abdominal pain and frequent (and confusing) diarrhoea and constipation. Only when I lost weight, grew pale and ended up drenched in sweat each night did I accept that maybe something worse was happening.

At the time I was living in Beijing and had just met the love of my life. I was also trying to get a science communication business off the ground. This was after the Olympic Games, when China was throwing money at everything, including science. Being a zoologist, the clients I attracted were other zoologists; and being in China, I mainly attracted giant panda researchers. I was trying to carve out a role in China's scientific revolution, but a big bleeding tumour in my colon had other plans.

On a quick trip to Australia, I squeezed in a colonoscopy. A year of cancer treatment and upheaval followed. Treatment was long, dark and marred by complications. I'll get to that later – suffice to say, bowel cancer is shit.

On the other side, spat back into somewhat normal life, I tried returning to work, though not to my business – I may have survived cancer, it hadn't. I found a job communicating medical research in Sydney, but something didn't feel right. It wasn't just my numb hands and feet from chemotherapy, or the bag stuck to my abdomen collecting faeces – something deeper had shifted inside me.

While slogging away at pretending I was back to normal, a memory resurfaced. The memory was from chemotherapy, when steroid-induced insomnia had me wide awake and baking at 2 am. As a banana bread rose in the oven, I typed 'How to become a doctor' into Google and attempted an example medical school entrance exam. The idea of becoming a doctor had trickled into my mind a few days earlier, as I lay in hospital watching chemotherapy trickle into my arm. The practice exam was as far as I got. I don't remember why – much of that time is fuzzy, something we cancer people call chemo brain.

Three years later, I again asked the internet how to become a doctor. It just happened to be the same day that applications to sit the medical school entrance exam closed. I put my name down for the exam.

I wanted to become a doctor, to help people like I had been helped, and make the health system better along the way. I don't want to sound selfish; I am deeply grateful for all my treatment and care (I even had a t-shirt printed for my surgeon one Christmas that read 'Superstar Surgeon'). But during my cancer treatment and hospital stays I noticed lots of stuff that needs fixing in healthcare.

Rushed ward rounds where strangers loomed over me, discussing my body as though I wasn't there; being scolded by nurses for wanting to look at my medical record; being threatened with a tube in my stomach because I gagged every time I took a mouthful of food; having no way to digitally communicate with any of the doctors looking after me; waiting for hours at clinic appointments; feeling too intimidated to ask questions; no wi-fi; hospital food; having to pay to watch free television . . . the list goes on. Some of these may seem trivial – I assure you, when you're sick, desperate and sometimes alone in hospital, they are not.

I figured the best way to make things better for patients was to become a doctor, perhaps even an oncologist. And so I went to medical school, ready to learn about cancer and change the world. I was quickly hit over the head with hundreds of years of medical knowledge and tradition.

At thirty-two, I was older than most other students. I had also almost died, so I kind of 'got it' when it came to illness and patients. While studying, I was still a patient with a separate busy schedule of check-ups, scans and scopes. During the long hours of study and isolation I feared my cancer would return and end it all.

At times it just didn't feel worth it: modern medicine seemed to be about chronic disease, dodging egos and ducking from bullies. If not for the patients, I'd have called it a day. I was still one of them, after all, and I knew they needed us. Patients don't just need doctors good at diagnosis, they need empathic and compassionate doctors willing to talk, listen and advocate for them.

It is approaching a decade since my cancer diagnosis and treatment. Although I'm now a doctor, I'm still working out what it means to have started this journey as a patient. I'm frequently told that I have crossed the line from patient to doctor, but I don't believe there should be a line. Patients and doctors are the same: they're both people. Keeping this in mind is critical to the relationship between the unwell and well. It's a relationship that plays out inside my head every day.

This is my personal perspective, as a patient and a doctor, on how to make medicine better for both. There are countless amazing doctors – junior and senior – practising with heart. I was cared for by many when I was sick, and met many more as a medical student and a doctor. But that doesn't change the fact that the patient–doctor relationship is less than ideal most of the time.

This is my experience of health – and, to be blunt, I'm a tall white man. We know things are worse for women, First Nations people and others of colour. I hope to use my privilege to highlight these issues.

Becoming a doctor is a long process with an entrenched and strict hierarchy. Some may question whether a junior doctor can meaningfully change how we do things – especially when I'm calling for big changes to how doctors are selected, educated and trained, and how patients are treated, viewed and communicated with in healthcare. But it's precisely because I'm still learning to be a doctor that I question how the healthcare system currently functions.

As I mentioned, I went into medicine older than most, after a career spent thinking about ecosystems and *because* of serious illness – this gives me a unique view. I approach medicine as an outsider, though I now possess insider knowledge.

Recently, the pandemic has exacerbated existing issues, strained already insufficient hospital budgets, taken hospital systems beyond their breaking points and stressed already strug-gling doctors and nurses. Globally, millions of people have died and millions more will suffer from long-term health conditions. Will we learn the lessons from this once-in-a-century event? I worry not – the status quo often prevails.

The pandemic brought out the best in healthcare workers. They have been brave, selfless and cooperative under awful conditions. This is the ultimate expression of humanity, but it has come at a cost. Surveys showed that healthcare workers were stressed and dissatisfied *before* the pandemic, but when Covid-19 hit they buckled down and saved us.

How the pandemic has affected healthcare systems and withered already strained patient–doctor relationships could be a book in itself. The events in this book mostly predate Covid-19, but the deeper issues those events highlight go beyond any pandemic. The health system knows that doctors and nurses lean in – in fact, the system is built to exploit that. The need to restore humanity at the centre of healthcare is as important as ever.

Covid-19 has been a shock to the healthcare system; cancer was a shock to me. My scans tell me there are no tumours now, but cancer changed me forever. I feel neither well nor unwell, not fully a doctor nor fully a patient. This book is about my place in these two worlds and the things I've learnt. My hope is to empower both patients *and* doctors, to better understand each other, and to demand a better kind of medicine.

PART 1

BECOMING A CANCER PATIENT

1

BLOOD AND SNOW

Two hours outside of Beijing there is a small mostly artificial snowfield. Beijing in winter is extremely cold, but also extremely dry, so if you want predictable snow in China you need to venture further north to the border with Russia and Mongolia, or south-west to the mountains of Sichuan and Tibet. The Chinese are extraordinary when it comes to modifying their environment and weather. Think of the massive Three Gorges Dam in central China that actually creates its own weather systems, or the Great Green Wall which aims to create a belt of new forest five thousand kilometres long to halt the encroaching Gobi Desert in northern China. Making a bit of snow for Beijing's residents is easy.

I decided to test out this winter playground with Ian, the man I had come to know later in life and treated as though he was my father. We had both only skied until that point, but I convinced him to try snowboarding after a couple of days on the hills. Under endless blue skies and over icy man-made snow we rented snowboards and boots and enrolled in a class with an English-speaking instructor.

Snowboarding friends warned me that I would spend a lot of time falling, sitting and resting on my bum. They were right. Ian watched on, balanced perfectly on his snowboard. He was more cautious than me, and fell less.

After our first day of snowboarding, we returned to the cabin exhausted. I felt the need to go to the bathroom, a feeling that had become more frequent, painful and fearful the last few months. I sat down on the toilet and, while it was a little explosive (not uncommon in China), it didn't feel unusual. What I saw in the bowl was anything but usual.

The white ceramic was painted with bright red blood. There were also bits of blood clot mixed in. For several months, I had been noticing small amounts of blood in the toilet bowl, but nothing like this. To be frank, and a little gross (but this *is* a book about a guy who got bowel cancer), it looked like the floor of a slaughterhouse.

After living in China for years, I had become comfortable with diarrhoea – I often ate at suspicious restaurants and paid the price a few hours later – but in recent weeks, bog standard (that's the last poo pun, promise) runny poo and nausea had given way to serious episodes of cramping and bleeding. The result: I'd become much less comfortable with diarrhoea.

I was finding it harder to explain away what was going on with my bowels. I started having clean drinking water delivered to my apartment; I became choosier about restaurants; I ate more fibre. But, no matter what I changed, the attack on my gut continued.

Up until this point, I had only told my partner about these occasional bloody bowel movements, and even then I downplayed how sick I felt. The symptoms were gross, embarrassing and worrying, and I'd hoped they'd just disappear. I wanted to believe nothing was gravely wrong. But there was no ignoring this amount of blood.

It was time to confide in Ian. I came out of the toilet and found him glued to the TV, watching a local period drama set during World War II. He couldn't understand what they were saying, but he was able to follow the action. During his visits to China to see me, he had grown fond of these war dramas. They played continuously and always carried the same message: Japan is bad. Ian was sipping a warm local beer (it was often hard to find cold beer in China).

'They really have gone to town styling the Japanese general, even his moustache looks like a war crime,' he said.

On any other day I would have popped the top off a beer and grabbed a seat next to him while we tried to work out the show's plot. Instead, I told him about the toilet bowl.

'I've been bleeding from my bum,' I said. 'It's been happening off and on for a few months now.'

'Okay,' he said. Conversations with Ian involve long, pregnant pauses. He takes great care when choosing his words. This frustrates a lot of people, but I find the pace comforting.

'There's more,' I said. 'I get really sweaty at night, sometimes I need to change the sheets. And I've been having bad stomach pains.'

I mentioned being tired all the time, and how one day I'd be constipated and the next day have diarrhoea. He held his warm beer and listened. After a few seconds, he took a sharp breath.

'It's probably just haemorrhoids, but I'm worried about the sound of that. I think you need to see a doctor,' he said.

It was a relief to finally tell someone other than my partner.

The next day we returned to the slopes. A fresh layer of fake snow had been made and our instructor wanted us to be among the first on the hills. My excitement and bravado from the previous day had dissipated. Now, after each fall, I felt anxious. Did I really just have haemorrhoids? I kept seeing all that blood in the toilet bowl. Was each fall causing more bleeding? Was all of this making whatever was going on inside me worse? I dreaded the next time I had to go to the toilet.

We returned to Beijing a few days later, bruised and more anxious than you'd hope to be after a holiday. It was close to the time I had to travel back to Australia on a visa run to renew my Chinese paperwork. I rang Mum to let her know I was coming to Melbourne, and to share my growing list of symptoms.

Now, a word about my mother. Mum has no health training, but she has spent hundreds of hours watching Oprah and Dr Oz, and obsessively buys potions, herbs and supplements online. She is also a hypochondriac. New symptoms are always popping up, alongside new pills that, this time, are the ones she claims she should have been taking all along. Mum loves having X-rays and will rush off for any type of scan recommended to her, whether it's a GP or a naturopath making the suggestion. All of this has provided my family with endless entertainment and gags.

But soon Mum's enthusiasm and confidence navigating the health system would save my life.

'I'm booking you in for a colonoscopy,' she said, mere seconds into my description of symptoms.

This felt like overkill. 'Whoa, hang on. I've just had bleeding every now and then and a bit of pain. The tiredness is probably from working so hard,' I said. 'It's just haemorrhoids.'

'Benjamin, you need a colonoscopy and you'll be having one next week,' she said, with all the confidence and authority of her mentor, Oprah MD.

I still had my doubts. Organising a referral for a colonoscopy usually requires you to see your GP first – it's not something that can typically be arranged by a third party. But in the coming days, Mum popped down to the GP she'd been seeing for years (whom I had never met), told him my symptoms and how I was only going to be in Melbourne for a week while my visa was being processed. She secured a referral for me, and booked an appointment with a gastroenterologist. I was going to have cameras inserted down my throat (a gastroscopy to inspect my stomach) and up my bum (a colonoscopy to inspect my large bowel).

•

I landed in Melbourne a few days into the new year. I was looking forward to a week of summer and on the plane changed out of my thick puffer jacket and thermals into shorts and thongs. Mum and her partner, Graeme, picked me up from the airport. Mum had met Graeme a year ago and now lived with him and two of his children in his large home, where I would stay.

I spent the first few days in Melbourne chasing documents I needed for my visa back to China and queuing outside the consular office for hours at a time, fanning myself with a manila folder, wishing I carried a proper fan with me like everyone else in the queue. In between all this, I worked on projects in Beijing and regularly spoke with Tim, my good friend and business partner back there, to keep our fledgling science communication business on track.

Ian flew down from Queensland mid-week. He was worried about the upcoming colonoscopy and wanted to be nearby in case the news was bad. There was room enough in Graeme's big house for him to stay, too.

Mum and Ian had met lots of times over the years. Mum could be territorial, but Ian was always extremely careful not to let his relationship with me threaten hers. They got on fine, but had an awkward air about them – the kind that develops when two very different people are forced to hang out. I was so busy with the visa, work back in Beijing and keeping one eye on Mum, Graeme and Ian that I didn't think about the gastroscopy and colonoscopy until it was time to get ready for them.

Prepping for these procedures involves drinking laxatives and fasting for twenty-four hours beforehand. It's miserable, but in recent months I'd become used to suddenly losing my appetite and then having diarrhoea.

As Mum was an expert in preparing for colonoscopies, having had too many for no real reason in private clinics, she guided me through what to expect and I followed her instructions carefully. Knowing that the laxatives – and not something more sinister – were making my gut expel everything was only mildly comforting. I had experienced too much toilet trauma not to worry. And, as I had done for the last few months, I kept my worst fears to myself. The full extent of my problems were a secret shared between me and the toilet bowl, but not for long.

I woke early the next morning feeling nervous, hungry and tired. Mum was a stoic, reassuring presence; Ian remained quiet. At 9 am we arrived at the clinic, punctual and pensive. The gastroenterologist spoke with Mum, Ian and me before I went in for the colonoscopy.

'Deep down I'm worried I have cancer,' I said. Mum looked straight at the doctor; Ian looked at the ground.

'I'm not expecting to find cancer,' the gastroenterologist replied. 'You're so young and there's no bowel cancer in the family.'

An hour later, my world was torn apart.

•

I don't remember much detail from the day I had the colonoscopy, which I put down to sedatives and emotional shock, plus the chemotherapy I've since endured.

I woke from the anaesthetic and was led to the gastro-enterologist's office. Mum was already inside. Ian had remained in the waiting room, reading a novel, not wanting to tread on Mum's toes. She looked confident, having attended several post-colonoscopy debriefs of her own, always with good news. Yet the fact Mum was there made me uneasy. *I'm twenty-eight*, I thought, *I don't need Mum in the room, unless . . . oh, shit.*

Now, as a doctor myself, I realise that the gastroenterologist had made sure a support person was present. This is part of the breaking-bad-news protocol that doctors learn, and that I have since learnt.

I'm glad Mum was there with me.

The doctor said that there was a mass in a part of the large bowel called the sigmoid colon. *Fuck*, I thought. Then, *What the hell is a sigmoid colon?*

He had found it impossible to get the camera past the mass because it was big and almost blocked the bowel. My mind jumped to all those times I'd keeled over in pain, or spent a half-hour on the toilet trying to push out a poo. Using a much smaller camera designed for the mini colons of kids he had managed to squeeze through and examine the rest of the large bowel – which all looked okay. *Phew*, I thought, *some good news.*

He asked about my symptoms again and told me that the bleeding was from this mass, which he described as ulcerated. I was shown pictures of it. It looked ugly. It was lumpy with dark patches, like rotting meat. Parts of it were bloody, appearing red and wet like a fresh wound.

Samples of the mass had to be sent off for analysis to confirm what it was. He stopped there, inhaling slowly.

'But this looks like a cancer,' he said.

He'd found the exact thing he had told me not to worry about, because it was so rare in someone my age. But having cancer, he went on, explained my night sweats and weight loss. It was all starting to make scary sense.

I realised Mum was squeezing my hand. I hadn't been aware of this, or anything else, since the gastroenterologist first mentioned the tumour. I wasn't sad, my heart wasn't racing, my head wasn't spinning – I was numb. The doctor asked if I had any questions. I had a hundred questions and no questions, so nothing came out. I thought of Ian, a few metres away in the waiting room, oblivious to the bad news. I looked at Mum, expecting to see a weeping mess, but she was saving that for later.

'What happens next?' she asked the doctor.

A lot, it turned out.

•

An urgency descended over the consultation, perforating my numbness. The doctor had so far been measured and slow as he presented what he'd found inside me. Now it was go time.

A kind of race was underway to check for other tumours. The fastest way to survey my body for more cancer was to have a CT scan – where I would be X-rayed from lots of angles and a computer would organise the images, allowing a radiologist to literally scroll top to toe through my body. I needed one of these, and quickly.

The gastroenterologist started calling hospitals, looking for one that could fit me in that same day. I didn't understand why everything needed to happen so quickly. After all, I'd had gut problems for the last six months. Why couldn't this wait until next week? It was Friday afternoon, clearly my cancer wasn't getting the weekend off.

Tumours that start in the large bowel love spreading to the liver and lungs. This was why the race was on to work out whether I had one tumour or multiple tumours. Finding other tumours in the liver or lungs would mean that I had stage four cancer, the most severe, straight up.

While most people know that stage one is better than stage four, staging cancer is complicated. Even more confusingly, there are two different systems for staging bowel cancer and yet another system for grading the tumours. Basically, the initial staging is based on the colonoscopy, tumour biopsy and scans. From this, doctors work out how much of the bowel the tumour has eaten into, whether any lymph nodes have cancer in them, and if cancer has spread to other parts of the body. Each of these aspects of the cancer are described in as much detail as possible to arrive at an overall stage. As simply as possible, stage one and two means the cancer is in the bowel only, stage three means that the tumour has grown through the bowel and that lymph nodes are involved, and stage four means the cancer has spread to another organ.

Bowel cancer remains rare in young adults, despite recent increases in people under the age of fifty. While it is less common in my age group, we tend to get diagnosed a little later and with more advanced disease than older people. Given how big and ugly my tumour was, the doctor was worried that it had already spread. I relayed all of this to Ian in the waiting room while the doctor tried to find me a CT machine. I talked, Ian nodded – he gets even quieter when he's stressed, but always manages to say the right thing, just at the right time.

'Well, this is unexpected, my boy,' he said. 'Thank you for choosing to have the colonoscopy now and not later, at least something good will come from all that time we spent falling off our snowboards.'

Thirty minutes and numerous calls later, I was booked into a scan across town. But before we could go, I needed to make an important call. My girlfriend of five months, Sana, was back in

Beijing, likely on her way to work. With nowhere to talk privately in the clinic, I made my way outside, ending up in the parking lot. By now it was lunchtime. I hadn't eaten since breakfast the day before, but I wasn't hungry. I was scared and, for the moment, alone. My hands shook, and I knew my voice would too.

I leant against a car for support. It was a warm summer's day and the cloudless sky, so cheerful and optimistic, felt too expansive to appreciate. I looked at the ground instead, closer and safer. I thought about life: family, work, science, living in China. I thought about being in love. I thought about losing it all. As Sana answered I realised that I was not only about to ruin her day, but possibly her life.

I felt as though I ruined many people's days that day.

2

A YOUNG MUM WITH OLD IDEAS

My mum is the exact kind of person you want by your side if you find out you have cancer. She's solid under pressure, with a strength that can only come from single motherhood and dipping below the poverty line, more than once. That it was her and not another woman with me that day is not to be taken for granted – she had planned to give me up for adoption.

A month before my birth, my eighteen-year-old mother packed a bag and left Ballina, a small surfside town in New South Wales, for the Gold Coast, a much bigger surfside city in Queensland, hoping for better opportunities. She was also escaping the mess created when she fell pregnant to a friend's boyfriend.

I'm told my biological father, Wayne 1.0 (the first of two fathers called Wayne in my life – imagine being a child and trying to make sense of that), was a handsome bronzed surfer popular with women. He had tousled blond hair and broad shoulders, honed by hours of laying concrete. My mum's friend was in love with him and they'd been dating a while, but he and my mum had a connection too. They started an affair.

At the time, Mum was working in a grocery store. She hadn't finished high school, preferring to make money. When she found out she was pregnant with Wayne 1.0's baby, she drank tequila by herself and cried. She was terrified of telling her friends, certain they would abandon and condemn her. So, she did something people often do when trapped: she lied. Mum told people that my father was a traveller who had passed through town a while back. They'd met in secret. Then he'd moved on to the next town and she had no way of getting in touch with him.

This bought her time, but did nothing to fix her shame. She had been raised by traditional Catholic parents and spent time at a religious boarding school run by nuns. Nan and Pop had always threatened her, joking but stern, 'If you get pregnant we'll cut your legs off.' Mum believed that having a child out of marriage was not only sinful, but cruel. She was also worried about losing her legs.

The conflict between what she knew to be right and the situation she had created for herself festered as her belly grew. When my grandparents' business folded they decided to head north, and Mum upped and left with them. They crossed the border from New South Wales into Queensland for a new start. The state offered palm trees and new business opportunities. Best of all, no one knew Mum there.

Mum planned to start over, without me. She had been meeting social workers during her antenatal visits and the intention was to put me up for adoption. Everything was in place. All that was left to do was give birth and sign one final form.

I was born on a sunny autumn day in March 1982. The birth itself was easy, Mum says, at least compared to what would come next. In those days, babies for adoption were removed from their mothers immediately. 'It's a boy,' she was told, as I was carried straight out of the room.

I was swaddled and placed in a nursery. Mum was left to recover on the ward with the other new mothers. She was not allowed to see me, let alone hold me. A couple of midwives felt sorry for Mum and found her a single room so she didn't have to sit and watch the other new mothers feed, kiss and cuddle their babies.

There were strict rules about keeping Mum and me apart in hospital, as if the system knew that any bonding between us could cloud her decision. I spent my first few days mostly alone, wrapped in a hospital-issued blanket wearing state-provided clothing. I was fed bottles of powdered milk while I awaited final bureaucratic processes and my new parents to collect me.

The midwives grew increasingly sympathetic to Mum's situation. To one nurse in particular, Mum voiced doubt about the adoption. 'Will he really be better off with someone else?' she asked.

Late one night, a nurse snuck Mum down the fire escape to a set of stairs that led to the nursery. There, she held me for the very first time, bursting into tears and smothering me with kisses. She stayed for only a few minutes, in case one of the stricter midwives walked past the nursery. It would have meant trouble for both Mum and her accomplice.

She managed to return the next night too. These nocturnal, clandestine visits continued for three nights, by which time she'd seriously started to question the plan to give me up for adoption. That third night together was to be our last as the authorities were due to collect me the next day.

Mum was sleepless and anguished. At 5 am she used the hospital payphone to call her parents. She'd made her decision: she was keeping me.

That morning, as she waited for my grandparents to pick us up, the adoption team arrived first. With a knock on the door, the moment had arrived. Mum's nurse marched over and, through the door, informed the social workers that Mum had changed her mind and that I was no longer up for adoption. More knocking followed. The collector had a job to do, and they'd seen a hundred young women panic at the last minute.

The knocking turned to banging. The nurse barred the door with her arms. 'Go away! She said she's keeping the baby!' she yelled, forming a barricade.

Nan and Pop arrived soon after. They, too, had had a change of heart. Years of threats to cut off Mum's legs should she get pregnant out of wedlock dissolved into acceptance and support.

But deciding to keep me at the last minute had created a unique problem – I had none of the stuff newborns needed, including clothes. Pop rushed from the hospital and attacked the nearest department store, returning with a bag full of clothes. 'No grandson of mine is leaving hospital without his own clothes,' he said, thrusting a bag of tiny onesies into Mum's arms.

Mum compensated for our early separation by holding me constantly. By now she was totally infatuated, and I was more than just her baby. The decision to keep me was the exact moment she became an adult, she says. In some ways, I was her ticket to the love she had been craving. I was her son, but she also wanted me to be her friend – one who would accept all her flaws.

I felt this pressure from a young age. Sometimes it still explodes to the surface, usually when the magnitude of that decision and her endless want from me becomes suffocating. This bond, formed under traumatic circumstances, has endured though. When she jokes that she made me into the man she'd hoped to find one day, I reply that 'the bar wasn't very high'. Mum has had a rocky history with men, often falling in love with people she probably shouldn't fall in love with. And in a weird quirk of the universe, those men are often called Wayne.

•

Wayne 2.0 is my sister's father. He was a good-looking footballer and the star of a local team, who met Mum at a pub where he was celebrating a win. He was short, with a superhero jaw and stocky legs. He made up for his height with charisma. Their relationship was volatile from the beginning. I was a few months old when they met, but my existence never put him off. Maybe it was because his mother had also been young, around sixteen years old, when she had him. Or maybe he was so chill because he and Wayne 1.0 had actually been friends back in Ballina. Either way, he and Mum were hopelessly in love and, within a year, Mum fell pregnant with my sister, Kim. It was then that they agreed to tell people that I was also his child. This helped relieve Mum's shame and finally gave her the nuclear family the Bible told her she needed. They kept up the lie, even though Kim and

I ended up looking totally different: me, tall and lean with olive skin, dark hair and a big nose; Kim, short and stocky with pale skin, blonde hair and a button nose.

Being a young handsome athlete, Wayne 2.0 had many of the unfortunate habits of young handsome athletes. He was obsessed with sport, drinking and women, usually in that order. Mum still married him. She was a sucker for love. She also needed a husband to feel whole and was prepared to put up with a surprising amount of crap.

I was four years old when they got married in a ceremony at Nan and Pop's house. Wayne 2.0 and I wore matching pink shirts and grey suits; Mum and Kim wore puffy pink dresses. I was the ring-bearer. The four of us looked perfect, but we were far from it.

Apart from the wedding, I have only one memory from those early Wayne 2.0 years and it's not a nice one. I am four years old and Kim is two years old. The two of us are seated in the back of a car; flashing blue and red lights reflect off the thick glasses Kim has to wear to correct a badly turned eye. Wayne 2.0 is standing outside the car talking to two police officers, while his brother sits in the passenger seat. Wayne 2.0 took us to his cricket practice earlier that evening, and to the beers that followed. He is over the blood alcohol limit and is being busted for drink-driving. Suddenly, he shoves one of the police officers and the three of them wrestle to the ground. There's yelling, probably swearing, then he's handcuffed and taken away. I don't make a sound and neither does Kim, even as Wayne 2.0's head is rammed against my window before he drops to the ground. I look across at Kim to make sure she is okay, a habit Mum says started the minute she brought Kim home from the hospital.

Wayne 2.0's brother hops into the driver's seat and takes us to a large suburban mall where Mum manages a shop selling affordable fashion to middle-aged women. He dumps us at one of the entrances and drives off – whether he says anything at all, I can't remember. Now it's my job to navigate us to Mum's shop. I'm only four years old, but I know the way and take Kim's hand, winding us to safety. She holds on tightly. Over the years, when things around us grew unpredictable and volatile, like on this night, I was always there to hold her hand.

When we enter the store, Mum rushes up and asks what's wrong, why we're there, what's going on?

'I don't want to tell you, Mummy, it will make you sad,' I say. I am too busy beaming with pride that I've made it to the shop to notice her tears. Kim and I sit in the cramped staffroom until closing time, drawing on the back of discount signs.

Wayne 2.0 reappeared a few days later. We were living in a caravan park in Logan, beside the highway connecting Brisbane to the Gold Coast, and Kim and I played in the park's sandpit most afternoons. We looked up from the sandpit and ran to him. He asked if we wanted a lolly, Kim screamed yes as she jumped into his arms. We wandered to a small shop a few hundred metres down the highway and each picked a lollipop. Kim talked the entire walk there and back, yelling above the highway hum.

Things between Mum and Wayne 2.0 never fully recovered. A few months later, Mum ordered us out of the sandpit and into the back seat of our car – fully loaded with clothes and stuffed toys. I noticed that her eyes were red and puffy as she slammed the door. I put my seatbelt on, but Kim stood so she could look out the back window. She stared at Wayne 2.0 as he watched us zoom off.

'Daddy crying,' Kim said.

Soon after our sudden departure, Mum and Wayne 2.0 divorced. He tried to visit us, but Mum was too angry to let him back into our lives, especially when he settled down and remarried. Our contact with him became patchy over a couple of years, before stopping altogether when I was around six years old.

•

Even though we didn't see Wayne 2.0 for years, the secret that he was not my father was preserved until I was eleven. Everyone in the family – mum, her three sisters and my grandparents – was in on the secret. There was no long-term plan for disclosure, and my mother fretted constantly that I would find out one day and hate her. I did accidentally find out one day, but I didn't hate her. Sadly, I was kind of relieved.

The big secret that Wayne 2.0 wasn't my dad came undone by a pair of jeans. I wanted new ones, but Mum said no – money was always tight in our house. We fought and I stormed off to my room to feel sorry for myself. Half an hour later I emerged and heard Mum on the phone. She was perched on a stool near the landline in the dining room, holding a glass of cheap red wine. She looked upset and was talking so quietly no one more than a metre away would be able to hear her. My eleven-year-old mind figured that this conversation had to be about me. After all, we'd just had a fight. As I turned to storm back to my room I caught a few words 'but if he ever finds out' . . . Ah ha, this *was* about me!

How dare she talk about our fight, I thought. It felt like an enormous violation. I sulked back in my sanctuary.

A little while later, she knocked on my door. I was reading a magazine full of *Beverly Hills 90210* gossip and did my best to ignore her.

'Benny, don't be mad at me,' she said.

'I heard you on the phone,' I said.

She stood silently for a while, watching the carpet. I was confused, I was the one who was supposed to be upset.

'What's wrong Mum?' I asked, 'Why are *you* upset?'

'I didn't want you to find out this way, but I was just never sure how to tell you,' she replied.

'Tell me what?' I asked.

Mum sat on the end of the bed, her hands shaking.

'I need to tell you who your real dad is.'

My little brain was even more confused. I had wanted new jeans, and instead I was getting a new dad?

Mum went on to tell me that Wayne 2.0 was not my father. She said that Wayne 2.0 had decided to treat me like his son when they got together, a decision made when they were just nineteen years old.

'I'm so sorry I lied to you all these years,' she said between sobs. 'I just didn't know what else to do. I always wanted you to have a dad.'

But by then I hadn't had a relationship with Wayne 2.0 for years – he had remarried and moved on. I wasn't very fond of him and had no real attachment to him. Kim felt the same. He was more of a name that was thrown around than a father.

The fact that I had a different dad somewhere else was exciting and I was immediately curious about this new, mysterious man.

When Mum told me that his name was also Wayne I wondered whether I was actually asleep and in a strange nightmare that would end with me surrounded by Waynes of all shapes and sizes. The next reveal was even more shocking. She was sometimes in contact with Wayne 1.0, and he lived nearby. Mum arranged for me to meet him the very next day. All of this felt especially dramatic as I got to skip school. I only missed school for serious things.

Pop picked us up in the morning and drove Mum and me to the meeting spot in a seaside suburb on the Gold Coast, a stone's throw from the hospital where I was born and where Mum had nearly given me up for adoption.

The first thing I noticed about Wayne 1.0 was that he was tall. This is important because I'm tall – much taller than my mum, sister and Wayne 2.0 (I'm 198 centimetres, and no, I do not play basketball). Until then, it had never struck me as odd that I was taller than Wayne 2.0 and looked nothing like him.

Wayne 1.0 shook my hand and we walked over to a park bench overlooking the ocean. His face was framed by sandy blond hair that seemed to sparkle like the white caps of the breaking waves nearby. I had no idea what to say so I stared at the blades of grass poking up through the sand.

He asked me the usual things adults ask kids, how school was going and whether I played any sports.

'School is good,' I said. 'I don't play any sports.'

He asked if I liked or followed rugby league.

'Nah,' I said.

This felt like the beginning of our mutual disappointment. I think he was hoping for a footy-playing kid, the kind who got into fights behind the oval after school. I wasn't that kid. I was more of a book nerd who enjoyed talking on the phone. I had a few football cards, but mainly because I liked the cartoon mascots and thought they were cute. And I used to watch football games on Friday nights with my family around the TV, but mainly because I liked the way Pop yelled at the referees and because we got to order pizza.

Our conversation limped on like this, him trying to connect with me and me never sure what to say, until it was time to head home. On the drive back, Mum and Pop grilled me about what we'd talked about and what I thought of him.

'I dunno, I don't think we have much in common,' I said.

I think that put their minds at ease. Maybe this was the confirmation they needed that I was better off without him, or proof that they'd been right to keep this secret for eleven years.

Either way, I didn't see or hear from Wayne 1.0 again for the next ten years. He called me a week before my twenty-first birthday and we met for lunch at a local pizza place. We both took our girlfriends. It was less awkward, but we still didn't gel. That's the last time I saw him.

Over the years, Kim had been slowly reconnecting with Wayne 2.0. His football days were behind him – after remarrying, he'd had three sons and worked for a major property developer. Incrementally, Wayne 2.0 proved to Kim that he could be trusted, and Kim lowered the walls she'd put up after being repeatedly let down.

Mum's choices hadn't been working out for me so it was time to take things into my own hands. I set about finding a man worthy of being my father. For years I evaluated any older male

I crossed paths with against a set of criteria. The first condition was that they weren't called Wayne. Second, they hadn't dated Mum. Third, they did not have children – I didn't want to cut anyone else's grass. Fourth, they needed to be a calm pacifist. Last, they didn't play rugby league.

When I was sixteen years old I started dating my best friend, Cassie. We'd met in year three and became closer the older we got. Cassie was tall with long brown hair down to her lower back. She was one of the smartest people I knew, and still is. She described herself as the least funny person ever, but when it was just us two hanging out she would make me roll around in laughter. Her family was different from mine: they'd gone to university, the house was full of books, her mum and dad remained nice to each other even though they'd separated, and her dad was actually her dad. We dated for five years from the age of sixteen, and for a few of those years we lived together in her family home while at university in Brisbane. Mum's company offered her a job in New South Wales during my final year of high school and so she left Queensland. Kim was already living on her own, having left school as soon as she could.

Cassie's mum had a boyfriend who was a childless social worker living alone near Bundaberg, a town surrounded by sugar cane about four hundred kilometres away. He visited occasionally and called often. If I got to the phone before Cassie's mum we'd exchange a few words, eventually expanding into proper conversations. During his visits I'd suss him out further: his name was Ian (tick); he had never been in a relationship with my mum (tick); had no children (tick); he was so calm and quiet that he made koalas look frenetic (tick); and he didn't play, or watch, rugby league (tick). We got to know each other slowly; his shyness meant that I had to push things forward.

In between semesters during my first year at university I invited myself up to his place. I planned to stay a week. We'd never been around each other for more than a couple of days – when he popped down to see Cassie's mum – and we were rarely alone together. I was nervous about spending so much time with him. What if we annoyed each other? What if we just didn't click when it was only the two of us? What if he wasn't good dad material after all?

My fears evaporated on the first night. After dinner, we played backgammon for hours while he put on his favourite music for me, alternating between Nina Simone, Edith Piaf and opera. We drank beer and, amid our shouting accompanying double sixes, he taught me about history and sociology and I explained genes and how cells organise themselves.

Despite being different on the inside, and looking unrelated on the outside, our personalities complement each other. He hadn't been seeking a child, in the way I was seeking a father, but he was happy to go with the flow. He was careful not to push us in a particular direction, mindful of the type of men I'd grown up around. It was me who needed to pull back sometimes, so I didn't smother him and interrupt his relatively solitary life. I visited again during the next break from university, and the next.

Slowly, we evolved into something more than friends. Our father–son relationship has become so normal that we forget to tell people it's not biological. Every now and then people comment that they can see the family resemblance. We always chuckle when that happens. No single conversation or event made us feel like father and son. Unlike the actual birth of a child, our love has no time stamp. It was the result of hundreds of small actions. Like when I made him a stubby cooler with a picture of me on it for Father's Day, or when he put a framed photo of me on his work desk. Eventually, 'He's like a father to me' became 'This is my dad, Ian'.

Ian says I keep him young. We've travelled to a dozen countries together. He visited me each year that I lived in China. It was during one of these visits that we went snowboarding outside of Beijing, and, well, you know how that ended.

●

As a kid, at the start of each week, I would highlight all the nature documentaries in the TV guide for the next seven days. When I was ten years old, I watched a particular documentary about dolphins. In one scene, the filmmaker focused on the tuna industry and how dolphins were caught and killed by fishermen, who viewed them as pests. A grainy shot from a distance showed a fisherman hauling dolphins out of a tuna net and slicing them open right there on the boat's deck. My little brain wasn't ready to see the brutality humans could inflict on animals. I burst into tears, but I couldn't look away. Mum heard me crying and grabbed me, holding me so close that my tears soaked the front of her jumper.

'The dolphins . . . killed . . . tuna,' was all I could manage. She held me until the commercial break and then turned off the TV.

After seeing those dolphins die, I made it my mission to convince people that animals needed our help. In year seven, we were meant to do an oral presentation about our favourite hobby. I thought this presented the perfect opportunity to share the horrors of factory farming and animal experimentation with my classmates. Our encyclopaedias had nearly nothing on animal rights, so Mum went to the local RSPCA office and collected pamphlets on the cruelty of the cosmetics industry and battery chickens. On my poster I included pictures of rabbits with their heads in vices and mother pigs trapped in concrete pens separated from their babies.

No one raised a hand to ask a question after my talk – I had failed to convince my class that they should eat less pork or avoid certain shampoo brands. When the teacher stood from her seat I looked at my shoes, expecting her to scold me for not choosing something like cricket or football to talk about.

'That was a really good presentation, Ben. Have you seen the movie *Born Free*? I think you'd really like it,' she said.

As my class sat cross-legged on the carpet waiting for the next talk on soccer, my teacher told me that the movie was about a couple with a pet lion, which they release into the wild. This movie sounded like the next best thing to a nature documentary.

I saved up birthday money to subscribe to *National Geographic* so I could read about wildlife. I would cut out the best pictures – a large herd of wildebeest around a watering hole, a school of sharks in deep blue water – and take these to school to be hung in our classroom. I became interested in conservation, but my family weren't on the same page. When we stayed with my grandparents, Pop would head out to the backyard after dinner to whack cane toads with golf clubs, shouting 'Four!' as they flew through the air. When he handed me a golf club, I didn't take it – explaining that removing this pest was important, but a more humane method was to gently catch them and put them in the freezer.

'That's disgusting,' he said. But I thought hacking at them with golf clubs was worse.

Nan agreed to let me use a chest freezer in the garage. When Pop went to fetch his golf club I would run into the backyard with a handful of plastic bags and a bucket. The toads' warty skin felt gross through the plastic and the really big ones needed two hands to stop them squirming free. I froze them straight away. I'd heard tales of cane toads waking up after defrosting (this was before I had a good understanding of biology) and the thought of one coming back to life, stressed and in pain, was too much to bear. So, after two days in the freezer, I'd remove a batch and chop their frozen bodies in half, just to make sure they stayed dead once they defrosted in the bin. I'd never catch them all before Pop reached the backyard, so a couple ended up getting the club each night, but then he eventually gave up and let me control the cane toads my way.

We had a couple of cats and dogs growing up, but we moved around a lot and would sometimes end up in a new flat with no room for them. When I was twelve we had to move from a large house to a small unit after Mum's partner at the time hocked our stereo and some furniture for gambling money and fled. I begged Mum to find somewhere that would allow us to keep Arnie, our Maltese terrier, but we needed to move quickly and her single salary meant we couldn't be choosy. He went to a good home, but saying goodbye to him was especially difficult. I cried most of my first night without him and swore that I would never again have a pet. It seemed hypocritical for people to say they loved their pet animals, but then put them down or get rid of them when things got too hard. Animals were better off without people, I decided.

Around the same time I stopped visiting zoos. I found them miserable, even the so-called 'good' ones. Wombats, giraffes and parrots deserved to be free. While at the zoo, I felt the same awe that everyone feels making eye contact with a dolphin or looking into the mouth of a yawning lion only a few metres away, but this wonder was accompanied by a sadness. They were trapped and on display, at the whim of people who decided when they ate, where they slept and which other animals they interacted with.

Closer to home, I wanted us to eat only free-range eggs, but Mum said we couldn't afford them. There was never spare money lying around; when things were tough Mum raided our piggybanks to pay the electricity bill.

Money was a constant preoccupation in our life because we never had enough. Mum raised us on her own for the most part and worked up to three jobs. She would do anything for work – wait on tables, wash dishes, drive an ice-cream van, manage a fashion store, run a restaurant. After her divorce from Wayne 2.0 she sometimes skipped dinner so my sister and I had enough food to eat. Even though this was before the days of child support, when men were made to pay for their children, I'd have liked to think both Waynes would have supported us. But Mum tells me that was not the case.

At times we lived below the poverty line. During one episode, Mum desperately emptied my savings account to cover a debt. It wasn't a huge amount, accumulated from birthday money mostly, but it was enough to prevent her defaulting on the loan. She asked me, of course, but there was only one possible answer – we three were in it together.

We weren't entirely alone, though. My grandparents and Mum's three sisters always lived nearby – all of us frequently shifting among different suburbs in the northern Gold Coast and Logan area. Nan watched us after school, and if Mum had to work late at one of her jobs we would spend the night. My grandparents and aunts were generous – when Pop's business was booming we got new clothes and toys. When money was tight they were generous with their time instead, having us over for the whole weekend or taking us on a drive to the beach.

My nan and her four daughters talked to each other nearly every day. They loved each other intensely, but it was a kind of fragile love. If Nan, an aunt or Mum felt slighted, they could fly off the handle. And if one party was sufficiently offended, we might not see them for a few months. Kim, our cousins and I never knew when our mums were going to stop talking to each other. In a way, I learnt to trust that only Mum and Kim were a constant in my life.

My family was made up of self-made people who worked hard and didn't trust anyone with an education. Only one of my aunts had completed high school, and no one had been to university, because school was something you did until you were old enough to work – earning was better than learning.

This way of thinking played out regularly around the dinner table when my grandparents ranted about architects. This topic came up a lot because Pop was an old-school draftsman, the kind who learnt how to draw building plans on the job. He drew on drafting paper and could slip between metric and imperial measurements with mastery. He was good at what he did, and at times had successful businesses and loads of cash. But he didn't like architects.

'They may have been to university,' he would pontificate from the head of the dinner table, 'but I can knock out a set of plans faster than any of 'em.'

Every lecture started with something about them having gone to university and ended with how an architect could charge double or three times what my poor pop could charge for the same job. University produced greedy snobs. So, as soon as I was old enough, Mum sprung a job on me.

At fourteen, I arrived at my grandparents' house after school and before I'd made it down the driveway Nan was yelling at me out the window.

'Your mother has left clothes up here. You've got fifteen minutes to get ready for work,' she called.

'I don't have a job Nanna!' I said, hoping to sort this out from the driveway.

'Your mother's got you one. Just come up, quickly!' She was not in the mood to explain – Nan provided day care for up to twelve local kids and this was her rush hour.

Laid out on the bed before me was a new pair of jeans and two sweaters. The tags revealed they had been purchased from the local grocery store. I didn't care about that, they looked nice and I didn't get new clothes unless it was a special occasion.

Nan said that I'd be working for Mum's hairdresser. I was to sweep the floor, clean mirrors and shampoo dirty heads. I had set foot in this salon only once before and the owner, Bernard, had frightened the hell out of me, burying his clippers into my head like an angry landscaper.

I walked into the salon on that first day with fear, but also pride at my new outfit.

Bernard told me I'd be working two shifts a week and earning six dollars an hour. It was the most money I'd ever made, which was none.

I had no experience, but I quickly developed a reputation for giving great head massages and clients heaped praise on me after every shampoo. Bernard seemed to like the fact that I knew my way around a broom and would polish the mirrors until they sparkled – skills honed from needing to keep the house in order when Mum was at work.

You can learn a great deal about people in a salon. Bernard had a way of making people feel so comfortable they revealed parts of their lives they never shared with others. I watched him extract updates on his clients' health, marriages, children and money problems. He struck an artful balance between listening, validating and sharing his own experiences.

I worked for Bernard for six years, but had other jobs, too. I wanted money and lots of it. I worked at KFC (this was a family tradition) and then got another job delivering junk mail in my neighbourhood. At fifteen years old I was working three jobs multiple nights per week and spending most of each weekend folding junk mail and then cycling it all over town. My bank account looked great, but my report card did not. I even failed mathematics in grade ten.

It would have been easy to continue this way – making money at the expense of school. My family had done that, and were happy.

But I wanted something different. Despite my grandfather's criticism of people who went to university, spending time learning about animals, and then charging money for that knowledge sounded very sensible to me. Going to university also seemed like a way to get out of my hometown. At the key juncture between year ten and year eleven, when many people dropped out, I decided to stay. But there was no way I was going to get the grades needed to enter university while working three jobs. I quit the junk mail route and cut back at the hairdressing salon and KFC.

Half the kids in my grade disappeared after year ten. On the first day of year eleven my friends and I had great fun working out who hadn't returned. It seemed those we'd long ago dubbed dickheads were the ones now absent. We were elated, and the teachers seemed to relax too. Finally, class was actually about curiosity and not crowd control. I thrived in this new environment and started to get serious about science. A decade of religiously watching nature documentaries and reading *National Geographic* articles about wildlife had given me a good grounding in the natural world, but it was time to dig deeper. I could still freeze cane toads, boycott zoos and insist we eat free-range eggs, but to really make a difference I needed to know more.

I told my family that I wanted to study zoology. I'd be at the same university as Cassie, who was taking psychology.

'What job will that get you?' said Mum.

'Don't you want to earn money and get ahead in life?' said Pop.

'Will you still talk to us when you're a fancy professor?' said Nan.

'Awesome,' said Kim.

Because zoology has the word zoo in it, they assumed that I was using a fancy word for zookeeper. I should have seen it coming. For the next fifteen years I had to correct nearly everyone I met that I was neither a zookeeper nor worked in a zoo. Even now, I have to tell people that I have never worked in a zoo. They almost always look disappointed.

3

WILD LIFE, WILD CHINA

The zoology building at the University of Queensland was a wonderland for anyone who loved animals. A seven-metre model of an actual saltwater crocodile hung from the atrium. Colourful, detailed pictures of wildlife lined the corridors. The department's museum housed all kinds of taxidermic models, fossils, coral and jelly fish specimens and endless rows of insects. Every available space contained animals, even the roof, where the reptile department kept live crocodiles. It was everything I'd ever dreamt of.

I bounced from an ecology class on how to count kangaroos from an aeroplane, to a modelling class on predicting how a frog species would respond to climate change, to an evolution class comparing dinosaurs with living animals, to a behaviour class on why nesting insects choose to help each other out. The more I understood, the deeper my love for the natural world grew.

Love might seem like a strange word, but it best summarises my feelings towards biology. Perhaps if I were German, or Japanese, I might have a better word, one of those beautiful terms with clunky English translations like 'the feeling you get on a Tuesday when studying biology and you are not hungry because you are full of wonder'. English only offers words like love, joy, awe – none of which fully capture how satisfied I felt when watching, studying or talking about animals.

No topic hit the spot more than animal behaviour. When I learnt that working out how and why animals interact with each other was its own scientific field, it seemed too good to be true. Like when you learn that some people get paid to taste new types of lollies for a living. At the end of my three-year science degree I had the option of going to work as a zoologist or sticking around for an extra year of research. I chose the latter, desperate to home in on a single species and learn as much as I could about it.

Research on wildlife is painstakingly slow. As the term implies, wildlife live in the wild, and this makes them hard to watch, catch and record. Scientists often have to resort to examining the signs that an animal leaves behind, like scratch marks on a tree, droppings or footprints.

The animal I chose to study during my final year was the satin bowerbird. They're easier (and amazing) to research because the males build an elaborate bower on the ground out of hundreds of sticks and decorate it with blue objects to attract females.

Over hundreds of hours under camouflage netting deep in the Bunya Mountains, north-west of Brisbane, I watched bowerbirds as they tended their bowers. I recruited a small team of volunteers to help me and we squeezed into a two-bedroom cabin dwarfed by enormous pine trees. When I fell short of volunteers, Ian would drive four hours from his place on the weekend and pitch a tent in front of our cabin, even taking time off work for longer stints.

It was cold, uncomfortable work, but everyone appeared to love it. Sitting alone in the forest for hours every day for over three months with no mobile phone reception was meditative. Nan and Pop even made a trip to the mountains. They were both curious about my project – their attitude about university had certainly changed – and so I showed them the more impressive bowers we'd found, some with over four hundred decorations.

•

Six months later, as a freshly graduated 22-year-old zoologist, I traded hiking boots and binoculars for the drab office attire favoured by bureaucrats in the nation's capital, Canberra. Moving away wasn't difficult. As a kid I had moved house a lot – by fifteen years old, I'd lived in eighteen different places across two states and three primary schools. This meant that I was adaptable, but that no one place really felt like 'home'. Mum had already moved to Melbourne by this time and Kim had settled in Sydney. Cassie stayed in Brisbane and enrolled in further psychological study, but she and I had grown apart during my research year at university, and over a course of very painful conversations we decided that our relationship had run its course.

In Canberra, I was going to work for the federal environment department. I was outrageously naïve. I wanted to help protect Australia's animals and plants through federal policy. Instead, I rotated through a few listless teams, the most depressing of which was responsible for rubber-stamping applications to develop, bulldoze and blow up natural areas.

The system was geared towards bolstering the economy at the expense of forests, rivers, coasts and oceans. I processed paperwork and read developmental applications, frustrated at a lack of proper protection for the environment. There was one highlight: I convinced my bosses to let me relocate to the Northern Territory to spend four months with the team monitoring the environmental impacts of Australia's only uranium mine. The mine sat in the middle of the magnificent Kakadu National Park, a place so rich in biodiversity and cultural significance that the United Nations named it a World Heritage Site. A mine within a national park was a perfect summary of Australia's environmental policy.

As the deadline to return to Canberra loomed, I started to think about ways that I could help people understand the environment and demand that the government do a better job looking after it. The answer was education. I took myself back to the capital, walked past the environment department and instead joined the circus next door.

The Science Circus was an outreach program operated by Australia's National Science and Technology Centre and for several months of the year it travelled across the country spreading science fun. With a semi-trailer full of science experiments, toys, games, props and costumes, we drove from school to school, running science shows and workshops. We made bubbles so big that kids could stand inside them, exploded tins with liquid nitrogen and created soda fountains.

When I wasn't on tour with the circus, I was studying a postgraduate degree in scientific communication at the Australian

National University. Both the circus and uni taught me how to talk about different scientific topics to people of all ages and backgrounds. I began to appreciate that reaching as many people as possible was the key to effecting change. But information had to be relevant and targeted to each new audience. I was also feeling resigned to the fact that Australia seemed enamoured with economic growth above environmental protection. Perhaps I could better apply my passion for animals, conservation and communication in a country that was still developing.

•

After a year with the circus, my studies completed, and with a few weeks of Chinese lessons under my belt, I headed to a tiny town called Dongfang, on the west coast of Hainan Island in China, to work in a nature reserve set up for endangered Eld's deer. During my ten-month conservation mission I watched some deer get turned into wine and massive Burmese pythons turned into moisturiser, and realised I was completely out of my depth. I hadn't understood the context within which I was working and I hadn't grasped the values of the people I was working with. Our ideas about animals and conservation didn't align, so I left to take up a position with China's national zoological research institute in Beijing.

I arrived in Beijing a few months before the 2008 summer Olympics. The city was energetic with potential and hope. Tech start-ups were launching, art galleries were opening, bars and clubs heaved every weekend. Science budgets were growing (whereas elsewhere in the world, they were shrinking) and the country's research institutions were bulging with scientists and graduate students. Big-name Chinese scientists who had established labs around the world were being lured back with huge grants and prestigious academic postings. These science rock stars were part of a wave of Chinese-born experts returning to the mainland. They were dubbed sea turtles – they were finally making their way home to the beaches from where they were born.

Then, as now, scientists in China were encouraged to publish in English, as the official language of science. Their salaries and promotions were tied to the number of English publications they produced, and so the message from the very top was clear: doing science was important, but promoting that science across the world more so.

With my biology background and science communication experience, I was well placed. I was still learning Mandarin, but the professors all spoke English well. After eighteen months at the research institute running one of their journals, I left and started my own business focused on science communication, editing scientific papers for researchers, lab groups and other journals. My clients included several giant panda researchers. I became something of an expert on topics such as panda bear digestion and what types of male urine was most likely to attract female pandas. A friend from the science circus back in Australia, Tim, joined me in Beijing and we set about building science shows for schools and science-themed birthday parties. The business attracted a couple of science centres and we worked with them on their English materials and performances. It was going well, and we were starting to appear in local English-language media, even writing articles for China's international English newspaper *The China Daily*.

One Sunday in winter, a handful of Australian and British expats gathered for brunch at the home of a prominent lawyer. The guest list included the Australian ambassador to China and the newly arrived host of the *Beijing Hour*, an English language morning show on China Radio International. I attempted to entertain the table with fun animal facts, explaining an evolutionary theory for why people can't help wanting to cuddle giant pandas.

By the end of brunch, the morning show host had invited me to chat about pandas on the *Beijing Hour*, and a few days later, the show's producer, Sana, contacted me. We emailed back and forth, and then she called to scope out the interview topic. There was no spark over email or telephone. There was no sign at all that once I met Sana I was never going to be the same person again.

•

From the minute I met her I was hooked.

I was sitting in a far corner of the newsroom after my segment on pandas, when Sana came over to introduce herself. Her small face was framed by shoulder-length curly black hair, the volume of which threatened to completely overwhelm her face any minute. She had softly arched, perfectly shaped eyebrows set above large brown eyes. Her wide smile made her cheeks appear sculpted.

'So how does one become a panda expert?' she asked, in lieu of a standard greeting. She was the kind of person you knew was smart before they finished their first sentence. I thought she was beautiful and looked too glamorous for someone who had started work at 4 am.

I don't remember my reply because I was already in love. Only twenty-two years old, Sana had been born in Pakistan and raised in Canada, later working in the US, India and the UK. She'd come to China on a whim and a wish for adventure, and was now producing at China Radio International. She was only five feet tall – when I was sitting down, I was the same height as her standing up – but she had a booming laugh that sounded like the bray of a terrified donkey with a mouthful of hay.

I later learnt that the attraction I felt had been mutual. After a couple of minutes of conversation she returned to her desk and messaged a friend 'I've just fallen in love'. Her screen froze, just as I came over to ask a question (really, it was just an excuse to keep talking). Panicked, she half-stood, half-sat to block the computer screen, then quickly led me into the hall. This is what she recalls – I didn't notice the message or the awkward half-crouch, I was too busy falling in love.

Three days later we had our first and last date: we have been together ever since.

As a breakfast news producer, Sana's day started at three-thirty each morning. To maintain some semblance of a social life, she split her sleep into two chunks: four hours after her shift ended mid-morning, then four hours at night – with dinner and drinks in between. When she explained this complex sleep schedule, I said that she lived like a crepuscular animal – most active around dawn and dusk; she said that I was a nerd.

That summer we biked around Beijing, climbed hutong roofs, paddled around lakes and partied late into the humid nights. It was my best summer. Between falling in love and building my science communication business with Tim I was exhausted, or at least, that's what I told myself.

For months I had felt tired – as if my bones just couldn't get enough sleep. I was losing weight and would sometimes cripple over in abdominal pain.

I pressed on working. As summer drew to an end, my business partner, Tim, and I travelled to Guangzhou, a major city in southern China. The local science centre had invited us to perform science shows at schools. One day on stage, I was laughing maniacally while pretending to electrocute one of the Chinese performers when I began panicking. My bowels felt wrong – I struggled to hold everything in. Jumping around was not helping, and there, on stage, my bum won and I lost control. I'd pooed myself in the middle of the show. Thankfully, it was only a small amount. I made it through the last fifteen minutes, stilting my movements.

At another school later that week, I fainted between shows – falling back against the toilet and holding my head in my hands as I slid to the floor.

Uncooperative bowels are not uncommon for expats in China. All foreigners love swapping stories about poo emergencies, diarrhoea, food poisoning and squat toilets. In the four years I'd lived there I'd been sick regularly. When this pattern grew worse and I had pain, felt faint or looked a little pale, I attributed it to dodgy dumplings. And that was convenient, for a while. Then I started bleeding.

The blood accompanying my bathroom visits was getting harder to explain away to myself, though I tried. If blood was on the toilet paper? Well, it's not in the poo or in the bowl so it's probably a haemorrhoid. Blood in the poo? Well, that haemorrhoid must be getting worse. Blood on the toilet paper, poo *and* bowl? Wow, these haemorrhoids are really bad.

That I didn't have a history of haemorrhoids was irrelevant to me, I also didn't have a history of bowel cancer. I badly wanted these symptoms to be nothing.

As a scientist I was comfortable with percentages, risk and probability. I knew the probability of the cause being cancer was tiny, and the probability of it being a haemorrhoid was huge.

I also had no medical insurance in China and while I could speak a reasonable amount of Mandarin by then, I knew none of the words to discuss medical stuff. Going to a local clinic was not an option. So, I did what a lot of people do when they are in denial and accessing healthcare is hard – I ignored it.

Still, I had begun worrying constantly, panicking before using the toilet – I'd physically brace for pain, then emotionally brace as I peered into the bowl to check for blood.

Some people could tell I looked pale, but they didn't know about the bleeding. Tim knew I had pooed myself in front of an audience and fainted between shows, but he didn't know about the night sweats and fatigue. Ian knew of the bleeding, but not how consistent it had become. I told Sana I bled sometimes, and she knew about the night sweats, but not about the incontinence or fainting. There is nothing sexy about diarrhoea, poo pain and bloody toilet paper. I held off telling her the full story because I wanted her to get the best version of me.

This meant that only I had the full story; only I had the full horror.

PART 2

BEING A CANCER PATIENT

4

HELLO, I HAVE CANCER

Before my colonoscopy, I had been on a high because the doctor had downplayed my risk of cancer. Then, when he told me he'd found what looked like a big cancer, I felt nothing. Now that I was about to tell Sana, I wanted to cry.

Alone in the clinic parking lot, I called Sana in Beijing.

She'd left China Radio International a few months earlier and was hosting a TV show at a start-up news channel. She'd also just landed a bigger role: presenting for China's main English news channel, CCTV. She answered my call after one ring, sounding anxious. She was in a taxi, running late for work. I could hear her taxi driver chatting in the background, probably on a call of his own.

There's no good time to tell your partner that you probably have cancer, but I also didn't feel I could simply say, 'It sounds like you're stressed, I'll call you back later.' Things were moving quickly at my end and I needed her to know what I knew, regardless of the fallout.

'They found a tumour. It's big and they—' I began.

'What? Hang on, what? Cancer?' she jumped in. Being a news journalist, Sana likes to get straight to the point.

'The doctor says it's *probably* cancer, but won't know for sure until the lab analyses a sample. I'm about to head to hospital for a CT scan to make sure there are no other tumours,' I said.

She burst into tears. My eyes were already wet.

'How big is it? Are you okay?' she asked. 'I'll get on a flight today, I'll be there as soon as I can.'

'It's okay, wait until the end of the week, until we know more. You don't need to rush, you've got work,' I said, trying to soothe her. *God I love you*, I thought. *I'm so sorry to do this to you.*

'No. I'm coming,' she said.

Thirty minutes later, Sana walked into the studio and filmed her show. Then she told her bosses that she needed indefinite time off and booked a flight to Australia.

She boarded a plane that night.

•

Sadness gave way to fear as Mum, my self-appointed father, Ian, and I drove across town an hour later for a scan to show just how much cancer I was dealing with. Ian sat in the back seat, silent. Mum drove. She was very focused, creating lists of things we needed to do.

'You probably didn't bring many toiletries, so we'll have to go to the shops on the way home. And I've just run out of green tea. And I think your soy milk is almost done. I've got a good juicer, but we'll need to stock up on carrots and celery. What else do you want to juice? Tomorrow we start eating healthy, okay? I've got plenty of garlic, but we'll need to get ginger.'

Mum was talking, but not to me. She was off in her own world – her child was sick and she had work to do. I was only half-listening anyway, staring out the window. I tried closing my eyes, but each time I saw the tumour.

•

The gastroenterologist called me an hour after the CT scan. Ian and I were sitting at a café, waiting for Mum to get everything on her shopping list at the supermarket next door. Neither the gastroenterologist nor the radiologist (a doctor specialising in doing and reading scans) could see any other tumours outside the sigmoid colon. The rest of the bowel was clear, and, importantly, so was the rest of my body.

Over the weekend, my tumour samples would be analysed by a pathologist (a doctor specialising in tissues and cells). The gastroenterologist and radiologist were pretty sure I had bowel cancer, but all I could do now was wait for the pathologist to confirm it. I encouraged Ian to use his return flight to Queensland that evening – nothing new was going to happen over the weekend and I was expecting Sana to arrive the next day. Kim and her partner, James, were arriving the next day as well, having booked flights from Sydney as soon as they heard the news. They would all be staying with me and Mum at Graeme's.

For the first time since my colonoscopy, I could finally slow down and think. In a few hours I had gone from a 28-year-old with a funky gut to a 28-year-old with cancer. Then, for a short time,

I went from having one tumour to freaking out at the prospect of having loads of tumours, before settling back to dealing with having just one tumour.

People always say that cancer is a roller coaster, and it's true. I'd only had cancer for a few hours, yet I'd already completed one loop-the-loop.

Mum and I were spent. She didn't want to cook; she suggested we and Graeme head out for dinner instead.

'You pick,' she said.

This felt strangely special, like I was twelve years old and choosing where to celebrate my birthday. We settled on a popular Malaysian restaurant close to home. It was noisy and casual, with the right mix of distraction and relaxation that we all needed. I realised I was starving – I hadn't eaten all day. I devoured the first round of appetisers, hoarding the curry puffs and roti for myself.

Over seafood laksa and fried noodles we talked about the day, Mum and I taking turns to remember details the other person hadn't. We agreed that finding out that I only had one tumour was a real high point. Mum insisted on ordering a bottle of wine.

'Don't be stupid,' I said.

'Come on, we need this. We've got to celebrate – today could have been so much worse,' she said.

Mum, Graeme and I clinked glasses, celebrating that I *only* had the one tumour.

A quiet descended over us as we waited for dessert – banana fritters and sago pudding. Behind Mum's thick-framed glasses I noticed that her eyes were puffy. I'd not seen her cry, but the evidence that she had was obvious.

She held my hand as we walked back to the car. She had needed to end this day with hope. So had I.

That night, I struggled to sleep. I was alone for the first time since hearing the c-word. Staring at the ceiling, the magnitude of what had happened rolled up and down my body.

I. Have. Cancer.

It felt like everything and nothing. Everything, because the idea of cancer was terrifying – people died from it every day. Would it kill me too? I worried that everything was going to change. Would Sana get scared off? What would happen to my business in Beijing?

The cancer was also nothing – I was exactly the same person as before the colonoscopy. Little had changed on my inside or outside. In fact, for the last week I had felt pretty good. I pondered just closing my eyes and going back to life as I had planned it. I hoped to wake up tomorrow and realise that all this cancer stuff had just been a bit of fuss – I'd collect my visa and return to Beijing.

•

Four days after the colonoscopy I was back at the gastroenterologist's office. Mum, Kim, Sana and I crowded around his desk while he relayed exactly what we'd been expecting: the bits of the mass he'd sampled were bowel cancer. I held Sana's hand, Mum held Kim's.

This wasn't a shock. What the gastroenterologist had seen during the scope and what the radiologist had seen on the CT had looked very much like bowel cancer. And now we had proof.

Kim asked if they could tell how advanced the tumour was from the sample.

'Yes, they can grade the tumour. It says here that Ben's tumour is moderately differentiated,' he said.

'What does that mean?' Sana asked.

'It means that the tumour is intermediate, not high grade, which is bad, and not low grade, which is better,' he said.

I'd been reading about grading bowel cancer over the weekend, and jumped in. 'That's a good thing, yeah? High grade tumours grow quickly and spread.'

He nodded. 'The tumour is certainly a nasty one, but it's the not the worst possible type,' he said.

Kim let go of Mum's hand and hugged me. It felt like we were kids again, but it was her turn to make sure I was okay.

Now that it was official, I had to tell the rest of my family and friends.

I spent that week being the bearer of bad news.

Some people dramatically burst into tears. Others looked at me as though I was already dead, their lips pursed and forehead in a frown. Some went blank. There were people who focused on the action plan and others who bombarded me with questions.

I felt emotionally responsible for how each person coped with the news. I would rush to reassure them, 'It's fine, I'll be okay.' I felt guilt on top of guilt: first for getting sick, and then for upsetting the people I cared about. Some days I couldn't handle the burden of communicating my diagnosis. I found myself delaying telling some people, asking people who already knew to tell them for me.

The three responses I feared the most were silence, sobbing and blind optimism.

The silent people were grim. They'd drift off into their own world, picturing what they'd wear to my funeral. Telling these people could end up a real downer because it made me feel like I was already at death's door. Even normally talkative people could find themselves lost for words.

Tim, my business partner in Beijing, is one of the loudest extroverts I know but all his energy disappeared when I called to tell him that I had cancer. He didn't say a word on the other end of the phone. I was as shocked by his silence as he was by my news, but I recovered first.

'It's fucked, right?' I added.

More silence.

'Yeah,' he said, eventually.

The sobbing people didn't allow much space for any other emotion. I felt like I had a responsibility to validate these people, to put them at ease. Yes, Sana fell into this category, but with time she was able to talk. Aunty Cathy, Mum's older sister, is a well-known sobber. She doesn't just wear her heart on her sleeve – her beach-ball-sized heart is held atop her head by two anxious Care Bears straddling her shoulders. I asked Mum to ring Aunty Cathy, tell her, wait out the emotional flood and then pass me the phone.

Neither silence nor sobbing made me angry – but blind optimism did. It was minimising and invalidating. I wanted to scream, 'I'm not telling you about a fucking paper cut! Stop telling me I'll be fine!' It felt as though the person didn't hear (or didn't want to hear) the word cancer. My grandparents took this approach.

Mum and I called Nan and Pop together. Pop answered.

'Hi Pop,' I said. 'Hi Dad,' said Mum.

'Oh, hi you two, how are ya?'

'Okay . . . well, not really. I have some bad news – I haven't been feeling well for a while and I had a colonoscopy and they've found cancer,' I said.

He paused. I waited for him to ask questions, say that was awful, anything.

'Hang on, I'll put Nan on,' he said.

Telling Nan was similarly underwhelming. When Mum suggested that they fly from Queensland to Melbourne to see me, Nan responded as though we were discussing last night's lotto numbers and not that her grandson had cancer.

'Oh no, I don't think we need to come down, Ben will be fine. There's nothing much we can do, we'll just get in the way.'

I just wanted people to respond with compassion and curiosity.

•

The days after my colonoscopy and diagnosis were full of feeling let down, not by others, but by my own body.

As a healthy twenty-something, I'd never broken a bone or been to hospital. I didn't have any health problems, but that had changed overnight.

I felt betrayed by my bowel and disappointed in my body. The idea that I was fit and healthy evaporated, replaced with distrust. I no longer believed I was invincible – I wasn't even sure how long I had left to live.

5

WHAT GOES UP MUST COME DOWN

The surgeon sat at his desk, hands clasped, exuding confidence. He was good-looking, with bright blue eyes and a chiselled jaw. You notice these things when you meet the person you hope will save your life.

On his desk was a model of the large bowel. Pointing to the sigmoid, he said, 'This is what we'll cut out.' He was enthusiastic, full of hope, and said the surgery could happen as early as the following week.

According to the CT scan, only one section of my bowel had tumour. The surgeon explained it in terms of plumbing – the idea was to cut out the bit of pipe with the cancer in it and join the rest of the pipe back up. After removing my sigmoid colon, he would join the large bowel above (the descending colon) with healthy bowel below (the rectum). I was buoyed to learn that, when caught early, bowel cancer was highly curable and had a ninety-eight per cent survival rate.

He'd do the operation laparoscopically, meaning he would use small holes to get at my bowel instead of a bigger cut across my abdomen. He was optimistic about my chances of a full cure and said that I could get back to China in six to eight weeks.

This was exactly what Mum and I had wanted to hear – a quick surgery and I'd be on my way. I smiled as the surgeon talked. What had seemed life-threatening was now life-restoring. I felt lucky to have a cancer that was so easily cured.

The exact order of events in the immediate weeks after my colonoscopy remain hazy. Some moments from this time are crystal clear, others are blurry – worse, some details have been forgotten altogether, and not just by me. Mum and I remember attending the first meeting with that surgeon on our own. And I remember Kim and James had to return to Sydney for work, but no one can remember why Sana wasn't with us at the meeting – including Sana. She was in Melbourne, that much we know. She wasn't working yet. So where was she? Honestly, between the shock, cancer loop-the-loops, endless telephone calls, and sudden explosion in medical appointments, it is not surprising that some details have been lost.

Later that day I found Mum chain-smoking on the patio, something she only did when stressed. She was excited, her words rushed between drags. Her neighbour had overheard her talking to Aunty Cathy on the phone about my cancer. The neighbour had poked her head over the fence and suggested something that changed my life: 'Ben should get a second opinion.'

This neighbour had once been a nurse at a hospital in Melbourne dedicated to cancer.

'Speak to them,' she said, 'they're the best.'

A whole hospital for cancer seemed too good to be true. I could see the benefit of a one-stop-shop for cancer, but I already had a plan from the surgeon. Plus, this was all going to be over soon.

Getting a second opinion felt unnecessary, but as a courtesy to Mum's neighbour I called the hospital she'd worked at. I was put through to a nurse who spoke to me with the deliberate care afforded an old friend. She'd probably had conversations like this hundreds of times, and yet she spoke with a warm authenticity that I found contagious. Her reassuring words dripped down the telephone line like a tonic, as if it were hospital policy to start the healing process from the very first call. I was given an appointment to meet with a surgeon that same week and called Mum's trusty GP to organise a new referral.

I've reflected on this life-changing call more than once. The nurse at the cancer hospital didn't act as though I was a nuisance. She'd made me feel welcome, like a patient who deserved her help.

•

Entering the hospital felt like walking onto the floor of a cancer factory. There were people everywhere, all occupied by cancer. Doctors and nurses manoeuvred with purpose around patients walking with drips, others being pushed in wheelchairs. Families chaperoned their sick to and from the café.

Signs pointed to cancer clinics, cancer imaging, chemotherapy, the pharmacy, cancer surgery, the cancer library and the cancer information centre. I was overwhelmed.

Mum and I sat in one of the waiting rooms. Again, we can't remember where Sana was and why she wasn't at this appointment; and just like the meeting with the first surgeon, neither can Sana. She was at every other major appointment, but why she missed these two remains a mystery.

Mum nudged me. 'All these poor people have cancer,' she whispered.

'Well, it *is* a cancer hospital,' I said, unable to resist pointing out the obvious.

'Yes, but come on, Benjamin,' she said. She'd used my full name – this was a serious moment for her.

'It's sad,' I said. 'There are so many.'

As I waited my turn, I looked around the room, surveying other patients while pretending to look at motivational posters on the walls. The shock of sitting among so much cancer subsided. It became comforting. *Cancer is normal here*, I thought.

Patients and families chatted away. They swapped cancer tips freely, as if trading pieces of gossip. Magazines changed hands alongside nods of hope. 'Good luck with it all,' one carer said to another. Cancer wasn't a lonely thing in this waiting room.

The more I looked around though, the more I noticed something odd: while cancer may have brought us together, time was doing its best to separate us.

I nudged Mum. 'I'm the youngest person here,' I whispered.

'You sure are, my son,' she said. Again, Mum was a step ahead of me.

'I'm at least half the age of the next youngest person,' I said.

'But you're probably twice as fit and healthy,' she replied.

In this waiting room where cancer was normal, I was still an anomaly. Suddenly, I felt more isolated than ever.

Cancer waiting rooms are full of older people because age is the biggest risk factor for cancer, not smoking, alcohol or ultraviolet radiation. Someone's chance of developing cancer increases with every year of life, and cancer affects way more older people than younger people. So, wrinkles, walking sticks and grey hair always dominate cancer waiting rooms.

While bowel cancer is increasing in younger people, in 2011, when I was diagnosed, only eighty-nine other people my age (twenty-five to twenty-nine years old) were also diagnosed with bowel cancer. If you zoom out and look at all cancers in people my age that year, 1100 were diagnosed. For people sixty-five to sixty-nine years old, though, the number of those diagnosed with cancer was 16,700. In the older age bracket of people seventy-five to seventy-nine years old, over 40,000 people were diagnosed with cancer. That's thirty-seven times higher than for my age group. Cancer in people my age is plain rare, and bowel cancer rarer still.

It's no wonder I felt out of place.

•

Mum and I had been waiting at the hospital for an hour. Anticipation rippled through the people waiting each time a doctor approached. The doctors always stood still for a second before calling out, double-checking the patient file to get the name right. Us patients lowered our phones, magazines and books. All chatter paused. In that moment, tension spread across the room and people shifted in their seats. Some patients squinted up at the file, trying to discern if it was their name written in bold letters.

A tall man with short, cropped hair, thin glasses and an expensive suit approached and called my name. 'Ben Bravery,' he repeated twice. Mum got to the doctor before me. 'Hi, I'm Ben's mum,' she announced loudly.

We were shown to a small consultation room and the surgeon introduced himself. I explained the events of the last week.

Surgeons like getting to the point.

'Look, I'm still waiting to view your CT scan,' he said, 'but I have seen the colonoscopy report and pathology analysis indicating bowel cancer.'

He explained the general approach to bowel cancer at the hospital and that surgery, chemotherapy and radiation were all possible treatments. But he wouldn't be drawn on specifics, such as the type of surgery or how long I would need to remain in Australia.

'Look.' It was becoming clear surgeons liked starting sentences with the word 'look'. 'There are some things we have to do first. I need to see the scan, then normally we take cases like yours to a multidisciplinary team meeting where several different doctors discuss the best way forward.'

I was taken aback by how different this approach was. The other surgeon had presented a much quicker, more clear-cut option.

'I've already met with another surgeon and he says this looks straightforward,' I told him. 'He can do the surgery next week actually.'

Leaning back in the cheap hospital chair in his expensive suit, he paused and put his expensive pen on the cheap desk.

'Look, that's fine for you to get a second opinion,' he said, in a way that indicated it was not fine. 'I'm just telling you how we do things here.'

He called what I was doing 'shopping around'. *Ouch.*

I'd offended him, and he'd offended me. *Coming here was a disaster,* I thought – and all because Mum hadn't wanted to upset her neighbour.

Outside the room I rolled my eyes at Mum and she grimaced. We had both found the experience a bit prickly. It was such a contrast to the high-fiving jig we'd done after meeting the first surgeon.

On the drive home we assembled a pros and cons list for each surgeon. Surgeon one offered optimism and a friendly manner. He operated at a large general hospital and offered keyhole surgery and a quick recovery. Surgeon two operated as part of a multidisciplinary team at a smaller hospital that dealt only with cancer. Everything I might need – scans, blood tests, chemo or counselling could be done in the one place. He was older and more qualified, but that seemed to come with an unexpectedly healthier ego. Surgeon two didn't fill me with hope, but his approach was more cautious than surgeon one's.

This felt like the biggest decision I'd ever had to make. However, underneath it all was a simple question: did I have to *like* my surgeon? I mean, they did not have to be my friend, but did they have to at least be friendly? I didn't know.

I gave myself the night and the next day to think it over. Ian and Kim, free from any ill-feelings towards surgeon two, felt that he was the way to go. Mum and I were leaning towards surgeon one (and his smile). Sana said she'd back me either way.

Despite my initial misgivings, in the end we opted for surgeon two and the one-stop-shop for cancer. In my scientific career I valued experts and I wanted as many as possible working on the most important issue to me: keeping me alive. Perhaps I would grow to like the surgeon, or perhaps it didn't matter. The quick surgery and rapid recovery being offered by surgeon one was seductive, but surgeon two wanted a lot more data before committing to a treatment plan. I didn't understand exactly why, but I figured more data had to be better. Surgeon two obviously knew things I didn't.

•

A few days after my appointment at the cancer hospital, surgeon two called me.

'Look,' he began, 'we had the multidisciplinary team meeting today and the radiologist spotted something on your CT scan. It looks like your sigmoid colon is hanging lower in the pelvis than it should be.'

'Okay . . .' I said.

'This could be normal for your sigmoid, or the tumour may be sticking to another piece of bowel and anchoring it down there. To have a better look, we need you to have an MRI as soon as possible,' he said.

An MRI produces highly detailed pictures by using a magnetic field and radio frequency pulses to measure tiny differences between hydrogen atoms throughout the body.

'Oh, wow, okay,' I replied. 'But I thought the tumour was just in the sigmoid?'

'Look, we aren't sure what's going on yet. The tumour may have grown outside the sigmoid and invaded the rectum. If the MRI confirms this, we'll need to treat this cancer very differently.'

It felt like another loop-the-loop was approaching. I wanted off the roller coaster.

•

I had a few days before the MRI, so I used that time to brush up on the anatomy of the human bowel. So far, I'd been getting by on what I remembered from high school biology classes and what I'd learnt about the digestive systems of carnivorous animals from my zoology degree. It was time to make sense of my bowel.

I learnt that our digestive system is like a continuous tunnel that runs from the mouth to the anus. There are a few offshoots, like the liver, gall bladder and pancreas, but the rest of it forms one long conveyer belt of food, fluids, bacteria and gas. The bowel begins at the base of the stomach and ends at the bum. The small bowel is three to five metres long and absorbs ninety per cent of food; the large bowel, or colon, is only a metre and a half long – its main job is to absorb water and salt back into the body. The first section of the large bowel is called the ascending colon (named because it travels up the abdomen). Next are the transverse colon and descending colon, which then becomes the sigmoid colon. Last is the rectum, and very last are the anal canal and anus.

My tumour was in the sigmoid colon. I read that the sigmoid colon is S-shaped, folds back on itself and can move around, unlike other parts of the bowel which are anchored in place. This now made surgeon two's worry about the location of my sigmoid clearer. The last part of the large bowel is the rectum, whose job is to hold poo before it is squeezed out on the toilet. All these bits seemed important, especially the last bit.

What happens once these are cut out? I wondered.

The results of the MRI scan had far-reaching implications for my treatment. It showed that my sigmoid was stuck down in the pelvis and unable to move. The tumour had grown so big that it reached from inside the sigmoid through the bowel wall, and had attached itself to my rectum.

The tumour hadn't stopped there.

The scan showed that it was really close to my bladder, and closer still to my vas deferens – a tube that carries sperm from the testes. Worse, a seminal vesicle, a semen-producing gland tucked between the bladder and rectum, already had the tumour in it. A lymph node near the tumour also looked suspicious. This dodgy lymph node scared me the most. Cancer uses the lymphatic system – a network of tubes and ducts that collect waste throughout the body – to colonise other organs. Could my cancer have already spread?

Now that the rectum was involved, surgeon two wanted to treat me as though I had rectal cancer. Rectal cancer is still bowel cancer, but trickier to cure.

To give me the best chance of living a long life, surgery, chemotherapy *and* radiation therapy would be needed. Quick surgery and a rapid recovery was no longer an option. I needed a lot more treatment, and it would take a lot more time.

Before I could start radiation, the team wanted to double-check that I only had the one tumour – the MRI had spooked them and they didn't want any more surprises. They did this by sending me off for a PET scan, which is one way to look for small tumours that a CT scan or MRI may miss.

Tumours, busy trying to grow as fast as they can, light up in a PET scan. For my scan, a radiation therapist poured a metal flagon of radioactive sugar into a jug of water and handed it to me. I drank the whole jug and then spent an hour lying as still as possible. Tumours need lots of energy to grow, and so they suck up more of the radioactive sugar than the tissues around them. The PET scan sees where the radioactive sugar has accumulated because the sugar emits radiation that can be measured.

With great relief (again), my PET scan did not find any more tumours. This was the last test needed to be confident that I had only one tumour – but with the new information from the MRI, I was now classed as having a late stage cancer, stage three.

•

It was now a month after my colonoscopy. Surgeon two's plan was to start me off with six weeks of combined radiation therapy and chemotherapy. The chemo would be low dose, just enough to weaken the tumour while the radiation cooked it from the inside. The goal was to kill as much of the tumour as possible before going in for surgery. After surgery, I was to carry on with four months of high dose chemotherapy.

For now though, I had a couple of weeks before radiation and chemotherapy started. This was my last chance to live normally, before I officially became 'a cancer patient' and before any side effects emerged.

After a month of only thinking and reading about cancer, I picked an action novel from Graeme's bookshelf to read. I jogged in the mornings and meditated in the afternoons. Over turmeric smoothies, Sana and I planned out the rest of the year: staying at Mum and Graeme's place, Sana finding a job, my treatment. But as the radiation and chemotherapy start date approached, tension was rising at home.

At that dinner the day of my colonoscopy, Graeme had spoken of the need to fight, of 'going into battle against cancer'. His way of viewing cancer treatment didn't sit well with me, but it showed that he thought cancer was a big deal. These war metaphors became fewer, and within a couple of weeks, he spoke as though I had been diagnosed with a bad head cold only. I started to really resent this view.

Sana and I spent as much time as possible out of the way, but things came to a head anyway. One afternoon, Graeme sat us down to speak about taking on more of the household chores. We were picking up after ourselves, but the recent collapse of my world as I knew it meant that I wasn't doing as much as I could to help.

Then Graeme's speech took a turn for the worst, taking on a my-house-my-rules tone. It was a talking-to that made me feel eight years old, not twenty-eight. I badly wanted to point out that his sons, sixteen and twenty-five years old, contributed less than we did – but I was conscious we were only guests in Graeme's home, using a landing at the top of the stairs as our bedroom.

'My head is all over the place at the moment, I'm sorry,' I said.

Graeme was impatient, but Sana and I could handle it – we had bigger issues. Plus, I wanted to be physically close to Mum. The way forward was for us to bunker down and ride it out, but conflict in the house continued to escalate. Graeme wasn't just butting heads with us, he and Mum started to fight.

They had been planning a month-long trip to India when I was diagnosed with cancer. Graeme's visa forms were completed and ready to submit, but Mum wanted to delay the trip because their flight would leave the same day I'd start radiation and chemotherapy. Graeme wanted to go anyway.

One Saturday, while Sana and I were watching TV in the family room, Mum and Graeme's arguing about the trip to India exploded.

Sana and I agreed that we needed calm, not crazy. And not just because I was about to begin treatment, but for Sana's sake, too.

Sana had always been independent, but she'd recently found herself in a country where she had no friends or family, living under someone else's roof among strangers. Mum and Sana were slowly getting to know each other, which was already complicated because I was sick and neither of them wanted to make the other feel awkward. Added tension with Graeme complicated their relationship further.

There were simply too many adults under the one roof. Everyone reacts to cancer differently, but some react better than others and the house was becoming a hotbed of tension. So, we made the decision to find our own place and started looking immediately.

With no savings, furniture or references, our options were limited. But we found university accommodation in Carlton, a short walk from Melbourne's most famous strip of restaurants and eateries, and a twenty-five-minute walk to the hospital. Despite its location, the apartment was cheap and came furnished.

It had been empty for weeks because it was directly opposite a cemetery – the Chinese and Korean students who preferred this neighbourhood were too superstitious to overlook all that death. Their superstition was our lucky break.

We packed the suitcases we'd brought from China and moved in as soon as the paperwork was signed. Mum lent us bond money and filled bags with spare pots, pans and linen from Graeme's place.

We moved in a week before radiation started; Mum and Graeme went to India.

6

RADIATION AND
ALTERNATIVE ENERGY

To work, radiation must get from the machine to the tumour.

Radiation beams pass through everything and anything on their way to the cancer, and beams scatter and bounce around inside the body. This means that radiation can result in collateral damage.

While female pelvises are larger and shallower to accommodate birth, male pelvises are narrow and deep and jam-packed with anatomy. There's the sigmoid, rectum, bladder, prostate, penis and seminal vesicles, plus nerves, blood vessels and spermatic cords passing through it. So getting maximum radiation to the tumour and minimum radiation to everything else requires careful planning.

I was due to be zapped every day for six weeks, hitting the tumour with a bit of radiation each day. To know where to point and shoot, complex maps were made of my pelvis. Then, I was marked with a series of small, permanent tattoos. These tattoos worked like GPS coordinates for the radiation machine, helping it fire radiation right at the tumour every single time.

Six weeks after my colonoscopy, Sana and I set off from our tiny apartment to the hospital for the mapping and tattooing.

'Slow down!' said Sana.

I hadn't even noticed I was five paces ahead of her. If it were up to me, we'd have jogged to the hospital. I was itching to get treatment started and these scans were the first step. Every other scan until now had been aimed at understanding my cancer, not attacking it.

I'd been living with knowledge of my tumour for six weeks. That was only a fraction of the time that I'd had it. (The first bud of colon that would become the tumour probably sprouted five to ten years earlier, the doctors told me.) But I had been oblivious back then. I'd now seen a picture of the tumour and it had been poked, biopsied and scanned using CT, MRI and PET. I knew exactly where it was inside me.

I wanted it out of me, gone. It was everywhere I was – whether I was eating breakfast, jogging, talking on the phone, having sex. It heard everything I heard and saw everything I saw. It hadn't been invited into my world and it wasn't welcome. We cut diagonally through Carlton Gardens, an expansive park containing Victorian fountains, flowerbeds, lakes, heritage buildings and the Melbourne Museum. Normally, I'd have stopped several times to admire certain trees or point out interesting insects to Sana – not today. I tried slowing down for her; she tried speeding up for me.

At the hospital, the therapist told me to take off everything and put on a hospital gown. This was fine – I was getting used to taking off my pants for strangers and being prodded. One way to examine for bowel cancer, for example, is for a doctor to put their finger inside your bum. I'd also become fast at stripping down and throwing on a hospital gown.

Despite being one-size-fits-all, hospital gowns are not designed for people two metres tall – when I wear a hospital gown it looks like I've tried to wrap myself in half a pillowcase. They only just reach my thigh, and the partial open back becomes a very open back, plus bum. Worse, they expect you to walk, sit down and climb around in these things. I entered the scan room carrying a plastic basket of clothes in my left hand, while my right hand pinched the gown closed over my bum.

I lay facedown on a table in the middle of a large, cold room. The doughnut-shaped CT machine sat at the end of the narrow table I was lying on. The walls were bare and the lighting dim, giving the equipment an eerie glow.

Four (four!) radiation therapists positioned themselves around me. One used markers to draw crosshairs at different locations on my lower back. My eyes were still adjusting to the light, and for a second I felt as though I was in a B-grade science fiction film about to be experimented on by aliens.

The poor therapists tried to keep my gown closed above and below the points they were marking, without success. Each time they moved or adjusted me the gown sprang open in an entirely new spot.

Adjustment, more gown loosened, new crosshair drawn, re-scanned, more gown loosened: this went on for what felt like hours, but was only forty-five minutes. For each new sweep of the CT machine, I raised my arms above my head. The generous mid-thigh cover provided by the gown disappeared each time I lifted my arms, exposing my bum. Defensively, I slid my arms out of the gown so that it wouldn't move each time I put my hands above my head.

It was then time for the therapists to address the elephant in the room: my scrotum. My testicles would be in the radiation firing line and I had so far received mixed messages about whether they would be permanently cooked. Would I be able to have children in the future? No one knew for sure. To minimise the amount of radiation they received, one of the therapists explained a sophisticated safety technique to me.

'Reach round, grab your scrotum from behind and pull down as hard as you can.'

While trying to achieve this awkward pose my gown fell to the floor. A therapist lunged towards it, but I waved them away with the free hand not gripping my balls. *Why bother?* I thought.

I was now buck naked, trying not to fall off my precarious perch; pen marks all over my back; my hairy bum on display; and my dick squished between me and the very hard (and very cold!) table. One arm was above my head and the other was between my legs trying to yank my scrotum to my knees. *All right already, you win, cancer!* I screamed inside. I couldn't have felt more vulnerable if I'd tried. Once the tattoos were in the right place and sufficient scans had been done, I was free to scurry out of there and change back into my clothes.

I knew that being drawn on, tattooed and scanned over and over again were vital to ensuring that my tumour got hit with as much radiation as possible. It was also routine for the people at the hospital. It was clear that I was just another body for the professional team of radiation therapists to work on. While they were focused on their task, they were friendly and polite and showed some sensitivity. Yet the experience left me with more than just permanent tattoos. Each time I had to undress for this, or lie down for that, my mind returned to that day, and I was fearful I would end up being that exposed again. I carried the rawness I felt that day for a long time after the event.

It occurred to me much later that I often went into a procedure or treatment with little knowledge of what to expect and how I might feel. 'We're going to do scans and put small tattoos on you for radiation' in no way prepared me for the nudity and embarrassment I ended up feeling. Likewise, concluding the session with 'All done, you can head out and change into your clothes' did little to help me process having to part my legs, reach behind and pull on my balls in a large cold room full of strangers. While hospitals had become very good at treating people, their treatment *of* people was not nearly as effective.

•

I didn't trust the highly sophisticated grab and stretch system developed to protect my scrotum from radiation. One doctor in my treatment team had warned me that I was certainly going to lose my fertility. I had no idea whether or when I wanted children, but I liked the idea of having the option. So, prior to my radiation therapy, I deposited semen at a sperm bank.

This was yet another ridiculous conversation I had to have with Sana only six months into our relationship.

'So, do you want kids?' I asked her.

'Excuse me?' She looked shocked.

'I'm going to deposit sperm either way. I know we have no idea what the future holds, but now is a good time as any to chat about it.'

'I'm only twenty-three!' she said. 'I've also never seen myself as the mum type.'

'I'm not saying we make a baby now, I'm not sure I even want kids either,' I said. 'Actually, I don't even know if I'll be alive in a year's time, it's stupid to talk about this now.'

And so we didn't.

Instead, we made our way to the andrology unit so I could deposit some sperm. Andrology is the brother to gynaecology, making andrologists specialists in male reproduction, especially storing and analysing sperm at places called andrology units. This is important to know because the terms Spank Bank and Wank Bank do not appear on hospital floor plans or directories. Inside the cramped andrology office, I nudged Sana and pointed to a room about a metre from the front desk where I was filling out paperwork.

'Imagine if that's the room,' I whispered.

'That would be one awkward wank,' she said.

We laughed. We stopped laughing when the receptionist handed me a cup and pointed to the room.

I locked the door. Even with the door closed I could still hear the receptionist on the phone. *If I can hear everything out there,* I thought, *they'll be able to hear everything in here.* My stomach dropped. This was not conducive to an erection.

I tiptoed across the room and sat down, the vinyl armchair squeaked loudly. *Shit, they'll know I've just sat down.* I glanced around the room. It looked like it had been decorated using the Spring 1948 issue of *Nursing Home Digest*. The chairs were old and covered in beige vinyl; the walls were also beige. A laminated set of instructions (everything in the room was wipeable) stuck to the wall told me what to do and in what order. A sad set of drawers contained old male and female pornography magazines and a few DVDs. The only items in the room manufactured after 1970 were the DVDs and a TV in the corner. There was no laminated instruction sheet telling me how to work it so I gave up after a few minutes, and then panicked that I was taking too long.

After the quietest ejaculation in history, I exited the room and took the single step needed to reach the reception desk. I filled out more forms, answering questions like 'How much of the sample missed the cup?' and 'In the case of your death, what do you want us to do with your sample?'

'How long can the sperm last in the deep freeze?' I asked the technician who came to take my sample away.

'Ten years,' he said.

•

Eight weeks after my colonoscopy, my pelvis had been mapped, my skin tattooed and my sperm frozen. It was time to treat.

Radiation is invisible – for the first couple of weeks it felt like nothing was happening.

After lying down (and stretching my scrotum) on the radiation slab, the radiation machine above me buzzed, emitted a laser-like sound, then moved around me to zap again. Each treatment took less than a minute – the longest part was waiting for the lift down to the radiation bunker and weaving through the labyrinth of thick-walled corridors leading to the machine. Radiation treatment is always at ground level or underground – heavy concrete walls up to a few metres thick are needed to prevent radiation escaping.

The radiation machine was enormous, with a large base supporting a rotating head and three arms. It looked heavy, and moved liked it was. Lying on the table facedown, the head and arms of the machine hung above me like the claw of a giant skill tester. In some ways it sounded like one too, all mechanical whirs and beeps.

Over the six weeks, radiation became my routine.

Neither it nor the low-dose chemotherapy I was having at the same time caused any side effects. My skin didn't burn from the radiation and I didn't vomit from the chemo.

I did get tired halfway through, and then very tired towards the end, but if not for that I wouldn't have known I was having cancer treatment at all. This helped me regain some confidence that my body was going to cope.

My confidence didn't last long.

•

I went into cancer treatment as a person of science. I had been trained as a scientist and worked as a science communicator. I liked evidence and data. But people who are very sick, and sometimes dying, often choose to ignore expertise, evidence and treatments that work. Instead, they opt for alternative therapies that might meet their emotional needs, even though these therapies are backed by little more than anecdotes at best, and outright deception at worst. People do this because they are scared, feel alone, and are desperate to stay alive. Doctors are often oblivious to this.

As my surgery approached I grew increasingly scared. I found myself drawn to treatments that had little evidence of success in a bid to take back control of my body and do something that would help me beat this disease. This spiral away from science reached the point where I considered abandoning the conventional treatments that my head told me would save me, but in my heart terrified me.

The radiation had damaged the tumour somewhat, but the surgery to remove it was still epic. Given my floppy sigmoid, invaded rectum and proximity of the tumour to my bladder, the doctors were asking me for consent to remove all of the above – if needed.

There was a chance I might not survive such invasive surgery, but even if I did, it had the potential to leave me with erectile dysfunction and two bags permanently hanging off me to collect urine and faeces. These possibilities had propelled me headfirst into exploring other therapies like meditation, acupuncture, energetic healing and juicing. These had given me a sense of power over my body, as though I could have an effect on the outcome of my cancer – that it wasn't in the hands of others alone. These other strategies also have next to no side effects (except a lighter wallet).

Over my four years in China, I'd walked past a thousand Chinese medicine shops and never entered one. Plenty of my colleagues and friends had used traditional medicine. But I never did. Now, I was curious.

About halfway between my apartment and the hospital was a traditional Chinese herbalist who also did acupuncture. When I entered the shop, the smell sent me back to Beijing. Chinese herbs, en masse, have a distinct aroma: a mix of sweet soil and warm compost that hangs in the air, enveloping the nose but not overwhelming it. The doctor, Jack, was sitting behind a glass counter, wearing jeans and a polo shirt and smoking a cigarette. What was left of his hair had been dyed jet black, just like my neighbour back in Beijing. We exchanged pleasantries in Mandarin, before switching to English to talk about my cancer.

He asked about my appetite.

'How much do you eat for breakfast?' Followed by, 'Do you urinate often during the day, and what colour is it?' Jack wanted to know about whether I woke up feeling recharged in the mornings, and whether my hands sometimes felt cold. He felt the pulses in my wrists for several minutes. I left with three bags containing a bespoke mixture of twelve herbs, with names like sang ji sheng, yi mu cao and dang shen. These three bags equalled three days of 'treatment'. Each day, twice a day, I was to boil the contents in water and drink the resulting tea. The Chinese doctor said that these herbs would help me better handle the life-saving treatments I'd received at hospital.

Like a good patient, I cooked the herbs on my stove twice a day, in the morning and evening. The tea they resulted in tasted earthy and bitter – it was unpleasant, what I imagined boiled swamp water tasted like. Our small apartment quickly took on this scent, as did the corridor. Luckily, all our neighbours were Chinese and Korean students, so I didn't need to worry about complaints.

The herbs and acupuncture were expensive. I only had acupuncture once a week and I couldn't afford fresh herbs every day. Sometimes, I'd re-use the herbs for a second or even third day. I didn't tell Jack.

Kim was trying her best to help me from Sydney, where she was busy working for a big corporate company. She'd tracked down an energetic healer not far from me and paid for a package of sessions. I was sceptical, but the sessions had cost Kim a lot of money, so I went along.

Tanya's house was on a quiet, leafy street. The hallway inside her front door served as the waiting room. It smelt like fresh fruit salad. Gentle harp music wafted from speakers. A pile of soft, colourful cushions gathered in one corner. Small pink and purple crystals dotted the room, and a large salt lamp glowed from atop a side table. Its orange light warmed me from the inside whenever I stared at it, which was often.

As I followed Tanya into the treatment room I noticed that her left shoe was bigger than her right one, with a sole about double the thickness. The walls of the treatment room were covered with diagrams of the human body with lines indicating supposed pathways of energy flow.

Tanya explained that she used a 'hands off' method and asked me to lie on a table, fully clothed, in the middle of the room. I closed my eyes while she suspended her hands over my abdomen. I felt that this was bullshit. After a few minutes she asked me questions. Why did I think I had cancer? Did I find it hard to let certain emotions go? What was my childhood like? Did I feel loved? I answered her questions as best I could: some cells mutated and became a tumour; no; it was hard at times but I'm okay; definitely. I didn't feel any different after the first session, or the second. By the third session, I was sobbing as she moved her hands above me.

As Tanya and I got to know each other, we shared more. She told me about her own experience with a tumour in her leg and the multiple surgeries needed to cure her. She was supportive of my cancer treatment, and like the Chinese medicine doctor, wanted to support my body, and mind, through it. I told her about my childhood, how it had been hard moving around so much and how Mum, Kim and I had often been let down by people Mum had trusted, even loved. I opened up about Sana, how I wanted to be the best boyfriend in the world to her, but that I could be snappy and moody, leading to guilt and regret. During particularly heavy conversations, Tanya asked me to take my attention and burrow into my bowel, right up to the tumour.

'I want you to really feel this mass,' she said. 'Then will it away.'

I was sure the energetic healing wasn't doing anything, but I loved these sessions and continued them for months. The whole experience, from the waiting room to the table and then leaving back out the front door, was full of warmth and care. Tanya didn't just give me permission to be in my body and explore my mind, she encouraged it. I spent hours lying on that table, sometimes talking, sometimes listening. I still don't know if Tanya's hands changed anything inside me, but spending time with her definitely did.

●

Six months after my colonoscopy, and with surgery just a couple of weeks away, I met with surgeon two and a nurse in a small, crowded room at the busy cancer hospital.

'Can't you just take the colon, or rectum, and leave my bladder alone?' I pleaded with them. 'Let's delay the surgery. I promise to spend the next six months working out, drinking Chinese herbs, juicing and meditating.' I made this plea because I was petrified.

My team didn't like the direction this was heading – they looked me straight in the eye.

'People who try these methods always come back to us crippled by pain and by then it's too late to save them,' my surgeon said.

'It's normal to be scared,' the nurse jumped in, 'you're facing the pointy end of treatment now.'

Their opinion was clear: you have cancer and we have the treatments that cure cancer.

But I needed to feel like I was contributing, that I was playing an active role in my treatment. Besides, what else was I going to do? I had appointments once a week. How else was I going to fill my time? It made sense to do everything in my power to help the outcome, which was to stay alive.

In the end, I agreed to follow my doctor's treatment plan and consented to them removing any organ they needed to. I still did other things – meditating, drinking apple cider vinegar, and eating a vegan diet. I also continued to see Tanya, the energetic healer, and Jack, the Chinese herbalist. These gentle treatments seemed a universe away from the sickness and pain of chemo and surgery. They gave me hope.

I didn't abandon medicine, I just wanted time to try other things before conventional treatment started. Many people do walk away though. I've met a couple of them, but sadly, they aren't alive anymore. I tried to find data on just how many people abandon medicine but once these people opt out of the medical system, they are impossible to track. The few studies I did find tended to group complementary and alternative therapies as the same thing, even though they aren't. All the things I was trying to do outside the hospital were supposed to help, or complement, whatever treatment I was getting inside the hospital. An alternative treatment is just that, it's either one or the other.

There were lots of complementary therapies offered inside my hospital too, like massage, music therapy, meditation and exercise. In contrast, alternative therapies – things like chiropractic, high dose vitamins and homeopathy – operate far from the medical world.

People who had left mainstream medicine often told me that the alternative therapies were harmless, but that isn't true. Complementary and alternative medicines aren't regulated in the same way as conventional medicines, and very few treatments have been subjected to rigorous scientific analysis. Plus, these treatments can interact with conventional medicines, which is a significant issue for people undergoing cancer treatment.

My two treatment worlds came crashing together during chemotherapy when I was asked to stop drinking Chinese herbs and swallowing antioxidant pills. The herbs contained all kinds of chemicals that could have interacted with the chemotherapy, and antioxidants can actually undo the benefits of chemo-therapy and help the tumour fight back.

The people selling and promoting alternative treatments rarely discuss all the risks, especially the biggest risk of all – missing that small window of opportunity to hit a cancer with the best treatment possible, which is usually aggressive chemo, radiation or surgery. This is what surgeon two feared most in that meeting with me: that I had crossed over from doing things that would *support* his treatment plan for me to doing things *instead* of his treatment plan.

I stuck with medicine, but this conflict opened my eyes to the kinds of things that medicine can't offer and that may have benefits. Even though some treatments might not help people medically, they can help their spirit, sense of purpose and need for control. I was so scared in the lead-up to surgery that avoiding it started to feel like the only option. I longed for my friendly Chinese doctor, Jack, throwing herbs into paper bags, and more sessions with Tanya where we shared our stories. Back at the hospital I just wanted somebody to say, 'I know this sucks, and I know it's scary. Here's what we think you should do. What do you think about that?'

And, luckily for me, at that tense meeting with the nurse and surgeon two, that's just what they did.

7

THE POINTY END

The circles and arrows were dotted across my abdomen like a crude map. I traced the thick black lines, each one a different future.

One circle marked the hole that would divert faeces into a bag attached to my abdomen after surgery. The plan was to have this reversed in six months, once my large bowel healed – but there was a chance it could be permanent if the surgeon couldn't save enough rectum and anal canal.

Another circle showed the best spot to put a hole to collect urine. No one knew if this hole would be needed yet – whether the tumour was too close to the bladder wouldn't be clear until mid-surgery – but if it was, it would be permanent.

After months of discussing the surgery, Sana and I stared at this diagram on my stomach. She climbed up onto my hospital bed and we hugged. Visiting hours were up in fifteen minutes, but I didn't want to let her go.

'I'm doing the right thing, yeah?' I asked.

'Of course,' she said.

'And if I end up with nerve damage and impotent, what then?' I said.

'We'll cope. I'm not going anywhere.'

'Six months ago we couldn't keep our hands off each other. And now we're talking about what happens if I can't ever have sex again,' I said.

Sana lifted her head from my chest.

'We'll be fine. We'll deal with whatever happens, together.'

A nurse brought my first dose of laxative – my bowels needed to be empty for surgery – signalling that it was time to go it solo. I was on the home stretch and this last night was mine alone to face.

My water jug was removed from my bedside at midnight – the final fast before surgery had begun. Diarrhoea, thirst and fear kept me company until the morning.

•

I spent five hours on the operating table.

I emerged from surgery feeling that no time had passed, and for a second, like nothing had changed. And then I saw all the tubes coming out of me.

There was a narrow tube coming out of my neck, stitched to my skin. A longer tube started in a box attached to a pole and then disappeared behind my back. Another entered the bend of my elbow, attached to large clear bags hanging beside me.

I looked under the covers. Brown pigment had been painted from my chest to my thighs – a white rectangular dressing started above my ribs and ended at the base of my penis.

A tube emerged from a hole in my abdomen, collecting something dark and gooey from deep in my pelvis. A catheter carrying urine exited my penis and was attached to a bag somewhere below the bed. Two bright orange sticks, like fluorescent spaghetti, were sticking out of my penis too.

A bulb of pink small intestine poked through another hole in my abdomen, covered with a plastic bag to catch poo – this was my stoma; it looked exactly like the ones in the booklet I'd been given.

I'd been expecting the stoma – but I was yet to work out what the rest of my attachments were. I counted only one bag stuck to me – did this mean I'd kept my bladder?

Mum and Sana were brought in.

'The surgery went really well,' Mum said, through watery eyes.

'You didn't lose your bladder,' Sana added, knowing what I'd been most worried about.

They said that the doctors believed they'd removed all of the cancer. Apart from a partial vasectomy, because the tumour had grown too close to one of my vas deferens, everything had gone to plan: I'd lost a seminal vesicle, my sigmoid, rectum and some descending colon only. The vasectomy was no big deal because my attempts to pull my scrotum away from the beams during radiation treatment had not worked – all of my sperm-making cells had been destroyed. I was already sterile.

Mum and Sana stood a foot back from the bed. Sana glanced from tube to tube, afraid to get any closer. I manoeuvred my right hand towards her, she moved closer to hold it. She felt clammy, giving me a sense of how she'd felt the last five hours. Then Mum moved closer and gave my other hand a squeeze, still wiping her tears.

•

Recovery was slow.

The long tube that seemed to disappear behind me was an epidural. It entered my lower back and delivered pain medication to major nerves, numbing my abdomen and pelvis. The tube was stuck to my skin, but its tip – buried somewhere near my spine – moved if I moved. I realised that rearranging the pillows propping me up, or reaching to scratch a knee, caused the tube to move. Small shifts in its position meant the anaesthetic hit a different part of my spine, changing where I was numb. I couldn't feel the tip moving, only the aftermath.

When the band of numbness moved, the hurt was laid bare. The pain started deep in my pelvis, so deep that it felt below the bed, perhaps even beneath the floor. The ache began to limp around down there, building up to something broad and intense. It then became heavy and round: I couldn't tell where the pain started and stopped, I couldn't feel its edges.

Finding a position on the bed that blunted the pain, and then remaining frozen in that position, became my only goal. All other thoughts retreated into a blur – the radiation, nearly losing my bladder, returning to China, family. The pain consumed me. My life became an anticipation of the next hit of anaesthetic to my spine and the next round of pain tablets. I grew short-tempered and intolerant. I would snap at Sana, Mum, nurses. Pain does that to people, even nice people.

The most important goals after abdominal surgery like this are to eat, defecate, urinate and walk. These tasks, done mindlessly before surgery, now took effort.

The ability to eat and defecate was the crucial test for whether my digestive system was working. The gut really dislikes being poked by surgeons, and cutting it open can send large sections into a kind of paralysis called ileus. The need to go slow with food after surgery was paramount: too fast and I risked overwhelming the gut, causing a blockage and possibly damaging the surgical handiwork. My diet was slowly increased each day, from sips of water to clear fluids, thicker fluids and then actual food.

This slow and steady approach also gave the stoma time to get its act together. By detouring faeces, the stoma allowed the large bowel to heal properly. Sections of bowel that were cut and joined back needed time to fuse before they could handle faeces – otherwise, they risked bursting open and leaking it into my abdomen.

The bladder, like the bowel, doesn't like surgery either. Simple urinary catheters, like the one inserted during my surgery, aren't risk free – they can make the bladder lazy. Passing lots of urine after surgery would be a good sign that my bladder's ability to store urine and then release it hadn't been compromised. Before I could stand up and pee, though, I needed to be able to get off the bed.

Nurses told me that I needed to try getting out of bed as soon as possible. Getting the lungs upright improves breathing and opens up sections that can get boggy when people lie down too long. In those first few days, just getting up felt like a serious workout. I puffed with weakness and held on to anything I could reach, as I didn't trust my body. Any kind of movement, even taking two steps to a chair, would also reduce my chances of getting blood clots or having bits of bowel stick together. Why sections of bowel end up stuck together, called adhesions, after surgery isn't clear, but they can form U-bends or narrowing in parts, which can cause blockages later. Worse, they can lead to chronic pain.

Some of these reasons to sit out of bed and get moving were explained to me, some weren't. I like having a goal to work towards and taking advice from experts, so it might have helped if I could have understood all of this at the time. But the combination of having a bunch of surprise tubes sticking out of me and bad pain traipsing around my pelvis meant that the normal me was not around.

I resented being asked to get up, especially when I had just found a position on the bed that kept pain at bay. Those moments of relief were precious – they were the only times I could sleep. Getting sleep had become as important as avoiding pain. They were linked: sleep wasn't possible when the pain was bad. Two nights after my surgery, I gave up trying to sleep and instead moved to the chair. I spent the night there, neither more or less comfortable, but at least free from the expectation of sleep.

Each day, without warning, someone would appear to remove a tube sticking out of me. The tube in my neck was the first to go. I held my breath while the nurse carefully unpicked the stitches holding it in place. Later, the fluorescent spaghetti sticks were pulled from my penis. They had been inserted through the bladder and up into my ureters, the two tubes that carry urine from the kidneys. The spaghetti sticks had acted like high-vis cables during surgery, so the team didn't accidentally cut the ureters while trying to remove the cancer. I couldn't feel the nurse pulling them out, but I was in awe of how long they were.

The catheter came out next, and the tense wait to see if I could urinate began. Drink and wait; wait and drink. I smiled during that first wee, overcome with gratitude for my bladder. As uncomfortable as things were, I still had my bladder. I swore to never take simple bodily functions for granted again. I pushed the nurse call button, looking proudly at my first jug of urine. *What a symbol*, I thought, *of amazing medical research and surgical skill.* My greatest fears and hopes rippled across its yellow surface.

A nurse with gloved hands entered my field of awe and brought the jug to eye level. 'Good,' he said, and walked off. I heard him pour it down the toilet, and then anticlimactically shuffle off.

Of course, the nurse didn't know I'd spent weeks stressing over this moment. Nor was he around when I guzzled bitter Chinese herbs or cried alone in the shower. He probably didn't even know that I had consented to have my bladder removed during surgery. His job was to check that I had emptied my bladder – one of six bladders he was keeping an eye on that morning. A boring task for him perhaps, but one steeped in importance for me. The tubes were removed day by day, until I was left with only one in my arm. Getting to the chair and walking became easier – I no longer needed help carrying tubes and bags, or pushing IV poles. One lap around the ward became two and then three.

'You're doing really well,' said a nurse, each time I passed the nurses' station.

Then, suddenly, a week after surgery, I stopped doing so well.

I wasn't getting stronger. I grew tired, my face paler. The other three patients in my shared room got better and left. Not me – I was stuck, and getting worse. I didn't understand why, and neither did the doctors and nurses. Mum and Sana grew frustrated.

'Something's wrong. What time is the doctor coming?' asked Mum.

'We never know, they just turn up,' said Sana.

My stomach decided that it no longer needed food – I started gagging after the first mouthful, every meal. Unwelcome waves started in my abdomen and moved up into my stomach. My oesophagus, throat, tongue and cheeks joined in until I retched and heaved. Nothing ever came up, but not from a lack of effort.

These attacks were loud. The thin hospital curtain pulled around my bed did nothing to conceal the sound. I used one hand to protect the large wound running down my front, hoping to catch my intestines, which I was sure would erupt from it at any moment. My other hand held a sick bag over my mouth, catching spit and tears.

Mum had finally convinced Nan and Pop to come to Melbourne. One lunch they watched me gag until they could no longer stand it.

'We better give you some privacy,' said Pop. 'We'll go to the chapel and say a prayer for you, and come back tomorrow.'

This continued every breakfast, lunch and dinner for more than a week. I sent trays of uneaten food back to the kitchen, struggling to even drink water. I began to fear mealtimes. Mum brought my favourite foods, even fast food or chocolate – but everything triggered dry-retching. All the drama upstairs distracted me from the mess downstairs: my stoma was not behaving. After surgery like mine, the small bowel is supposed to start reabsorbing extra water and salt because the large bowel is on holiday. My small bowel had either not got the message or it didn't care – litres of green salty water passed right through it every day into the bag attached to my abdomen. I was taking the maximum amount of antidiarrhoeal medication, and still at risk of dehydrating. A new tube was inserted into my arm and I was given bags of fluid.

I didn't need to be a doctor to understand that if I was losing stuff out of one hole (my stoma) and not putting anything in the other hole (my mouth) that I was going to struggle to get better. I eventually lost fourteen per cent of my body weight, about twelve kilograms.

'Your skinny jeans are now baggy,' joked Sana.

Being healthy prior to surgery (apart from cancer) meant that my body was compensating and coping, but only just. According to blood tests the nurses took, I wasn't in the danger zone from malnutrition, but I was heading that way. I barely sat out of bed now. Hot flushes attacked from nowhere – I broke into a sweat day or night.

When I developed a fever, it became clear what was wrong: I'd sprung a leak. The surgery to remove the tumour from my large bowel was complex, and so was the plumbing solution that followed. Once the tumour and the tissues around it had been removed – in my case my rectum, sigmoid and some of my descending colon – tumour-free bits of bowel had to be sewn back together to create a seamless pipe. I had just enough anal canal left to attach the large bowel, and plenty of large bowel left to create a little cul-de-sac to replace my rectum.

Once the anal canal and large bowel were stapled together, the surgical team looked for any leaks or holes. This is critical – although the stoma will divert faeces, a small amount may still reach the large bowel. Moreover, the large bowel will continue to produce mucous, shed cells and house bacteria – toxic if leaked into the abdomen.

Checking for potential leaks in the bowel is done the same way a bicycle tyre is tested for leaks, using water and air. The pelvis is filled up with fluid until all the joins are submerged. A gas is then pumped inside the bowel. An intact bowel won't let any gas escape; any bubbles that form in the fluid indicate a hole. The hole can be repaired straight away, but holes can form later too, as the bowel is healing.

Getting a hole in the large bowel after surgery is a risk, but not a common one since surgeons started using stomas to divert faeces. Holes still occur in around nine per cent of patients though.

Unfortunately I was in that nine per cent. My fever was from an infected abdomen, caused by gunk that leaked out of my large bowel through a hole that formed in the days after surgery. The leak halted my recovery, prevented my small bowel from reabsorbing extra water, and made me too sick to eat.

I was rushed to the X-ray room and a dye was injected into my anus. I lay on my side, knees to my chest, under the X-ray machine. I watched dye swirl around my large bowel, in real time, on a screen in the middle of the room.

'There's the hole,' a doctor said, pointing to the screen. 'The good news is that it's almost healed itself, you won't need surgery.'

Instead, I was given antibiotics and a new tube. A rectal tube was inserted into my bum to drain gunk from the healing hole, anchored in place by an inflated balloon. It dangled from me like a smelly tail, attached to a bag to catch waste. I kept this bag strapped to my thigh, terrified the tube would get snagged on something and be yanked out of my bum. The rectal tube had to stay in place for a couple of weeks, even if I got well enough to leave hospital and head home.

I started eating, tiny amounts at first, then gorging on the chocolate bars Mum had been bringing in. My strength returned – I resumed laps of the ward. At first I walked in between Mum and Sana, worried I might fall.

'Nice to see you up and about again,' a nurse said, as I passed her desk.

•

The week before the leak was diagnosed was increasingly desperate and dark – not just due to the physical symptoms.

I felt that I'd been left to languish, and I was frustrated that I didn't understand what was happening. I felt that the doctors and nurses started to see me more as a problem, and less as a patient. Worse, no one seemed to be caring for me as a whole person.

The hospital did a good job of diagnosing and treating the leak eventually, but the setback had affected more than my body.

Behind my physical recovery from surgery, much more was going on.

I had spent nearly a month in hospital by this time and had come to know the staff well, and the view outside my window more so. The days had grown fuzzy. Stretches of boredom were punctuated by having my heart rate or temperature checked, meals arriving, watching the bathroom be cleaned, or Mum visiting.

At first, getting acquainted with my stoma had kept me busy – learning to empty it, measure the amount of liquid, change the bag. But even that had quickly become boring. Everything became predictable, except the one daily event that carried the most promise: the morning ward round.

I never knew precisely when it would occur, only that it would be far too early in the day. On most mornings the sun was barely up when the curtain would be pulled back, revealing my surgeon with a group of mostly strangers. They would be talking to each other. I usually understood about every third word. Suddenly, they would ask me questions. They would ask about the fluid coming out of my stoma, and if I'd farted. They would ask why I wasn't eating much. Someone would be writing things down; another would be on a laptop. The group was usually restless and distracted. I'd be asked if I had any questions for them. I would invariably lie and say no. They would then move away as one, responding to a signal I couldn't see or hear – the whole thing would be over in a minute.

This was how my day usually started in hospital. It's how most patients in hospital begin every day – at the mercy of the ward round. Patients – sleepy and confused, with unbrushed teeth and messy hair – stood over by healthy senior and junior doctors in positions of authority with perfectly combed hair, makeup and ironed clothes.

I began to resent the ward round during my month in hospital. I felt like a kind of intruder propped up on display. The hospital is the doctor's workplace after all – I was just visiting. There were actually lots of things I wanted to say and ask during ward rounds, but I got the sense that I was not supposed to take up too much time. I was also confused about which topics were up for conversation. Each morning, words would make their way to the tip of my tongue and then stop.

One recurring question I wanted to ask, but never did, was about my future and whether I was going to have terrible pain. I had become afraid of pain, partly because I had wrestled with it (and lost) in the week following surgery, but partly because of a man who spent time in the bed next to mine.

About two weeks after my surgery a man in his eighties, with thick grey hair and a thicker Eastern European accent moved into my four-person room. Pain kept him awake most of the night. He would repeatedly ask to see a doctor and beg them to euthanise him.

'Please, it hurts,' he'd say. 'I want to die, I want this no more.'

The medicines were no longer controlling his pain and his lung cancer was too advanced for further treatment. He was dying, it hurt, and there seemed to be little anyone could do.

After two nights of hearing him beg to die and then cry himself to sleep I started to panic: what if my pain never went away? What if I didn't get better? Was I going to end up like this poor man? I was supposed to have spent only five days in hospital, but I'd been there for weeks. The leak had not yet been diagnosed and I was getting sicker each day and couldn't eat.

The infection from the leak attacked me during the day; this man's wailing pain attacked me at night.

One morning, a few days into the man's stay, a ward round took place with more people than usual, perhaps around ten as opposed to the typical three or four. When they reached me, a woman I'd never met stood in the front row and scribbled on a notepad. My surgeon asked the usual things about the stoma. They looked at a computer screen. The woman lowered her notepad and with a tone reflecting her status at the front of the pack said, 'You need to start eating or we are putting a nasogastric tube in.'

The crowd shuffled to the next patient.

I'd seen what I assumed were nasogastric tubes in people around the hospital. They were white tubes coming out the nose, taped to the cheek for safety. I didn't know what they were for, nor did I want to know.

I'd also heard a few nasogastric tubes being inserted. As I now thoroughly understood, hospital curtains did little for privacy. Inserting the tubes seemed to take an eternity, mainly because of the loud gagging and horrible slurping that accompanies the tube's journey up the nose and down to the stomach. Sometimes it sounded like the patient was drowning. The tubes would get stuck on the way down, coiling in the back of the throat. Sometimes the only fix was to pull it out and start again, kicking off a new round of gurgles. I learnt to dread the nasogastric tube.

Of course, the woman from the ward round didn't know any of this. Nor did she know that I'd spent the last few nights next to a man weeping in pain. I appreciated that the ward round team didn't have time to sit down with me and unpack my understanding of what was happening to my body or how hospital was affecting me, but to use this valuable communication opportunity to imply I was choosing not to eat seemed grossly unfair. To feel ignored while suffering is one thing, to feel blamed for that suffering is another.

I later learnt that the woman was a hospital manager. To her, I wasn't a young guy with cancer and a life on hold, weak and confused, growing increasingly scared about a future dominated by pain and nasogastric tubes. To her, I was the problem in bed fifteen. The hospital needed me to eat so I could be sent home, but her message that morning lacked any compassion.

I didn't feel like a person, I felt like a problem.

I'd been reduced to a tumour and a surgery. At some point in the delivery of healthcare, they had forgotten I was a human. This depersonalisation is one reason that so much of a patient's experience in hospital is ignored. If you aren't inserting a nasogastric tube into an actual person then the need for that person's privacy won't be front of mind. If there are no other people, only patients, in the room when you do that, then why would you need to worry if anyone hears it and gets freaked out? And if you're addressing a problem, and not a person, you can threaten to insert a nasogastric tube without thinking twice about how a patient may be affected by that threat.

•

The shortcomings in my care, as perceived by a patient in pain and fear, were balanced by fantastic parts of the health system. Like the nurse who delicately explained how I could still have sex with a stoma bag attached, and the speed with which I was shuffled from radiotherapy to surgery to chemotherapy. However, the real touches of humanity often happened outside the patient–nurse or patient–doctor relationship. Like the porter who wished me luck when dropping off a meal, the cleaner who sung while wiping down the shower, or the person who guided me through meditation. There seemed to be a whole ecosystem of people in the hospital that remembered they were contributing to the care of people, not problems.

One of these people was Anne, a music therapist. Anne was part of a team who regularly performed music on different wards. On my ward, Anne usually set up just inside the door to our room.

She invited song requests, using the contact to strike up conversations with patients about musicians they liked. After playing a few songs she'd wheel her keyboard around IV poles and wheelchairs and perform for other patients down the hall.

Two weeks after my surgery, it was my one-year anniversary with Sana. We were a universe away from where we had expected to be on this special day. Instead of eating at our favourite restaurant in Beijing and boating around one of the city's lakes on a humid summer night, I was stuck in hospital on a cold Melbourne winter's day.

I didn't know where home was anymore, and Sana was a long way from hers. But we were together, and we had been through a lot in a short period of time. This was never going to be a fancy anniversary ending in hot sex against a hotel window high above the city, but it remains a deeply romantic and memorable one.

Anne and I hatched a plan. She'd come by when Sana was visiting that afternoon and play for us. Finding a song that Sana and I both knew that Anne could play proved tricky. Most of the patients were many decades older than me and tended to request songs written well before I was born. The music favoured by the clubs of Beijing was either outside Anne's repertoire or didn't translate well to a cancer ward.

Anne suggested 'The Rose', a song made famous by Bette Midler in 1979. Mum had played it often when I was little.

'That's perfect,' I said. 'I've ordered a dozen roses for Sana today.' When Sana arrived she smiled at the bouquet waiting for her.

'You're the one with cancer, in hospital, and somehow *you* organised roses for *me*,' she said. 'I love you.'

Anne arrived and set up on the other side of the curtains, so we could be alone. As she played Sana climbed onto my bed. The curtains did little to block the rest of the hospital out, but with them closed it still felt like our own little world. Cancer disappeared for those few minutes, and we held on to each other with all the strength we had left.

8

THE BLUNT END

If surgery is the pointy end of treatment, chemotherapy is the blunt end.

Eight weeks after surgery and four weeks after I left hospital, I started chemotherapy. The plan was to have it over three days every two weeks, for four months. Each cycle started with a day at the hospital, having several medicines slowly pumped into my arm. Then, a bottle of takeaway chemo was attached to a tube in my arm – over the next two days the bottle slowly delivered more of the cancer-busting drug. The bottle, about the size of a baby's milk bottle, went everywhere I went – bed, the grocery store, jogging.

Some types of chemotherapy target the tumour only, others activate the immune system – but my chemotherapy was old school. My medicines didn't only hurt the tumour – healthy bits of me were affected too. While this is a blunt attack, it is still clever: delivering just the right amount of chemo to inflict maximum damage on the tumour, and minimum damage on me. Chemo was wild.

I took steroids to control the nausea and vomiting from chemotherapy, which they did well – I only vomited once during those four months. But the steroids caused insomnia and made me anxious. I'd get waves of guilt about crimes I'd never committed but wondered if I would.

Many nights I'd be wide awake at 2 am, contemplating what to bake. Cooking and baking were how I distracted myself from the racing thoughts that never seemed to slow. Would chemo work? Would I get better? Would Sana get fed up and leave me? Being busy kept these questions at bay.

The baking wasn't just about being busy – I was always hungry. Again: steroids. I left hospital twelve kilograms lighter but put fifteen kilograms back on within weeks of being home.

Other medications in my chemo sent the nerves in my fingers, toes and mouth into a frenzy. When I touched anything cool, my fingertips would sting as if they were being screwed tight from the inside. Even drinking room-temperature water was like trying to gargle thumbtacks. Food straight from the fridge? No way.

This mostly resolved after I stopped chemotherapy, but not all of it. As I type this, a decade after my chemo, my fingertips still feel a bit numb. My toes feel worse, as if I've spilt superglue on them. At the same time as blunting the sensation in my feet, the chemo damage makes walking barefoot on roads or gravel painful. Walking outside feels like walking across a sea of ants, biting the soles of my feet.

The celebrity of side effects during chemotherapy is hair loss. In film and television, cancer patients are always bald. My chemotherapy didn't cause hair loss so I never really looked like a cancer patient on the outside. At most it caused a mild thinning – which my thick head of hair could tolerate and my hairy bum appreciated. Chemotherapy makes you feel blah – a mix of tired, poorly and just plain off. It would start during the infusion, build over the next week and then disappear in time for the next infusion.

While the medicines exhausted me from the inside, the schedule of infusions, blood tests, chemo bottle changes, maintenance of the tube in my arm, and medical check-ups were also demanding. I just wanted to lie in bed and eat chips all day long, and some days this is all I did.

Then, a couple of weeks after leaving hospital, I forced myself to start jogging again. I'd read research showing that exercise helped cancer patients cope with fatigue and other side effects from chemotherapy. My doctors encouraged me to keep jogging – the days of ordering cancer patients to rest in bed are long gone. Exercise has also been shown to reduce the chances of cancer coming back. So much of this experience felt out of my hands but this was one thing I could control.

My favourite place to run was the Melbourne General Cemetery across from our apartment. This enormous graveyard opened in 1853 and was one of the first to be designed as a public park, with tall trees, colourful gardens, winding paths and areas to rest. It was a beautiful, quiet and reflective spot to run.

After my usual circuit – forty-five painful minutes grunting from the Jewish section through Church of England, Roman

Catholic, Greek Orthodox and Chinese sections, and back – I'd pause at different graves, noting the occupant's name and age. Here, I'd get contemplative, as people tend to do in cemeteries. What had killed that person at fifteen years old? And this one at seventy-five? I wished their families had included this information on the gravestone for curious passers-by like me. Then I'd reconsider – would I want cancer to get the last word on my gravestone? Probably not, best to keep running.

At first, I worried that exercising in the cemetery was disrespectful, but I was quiet, avoided grieving families and stuck to the track. Plus, I was unlikely to offend the full-time residents. This worry was in vain – perhaps it was the bag of faeces bulging from under my running top, or the bottle of chemo taped to my arm – but no one said anything.

I actually felt safe among all the death in the cemetery. It helped me think about my own possibly imminent death and how people would react.

I thought of Kim, busy organising her wedding to James in Sydney later in the year, and how I didn't want to mess up her plans. I wondered about Ian and whether he'd be lonely if I wasn't around. I chuckled to myself, thinking that Mum would probably have to nag Nan and Pop to get the flight down for my funeral. Above all, I never stopped thinking about Sana. She had been there every step of the way, the idea of leaving her hurt the most.

The preoperative radiation and chemo had effectively shrunk the tumour, which had then been cut out in surgery. According to my team, I didn't have any more cancer. The long stretch of chemotherapy after surgery was given just in case – to mop up any rogue cancer cells or tumours too small to be seen on imaging.

This three-pronged plan gave me the best chance of surviving. Even so, my tumour had been advanced so my odds of living as long as the next five years were not much better than a coin toss – between fifty and sixty per cent. (Cancer survival rates and probabilities are calculated five and ten years from diagnosis.)

Death was on my mind all the time, and I became comfortable thinking about it. I didn't *want* to die of course, but a familiarity settled over me. This wasn't something I could talk about with anyone except my psychologist at the hospital. I'd started seeing her during radiation therapy, to help make sense of my diagnosis and everything that I was feeling. I tried to keep regular sessions before and after surgery, and even took Sana to one session so she could offload on someone.

Bringing up the idea of my death with anyone but the psychologist was tricky. This didn't feel like the kind of thing I could burden Kim or Ian with, and when I tried to bring it up with Sana she looked at me blankly – Sana shuts down when overwhelmed by a topic. Mum was the opposite – she'd start crying before my first sentence was done and then change the topic.

My death daydreams were mine alone, and the cemetery was my safe space to indulge these feelings.

•

As my chemotherapy neared its end date, I was beginning to think differently about life. And to help me along, the universe provided me with another scare just in time for Christmas.

Chemotherapy ended the week before Christmas, eleven months after my colonoscopy. But I needed one more scan before I could get excited about the holidays. Sana and I borrowed Mum's car – an old convertible – so we could swing by a mall afterwards and pick up some last-minute gifts.

This was my first CT scan in months. Now that treatment was over, this scan would check whether cancer had come back in my large bowel, or if new cancers had appeared anywhere else. We didn't speak on the drive to the hospital – I stared at the road, keeping both hands on the steering wheel; Sana stared out the side window, fidgeting with her seatbelt.

After the scan, Sana suggested we put the roof down. The sun on our bodies felt good and the wind made our hair dance – it was hard to stay sombre.

'I hope we get the results soon,' Sana said, raising her voice to be heard over the wind.

'It'll be at least a few days, I reckon,' I said.

A minute later my phone rang. Sana held it to my ear.

'Hi, am I speaking to Benjamin?' asked the caller.

'Yes.'

'I'm a radiologist looking at your scan. I'm afraid I need you to come back to the hospital.'

I looked at Sana, mouthing, 'Put it on speaker!' Her hand shook.

'What, like right now?' I responded.

'Yes, it would be best for you to come back straight away. There are no new tumours, but there are several large blood clots in your lungs and we need to start treatment.'

Sana watched my face, hers in a deep frown.

'Okay, I'll turn the car around and come back,' I said.

'You may need to stay for a few days for observation,' the radiologist added. 'Head straight to the ward – they are expecting you.'

I turned down a small street and stopped the car. As the roof was closing, I turned to Sana and hugged her.

'No more cancer,' I said.

'That's amazing. But that doctor sounded worried about these clots, let's get back to the hospital.'

•

Back on the ward, I was asked whether I'd ever had blood clots in my legs. No. Had I noticed swelling or pain in either leg? No. Had I been feeling short of breath? No. Dizzy? No. Any chest pain? No.

'You've got four large clots in your left lung. We get very concerned about clots like these,' the doctor said.

When my clots formed was unknown, but they were stuck in a mid-section of the left lung.

'You'll need to stay on a blood thinner for at least twelve months,' the doctor said.

'A whole year?' I replied.

'Unfortunately. Twice a day for the first three months, then once a day,' the doctor told me.

The blood thinner came in a syringe and had to be injected into my abdomen, thigh or bum. A nurse arrived with a box of syringes.

'Do you want me to show you how to inject him?' she asked Sana.

'Oh god!' Sana said, shaking her head. 'No way.'

The nurse chuckled.

'It's fine, I can do it myself,' I said.

Sticking myself with the needle wasn't the worst part – the medicine going in hurt more, stinging and burning the area, causing a bruise. Clots are a common side effect of both cancer and cancer treatment. Cancer cells release chemicals that cause clots, attack blood vessels and interfere with regular blood cells; cancer treatments like chemotherapy and surgery cause clotting because they increase inflammation and directly damage the body. When combined, these factors mean that people with cancer are four times more likely to develop a blood clot than other people, and account for twenty per cent of all clots found.

A haematologist I saw when the hospital reopened after Christmas was angry. She believed that cancer patients needed anti-clot medicine *before* they got clots – to prevent them forming in the first place. After all, she explained, one of the main ways people with cancer die is from blood clots like mine.

I injected myself for a whole year – the sting of the blood thinner a reminder that I had got too close to death for a second time. I felt like I was back at square one, having treatment and worried about getting sicker. But I was again lucky that a scan had picked up a big problem, before it became too big.

9

FALLOUT

The emotional fallout from cancer started the day I was diagnosed.

Cancer's impacts spread like a wound, inflaming old tensions and carving out new ones. Those closest to me were hit first. Later, other relationships were affected. At the centre of this wound was my relationship with Sana. We'd only known each other for five months when I was diagnosed with cancer. What had been a fresh and young relationship quickly warped into something old and tough, like a fibrotic scar that's had to give up its essence. Our young love didn't disappear altogether, but it had to mature very quickly. We became fused, in another country and in someone else's home, navigating a serious disease that endangered both of us by threatening to remove one of us.

Initially, we were dependent on other people for everything. I had no savings, job or insurance. Sana had little savings and no job either – she arrived in Melbourne on a tourist visa. I didn't own a car to get to appointments, let alone an apartment we could have moved into.

There were always plenty of cars around if I needed to get to the hospital though, so we were privileged in that sense.

Between appointments and tests we set about securing independence. My business in Beijing was still in its infancy and I had not yet drawn a salary from it. Plus, I didn't know how much actual work I was able to do – cancer had become a full-time job. The demands of treatment, tests and scans escalated alongside side effects like fatigue and nausea. Sitting down and working on the business was becoming impossible.

I applied for government support without realising the application process was itself a full-time job. The forms were some of the longest I'd ever seen, outdone only by longer wait times at my local welfare office. I found the support system hostile, peppered with small reminders that they didn't really want to help me. The whole thing felt like work, which would have been okay if the welfare payments resembled anything close to the amount earnt when actually working a regular job.

I didn't qualify for a disability payment (cancer is not disabling I was told) and was siphoned into the temporary payment given to people while they look for work. Don't worry, they told me, I didn't need to look for a job – another stack of paperwork for me and a doctor could be completed if I was too sick to go to job interviews. This extra paperwork had to be repeated every three months. Last, to work out whether the government could give me even less than the normal payment, itself below the minimum wage, they checked that no one else was helping me. Any money that Sana earnt would be deducted from my payment.

All of this felt like being kicked, while already down. The setback of getting cancer felt as though it was going to be made worse by money troubles, not only tomorrow, but further down the track. I didn't know when I would be able to work again, and Sana's visa status was impermanent. Mum helped out, but we didn't want to put any stress on her relationship with Graeme, meaning we felt that accepting more help from her would be awkward. Sana's family were far away in Canada.

The fastest way for Sana to work was under a working holiday visa. To apply for that she had to first leave Australia, file the paperwork, and then re-enter once approved. So, two months after first arriving she took herself back to Beijing on the cheapest flight she could. She spent the next two weeks packing up her Beijing life, undergoing requisite medical tests for the visa and saying goodbye to friends and colleagues. When she returned to Melbourne, she found work as a news producer. Any money she earnt slashed my welfare support, so Mum, Kim and Ian helped out again.

In addition to our meagre single income in Melbourne, we were bleeding rent in Beijing. An expat friend of a friend was subletting my apartment there, but soon stopped paying rent or answering my calls. *Who reneges on a cancer patient?* I thought, indignant but unable to do anything about it. While waiting for him to make contact I covered the rent. An email two months later informed me that he'd moved out. He never paid me back, and I never heard from him again.

Tim, my business partner in Beijing, was doing his best to keep our science communication dream alive. Tim is funny as hell, with good looks and a really big heart. In photos his smile forms a giant rectangle, like he's trying to create a window into his chest so people can see how big his heart really is. We had been friends for years, and he dealt with my sudden absence from Beijing well and continued to grow our reach among scientists and journalists in China.

Two months after my diagnosis he booked a trip to Australia to see his family. I asked if he was also coming to see me in Melbourne.

'No,' he said. 'I just won't have time.'

I was confused and hurt – Tim was a reflective guy who often used his spare time to help others. Couldn't he see I needed help? After our call I sent him an email asking him to reconsider and let him know that I was upset he was planning to skip Melbourne. I explained that even the shortest time spent with him would be enough to lift my spirits. I also asked if there was a reason why he had not planned to visit in the first place. *There must be something I'm missing*, I thought.

Three days later he replied, explaining that the cancer thing had really shocked him, and still did. He felt awkward at the idea of seeing me face to face – every imagined scenario involved him not knowing what to say so his instinct was to avoid me. I did my best to reassure him that I wasn't *that* different from the person I was before. A week later he rearranged his schedule to squeeze in a forty-eight-hour visit.

Tim's visit was one of my favourite moments that year. Among so much distress and upheaval, we hung out like old mates and made the same jokes we'd made for years. When things got really tough during treatment, I would draw on memories from that visit. I'd try to distract myself from pain by remembering sneaky beers we'd sipped in the sunshine. When lying in bed, anxious from steroids and panicked about sleep, I thought of how we'd chatted so easily about cancer.

As we said our goodbyes at the airport, he paused, looking at me intently. He grew serious and I braced for something heavy. Instead, he said, 'You may have cancer, but you're still the same dickhead!'

Tim went back to Beijing, but didn't last long. A few months later, he called it quits. He missed his family and wasn't enjoying running the business alone. What could I say? I had no idea when or if I would ever get back to China, and the business was largely based around me and the network of scientists I'd met over my four years there. Between the guy renting my apartment absconding and Tim resigning, it was clear that my time in China had drawn to an end. So, Tim and some friends packed a few sentimental items for me and sold the rest while I emailed our clients and explained the business no longer existed. Cancer hadn't killed me, but it had certainly killed my life in China.

Later, it dawned on me that perhaps I'd been hurt by Tim's avoidance of me because it mirrored my own angst: I really wanted to avoid cancer too. I was very familiar with avoidance – I'd spent twelve months pretending nothing was wrong with me before the colonoscopy.

All my plans – growing the business, cultivating new friendships, perhaps starting a family one day – dissolved after my diagnosis. I now had only one task on my to-do list: don't die.

My external world closed in as my internal world opened up. I became better connected to my body, and more in touch with its healthy and unhealthy parts. After years of worrying about a flat stomach, I accepted that it would never look that way after surgery. I took time to sit still and think – building my day around my own needs and less about what others expected of me. In this way, it was a selfish time – but it had to be. Things that didn't contribute to staying alive became less important. For the first time I viewed life through a laser-sharp lens. It was easy to determine what really mattered: relationships, love, joy and contentment. Nearly everything else was noise. Realising this was a kind of freedom.

But remaining free was hard.

Watching my friends and family get on with life was difficult. Each Instagram and Facebook post about travel, promotion, engagement or pregnancy was a reminder that I occupied a different world. It felt unjust, and that sometimes led to self-pity and despair.

I was lucky to have people around me who noticed when I was hurting and reached out to help. One friend put together a high fibre recipe book so I could look after my large bowel; another entered a fun run to raise money for cancer research. Kim was paying for the energetic healer and visiting Melbourne every month or so. Ian was paying for acupuncture treatments and came to stay with us for a week at a time, sleeping on a blow-up mattress in the corner of our small apartment. Mum was always dropping off jugs of pomegranate juice and taking Sana and me out for nice meals. Some friends travelled to Melbourne to visit me; others that couldn't sent books. Love came from all directions. And the most love came from Sana.

At twenty-three, she had become a carer, breadwinner and counsellor. For our first six months in Melbourne, Sana worked in breakfast television, her alarm going off at 1.15 am. By 2 am she was in the office. Out by 10 am, back in bed by 5 pm to do it all again the next day. The hours were brutal, but they allowed Sana to come to nearly all my medical appointments – spending hours by my side during chemo.

My insomnia meant that I was often awake to see her off at 1.45 am. I used the sleepless nights to bake muffins for her to take to work, hiding little love letters in her Tupperware. It was the least I could do – I had dropped her in this mess five months into our relationship, and she had dropped everything to help me. Sana and I were still getting to know each other, and I couldn't shake the feeling that I'd hijacked our relationship. I felt guilty, but also insecure. While mixing muffin batter late at night, I'd wonder if Sana wanted to be with me or felt obligated to because I was sick. When these worries overwhelmed me, I'd bring it up with her.

I gave her several genuine opportunities to leave – no hard feelings. A get-out-of-jail-free-card, I called it. I acted light-hearted, but my anxiety that Sana felt trapped by my cancer was serious.

Sana never wavered. From the moment I called her in Beijing to tell her I had cancer, she was loving and focused. She was amazing. There were times during cancer when I was not nice to be around. Sometimes this was because of discomfort, sometimes it was my resentment at having cancer. I could be snappy and demanding, lashing out over her shoes in the hallway or some other trivial thing. Carers get a raw deal – all the attention was on me, but who looked out for her?

Despite my moods, she remained steadfast in her support.

She was next to me when I got scared. She was there to hand me wipes when my bag leaked in bed, spilling faeces onto our sheets. She stood up for me when a taxi driver yelled, complaining of a smell coming from me – it was the rectal tube I was sent home with after the hole had been found. People congratulate me on how well I coped with cancer, but Sana is the real hero. That's not to say that I couldn't have done it without her, I just wouldn't have done it as well.

•

It took a year but finally my cancer was gone. With chemo finished, we could get on with our lives. Sana had exhausted journalism opportunities in Melbourne and wanted to move to Sydney. Moving away from Mum and my treatment team, still with a stoma and injecting myself twice a day with blood thinners, was a small price to pay. I felt like I owed Sana big time.

Leaving Australia and heading back to China was not an option – she'd turned down a big job there a year ago and my business had folded. Plus, I needed to remain in Australia for check-ups every three months.

We moved to Sydney in the autumn of 2012, into a small one-bedroom, half-underground flat in the city. I started applying for science communication jobs, hoping to return to the old me, and got the first role I interviewed for.

It was okay for a little while, and then it came crumbling down. It wasn't cancer this time, it was me – and in order to rebuild, I was going to need to lean on Sana, again.

10

STARTING OVER

Cancer took everything I was and whizzed it in a blender. Old ideas smashed into new feelings. The original me was sometimes recognisable in this new smoothie, but there was no going back – it is impossible to unmake a smoothie.

I was wide awake one night, three months into chemotherapy, at 3 am. I'd said goodbye to Sana an hour earlier, sending her off to the morning breakfast show she worked on, with the pasta and banana bread I'd cooked at midnight. For fifteen minutes I walked a loop from the bedroom to the lounge room and back. In our small Melbourne apartment that loop was twenty-two steps. My muscles were tingling. Tension spread all over me, as though each cell in my body was fidgeting.

I'd had my sixth chemo infusion two days earlier and hadn't yet crashed. The delicious steroid that blocked any nausea and helped me gain the weight I'd lost after surgery had really been messing with me that round. I wondered if a jog would help, but it would be pitch black in the cemetery across the road. I had decided to keep walking from the bedroom to the lounge room and let my thoughts jog instead. One idea kept racing around my mind – it had popped up a couple of days earlier, while I was lying in hospital attached to bags of chemo. The idea was so absurd that I hadn't told anyone. It was very different from my normal ideas and I was sure people would laugh.

There had been no lightbulb, no ah-ha moment. The idea just appeared. While watching the chemotherapy enter my arm, and waiting to feel like crap, it suddenly appeared between drips of life-saving medicine.

Drip . . . drip . . . drip – *I should become a doctor* – drip . . . drip . . . drip.

Huh, I thought, *that could be cool.* No rush of happy hormones had followed – I didn't even feel like sitting up. I kept watching the drips, waiting to feel sick.

For two days the idea had hung around, but not forcefully. Now that I was alone, doing laps in my lounge room in the middle of the night, the idea that I should become a doctor had become loud. It was all I could think about.

I peeled off during a loop and sat down at my computer, typing 'How to become a doctor' into Google. I clicked on links that explained the admission test and how to ace medical school interviews. I learnt that a medical degree was just the first, small step. More sites explained the actual work of doctors and how training was done in different specialties. Overall, becoming a doctor seemed like a lot of effort.

Even the first step of getting into medical school seemed hard. The day-long, marathon admission exam – the GAMSAT – was only held a couple of times each year. The test was expensive, and the scores needed to get an interview went up every year.

I found a sample practice test online. If the example questions had me totally stumped, I told myself, I would drop the idea. I expected the test to start with questions about science or medicine, but instead the first section reminded me of high school English. One question presented a poem and then asked about the use of metaphor. I grabbed a notebook and began scribbling answers. The sun was due to rise, and I still wasn't sleepy. Later in the exam a quote from a philosopher sat next to a related cartoon. A series of questions probed the 'creator's intent'. The questions in this section were dense, but I didn't feel too out of my depth.

The second part of the exam was an essay. The questions here again reminded me of high school English, a subject in which I'd done well. I jotted down the outline of an essay and moved on to part three of the exam – this was the science section. The biology questions were manageable, but the physics and chemistry questions had me stumped. I skipped several of those.

I looked at the clock, I'd been wrestling with the practice test for over two hours. I'd got less than a quarter of the questions right. The actual exam was nearly six hours long. *This is too much hard work*, I thought. Also, I already had a degree from the University of Queensland and one from the Australian National University, and a career (albeit on hold). Why start again?

I deleted the practice test and closed my laptop. I tore out the answers in my notebook and threw them in the bin. Becoming a doctor had hit a dead end. My tingling legs had grown heavy;

my eyes dry. The first signs of dawn emerged from behind the tall, gnarled trees that kept watch over the cemetery. Finally, I was ready for sleep.

•

My new job in Sydney was with the communications team at a neuroscience research centre. The research was fascinating and I quickly learnt a great deal about diseases like dementia, Parkinson's disease and schizophrenia.

It was nice to think about something other than cancer. I still had my stoma and bag, and I had to inject myself twice a day with blood thinner because of the clots in my lungs. The thumbtacks in my mouth had faded, but my fingers and toes still tingled. I still felt like a cancer patient as I took my broken body off to work each day.

A stoma can be messy business. My bag would sometimes fill up quickly with faeces or gas without warning. Unlike my regular bum, I had no control over the stoma: everything that made it to the stoma continued into the bag – it had a mind of its own. I could be in the middle of a meeting and it would start bubbling diarrhoea into the bag. Or it would dramatically fart, filling up the bag until it was rock hard like a helium balloon. One time the bag fell off in the middle of a busy footpath and poo ran down my leg.

Emptying the bag was tricky, and changing the bag even trickier. Bag changes required several components – like a plastic bag, wipes, new bag, scissors and medicine to protect the skin from digestive acids – which I kept in a kit concealed in a desk drawer or work bag. Juggling these in a regular bathroom cubicle was a nightmare, so I often sought out disability toilets for the extra space and shelves. Having a sink close at hand was also necessary because for the minute it took me to change between the old bag and new bag the stoma still ejected faeces. In fact, it often felt like the stoma chose these moments to do just that, catching me unaware and without toilet paper ready. After this battle with the stoma and runaway poo, sometimes I'd exit the disability bathroom to a disapproving look from someone waiting to use it. To them, I looked like a regular arsehole using a bathroom not meant for me.

My stoma and I never settled into a comfortable routine. I always found it difficult. This is not the case for everyone – many people get comfortable and go about their lives normally.

So, ten months later, when my surgeon said that it was time to have it reversed I was over the moon. I hadn't accrued much sick leave in the new job, so I promised my boss that I would work as soon as I was out of hospital and resting at home. I went down to Melbourne for the procedure and, despite another infection, it went well. The excitement of finally being able to use my bum blinded me to how hard it was going to be.

My bum was not the bum I remembered. Unsurprisingly, it had de-skilled while on holiday for ten months. It was now easily overwhelmed by eating too much of the same thing, eating too much of anything, not eating enough, skipping a meal, or catching gastro.

My guts were noisy too. For reasons I've never been able to work out, my intestines still occasionally generate a loud gurgle that resonates deep in my pelvis – like two elephants rumbling to each other. It comes without warning and repeats every few minutes. It's so loud that other people hear it. 'Whoa, you must be hungry,' they say, but then add, 'Or did you eat the wrong thing for lunch?' Embarrassed, I tell them I'm hungry and change the topic.

My new bum was also weak. I'd lost my rectum and sigmoid – these are very helpful holding pens for faeces. To replace these as best they could, the surgeons constructed a J-pouch for me – a kind of cul-de-sac out of large bowel – but it lacked the professional experience of my original rectum.

A weak bum is a leaky bum. Initially, it leaked a lot. Leaks could be easily managed at home, but I had to take precautions when I was away from home. A good day meant I could get away with a panty liner, a bad day would require a full nappy.

I was constantly worried about leaks because I wasn't always aware when I had one. This created anxiety, which was relieved only by frequently heading to the bathroom to check my underwear.

In my job at the neuroscience research centre, I worked in a kind of shipping container while a state-of-the-art research building was constructed next door. The container had very few windows and was always stuffy. I had to weave through half-a-dozen desks to get to mine in the back corner. This was the worst place for someone with a leaky bum to sit, but I didn't complain. I spent a part of each day worried that my bum was going to explode either at the desk or while I was awkwardly power-walking past my colleagues to the bathroom, butt cheeks clenched as my last line of defence. Sometimes I didn't make it in time. I began keeping deodoriser in my desk drawer and once all my colleagues had left for the day I would drown my seat in it, hoping to mask any smell, and my embarrassment.

•

After several months at the neuroscience centre I grew restless. This was more than jumpy legs and tingly toes from chemo-therapy: something was afoot. I had stopped enjoying the job, and wasn't having much fun outside of work either – my jogging had dropped off and I wasn't cooking much. It was getting harder to get excited about stuff, especially the future. I began to worry that the old me, the one before cancer, wasn't going to return. I also worried that the cancer would come back.

I floated through life, not really living. It felt like I was waiting to feel normal again. I wanted to be light and fun, not distrustful and cynical. *It must be this job*, I concluded, and so set about looking for a new one. If I could get back to something connected to animals, I thought, I would be happier.

I landed a dream job with a big environment charity, and was temporarily happy again. My colleagues were amazing, the office was full of plants and there were stuffed animal toys every-where. But after the initial rush of changing jobs I started to slow again. I got frustrated easily and I caught myself rolling my eyes when I was allocated more work. Everything took too much effort and I became oversensitive to feedback. This was more than the fatigue that can plague cancer patients after treatment. Something wasn't right, I was off kilter.

My mood was low. I dreaded locking in any kind of commitments, even those only a week away. And I would cancel plans at the last minute. I was supposed to catch up with friends from Beijing one night, but I cancelled only a couple of hours before. I was never invited to their place for dinner again.

Where I was heading in life seemed fuzzy and obscure – I was lost.

Less than a year into the dream job, I applied for extended leave. I asked for a few months to regroup and chill – the kind of time I should have taken straight after treatment. I'd rushed back to work too soon, and it had all caught up with me.

I began to focus more on myself and Sana. I read inspirational books and loads of science. Gradually, I resumed exercising, started cooking again and ate well. I let myself fully feel the way cancer had changed me. I started journalling, pouring what was swirling in my head into organised lines on paper.

My body looked different with its lumps and scars, and my bones felt old and tired, but something more profound had happened – cancer had changed my mind. I still valued many of the same things, but my life experience was richer now and new things motivated me.

Before cancer I'd always liked animals more than people. In fact, I had disliked people because of how they treated animals – chopping down their homes, hunting them, creating cruel farms. I'd studied zoology to better understand how special animals are; I had joined the public service to help protect them; I'd run off with the science circus and done further study to learn better ways to teach people about animals; and I'd gone to China to be part of saving an endangered species. In my work as a zoologist, I knew that people were critical to saving animals, but that didn't make me any more affectionate towards them.

Getting sick changed that. During chemotherapy I had become involved with a small charity that helped younger adults with cancer. When I'd been looking for help for myself, I'd discovered there was a gap in services for people my age with cancer. There were a lot of charities helping kids with cancer but then nothing much else until people hit their fifties and everyone is sent kits to test their poo for bowel cancer. The Cancer Council has an amazing peer support service, where people with cancer are matched to volunteers who have experienced similar cancers or treatments, but I was paired with a woman in her sixties. She was very supportive and friendly, but it was harder to connect given our age difference.

In the small charity, I helped out in the office and with events, and saw how the organisation struggled to secure funding, despite being one of the only organisations helping my age group. I met loads of other young people with careers, love lives and travel plans entirely upended by cancer. We faced many of the same challenges and were also annoyed by many of the same things: long waiting times, poor communication, people who didn't seem to care, noisy wards, a lack of privacy in hospital, communication systems based on letters and faxes. The list went on. Halfway through my chemotherapy I entered the City to Sea fun run so I could raise money for the charity. I wore a full-length orange leotard and stuck orange thongs to my head, inspired by the charity's motto 'Walk in their shoes' and ran thirteen kilometres. I was all smiles when a reporter interviewed me after the race, but spent the next four days in bed, exhausted.

I also helped other cancer organisations in Melbourne and later Sydney – sitting on committees, giving feedback on information booklets for patients, and speaking at fundraising dinners. At a medical research gala in a posh hotel in Sydney, I spoke about my cancer and how other young adults I met with cancer kept dying, despite being young and fit. The packed ballroom was dead silent during my talk. I realised that maybe people were interested in what I had to say.

I put my hand up each time the Cancer Council or Bowel Cancer Australia needed someone to speak to the media – I didn't care that every interview was about my bum. I also made myself available for research, volunteering to review funding applications and becoming a participant or advisor on everything from how lung cancer could be better managed to how to better treat pancreatic cancer.

Along the way, I started collating a list of things I wanted to change about the medical system and healthcare. And fundamental to the healthcare system, as I saw it, were doctors. To me, doctors were heroes, performing acts of bravery and skill everywhere they went. I respected them as principled sources of knowledge, but they also inhabited a separate world from me, with its own language and tools.

I could have stayed sitting on committees and speaking at events, but to change healthcare I knew I was going to have to enter it. My voice would only carry so far from the outside – inside, I would have more influence, and that meant becoming a doctor.

I thought back to the medical school entrance exam I'd attempted that long night during chemotherapy. It had been hard, and I'd got three-quarters of the questions wrong. *Cut yourself some slack*, I thought. That was without any preparation, during a mid-chemotherapy steroid-induced bout of insomnia. Maybe, with a little more effort, becoming a doctor was something I could achieve? I spoke to Sana first.

It was now three years since my diagnosis and three and a half years since we'd met. She'd already supported me financially and emotionally through cancer treatment, and then again when I needed a break from work. Returning to university in my early thirties wasn't a decision I could make alone – it affected Sana too. If I got into medical school, I would need to spend the next four years studying. Working would be nearly impossible, which meant that Sana would need to be the breadwinner again. Also, everything I'd read about medical school and medical training indicated it was brutal. The path I was proposing was going to be tough, for both of us.

Sana was such an amazing carer because of her consistency. She was always predictable and considered, and this gave me a sense of security I depended on.

One day during my break from the environmental charity I decided to discuss the idea of becoming a doctor with Sana. I prepared a picnic hamper and waited for her to finish work. It was a sunny Sydney day, a gentle breeze blew over the harbour, causing it to glisten like a carpet made of fairy lights. We headed to a little park on the water not far from our apartment. Once I had poured wine and set up the smoked salmon and olives I hit her with the whole doctor thing.

'A doctor? Really?' she asked.

'It definitely was not on the cards when you met me, but a lot has changed,' I said.

'You've been unhappy for a while. I don't know if this is what you need to do, but I think you should try.'

'But what about money?' I said.

'Medical school isn't forever. We've lived off my salary before and survived. We can do it again.'

'And what if I'm a crap doctor and can't handle it?'

She laughed. 'You survived cancer, going back to school is nothing.' The journalist in her always got to the guts of an issue. 'And maybe you'll struggle, but you'll be an incredible doctor. Your patients are going to love you.'

Talking to my family yielded wildly different responses.

'Oh god, not more university?' said Mum.

'Will you still talk to me when you're a fancy doctor?' said Nan.

'You will be excellent, just don't become too much like a doctor,' said Ian.

'Awesome,' said Kim.

•

Most people who get sick and spend a lot of time in hospital never want to spend time in one again – but now I wanted to work in one.

I thought that entering medicine would give me a way to channel all my experience with illness. When learning about a surgery, I imagined I'd remember what the staples holding my wound shut felt like. When it came time to study anaesthesia, I'd be able to draw on those first few days after surgery when the epidural kept moving and pain consumed me.

Becoming a doctor also seemed like the best way to tackle my own fear that my cancer would one day come back. I wanted to learn all about it – how doctors approached and treated it. Knowledge is power, I thought. Plus, I could help myself while helping other patients.

I figured that once I understood doctors, I would be able to talk to them about making things better for patients. I wasn't focused on the physical parts of medicine – correcting blood pressure or chopping out skin cancer – I wanted to change the parts of the patient–doctor relationship that seemed to matter more to patients than doctors: eye contact, body language, waiting areas, appointment times, communication. Hell, even greeting patients properly was a problem for many doctors. I wanted to enter healthcare to work out why so much humanity had been removed from hospitals, and how it was that patients were seen as problems instead of people.

The task before me was enormous, and long.

I was still a patient, with check-ups every few months and scans and colonoscopies yearly. My bowels remained unpredictable and temperamental, and my fingers and toes were still weird. Becoming a doctor meant I was also going to have to care for very sick people, some of whom would have cancer, probably even bowel cancer. I would meet people my age who were sick or dying. There was a risk this would upset me, but I believed I would be able to cope.

Remaining a patient would have been the easier thing to do. I wasn't as confident I would be able to handle medical school, but becoming a doctor seemed like the only way forward – I needed to try. I wanted to build on my experience as a patient with cancer and become something patients, doctors and hospitals badly needed – a patient doctor.

PART 3

BECOMING A DOCTOR

11

BAD COP/BAD COP

A buzzer sounds and I enter the first interview room. I've got two minutes before I am allowed to talk. Instead of greeting the person behind the desk I'm supposed to hand them a sticker containing my name and barcode, but my hands are shaking and I can't get one of the labels free. I scratch at the sheet with both hands, aware that I'm losing precious time. How long ago was the buzzer?

I get a label free and accidentally fold it in half as I hand it to the interviewer.

'Sorry, do you want another one?' I ask.

'No, this will do. I think you should take a seat,' says the interviewer. She salvages the label and attaches it to the top of a marking sheet on her clipboard.

I don't know how long I have left. There's no point asking the interviewer because she doesn't know either – the buzzer is controlled outside the room and there are no clocks. Plus, we aren't supposed to talk to each other.

On the desk between me and the interviewer is a written question and a photograph. 'Describe what you see in this photograph and what you believe occurred prior to it being taken.' The picture is of a uniformed soldier holding a child, a walkie-talkie to his ear. A tank sits in the background, surrounded by men in more camouflage, holding guns; smoke is rising from a distant hill. A kneeling woman looking at the child dominates the foreground, her mouth wide open, hands together at her chest.

This must be the 'reflection' question, or maybe it's the 'empathy' one, I think. *Actually it could be the 'ethical' –*

The buzzer goes off.

I have five minutes to talk. I start describing all the things I can see in the image and describing the emotions of the people within it – the soldier's focus, the child's fear, the woman's desperation. Then, after exhausting all the ways to describe a tank, I start wondering aloud about which war this –

The buzzer goes off. Time for me to rush to the next room.

I head for the door.

'Don't forget your labels,' the interviewer says.

I swipe them from the desk, and immediately start clawing to peel one off in time for the next room. I forget to thank her, or say goodbye. She doesn't notice, her head is down – ticking boxes on a marking sheet and recording my score.

•

I always had a knack for interviews – I'd got every job I ever interviewed for. But that track record meant nothing walking into the medical school interview. Most medical schools use an interview system based on speed dating – the interviewers stay seated in each room and the candidates rotate. Each room, or station as they are called, is focused on a different interview question. Medical schools love this system because it is supposed to reduce bias and is therefore more reliable than traditional interviews. Prospective students hate this system because it is terrifying.

It's a carefully and precisely controlled exercise. Once inside each room, I was allowed to make notes, but the pen and paper had to remain behind when it was time to leave – security is tight. The whole process was driven forward by the buzzer. Small talk with the interviewers was not allowed – they remain stony-faced and distant. It felt as though all the interviewers had completed identical interrogation training, and had all graduated as Bad Cop.

I walked into each station not knowing what I'd find. One station asked me to describe a major health issue in Australia, another presented an ethical dilemma about some misplaced anatomical specimens. There was the warzone photograph, plus a station on the challenges of group work. There must have been a question at one station about why I wanted to study medicine and one about the university, but I can't remember those. All that adrenaline, and racing from room to room, blurred my memory.

Afterwards, a dozen of us shell-shocked interviewees shuffled into a common room. The school organised two current students to debrief us. I put up my hand.

'What the hell was that?' I said.

The students chuckled.

'It's intense, right?' one replied. 'But it's the best way of interviewing lots of students. I don't know how many apply, probably in the thousands, but then they interview three hundred for only one hundred spots.'

'Plus, this is a model you need to get used to in medicine, it's how many of our exams are done,' the other student said.

That last point wasn't very comforting.

The first student was right, thousands more people apply to medical school than are accepted – rejection *is* the norm.

I'd done well on the marathon entrance exam (the GAMSAT) – despite only having two months between registering for the exam and sitting it. I'd spent every day of those two months summarising textbooks, writing practice essays and doing example questions.

My better-than-average marks on the science, humanities and essay sections had given me a good shot at landing interviews at a couple of medical schools. I was pleased, but this was just the first step in the long road to becoming a doctor. But I remained doubtful about actually getting in – I'd narrowed my options down to just one graduate medical school out of eleven across Australia.

We had to stay in Sydney, as Sana was rebuilding her career and working in a major newsroom. She wouldn't have the same opportunities in other, smaller cities. She'd dropped everything and moved hemispheres to support me, now it was my turn to support her. We decided that if I didn't get a spot in Sydney, I would have to rethink becoming a doctor.

There were two graduate medical schools in Sydney, but only one of them was an option for me. One school was old and famous, but a bit stuffy – it only interviewed the highest performing students from the entrance exam, perhaps the top two per cent. The other school was new, having only opened several years prior, and had a broader selection process: they considered a student's portfolio in addition to the entrance exam, as well as their previous degree and interview scores. I didn't bother applying for the stuffy school – my exam score was good, but not high enough for them. That left me only one option in Sydney.

A month after my speed-date interview, they emailed to offer me admission.

I read the letter twice, grinning. 'Yes!' I thumped the table.

It felt as though everything was falling into place. After chopping and changing jobs I had wondered if I would ever feel anchored to something again. And here I was, tied to a med school, on my way to becoming a doctor. I thumped the table again.

Sana was the first to know.

'Oh my god! I'm so proud of you. This is amazing!' she yelled, jumping up and down. 'I always knew you would get in, you were made for this!'

To celebrate, she took me to dinner at one of our favourite restaurants, a small Persian place where every inch of wall was covered in art, or artfully placed cutlery. Two saffron-flavoured beers arrived and Sana held her glass to cheers me.

'I am happy, but med school is going to be so hard,' I said, not quite tapping her glass.

'Shut up and cheers me properly, we'll worry about all of that later.' She was smiling ear to ear. I shared the news with my family the next day. I loved being able to call the people closest to me and deliver good news, for once.

'Are you sure you don't want to study back in Melbourne, close to me?' said Mum.

'I'm very proud of you, Ben,' said Nan.

'Excellent news, but not unexpected,' said Ian.

'Awesome,' said Kim. 'I'm throwing you a party.'

•

Three years after my cancer treatment, nine months after sitting the GAMSAT and two weeks before med school, Kim kept her promise and threw me a surprise party in Sydney. Sana was in London at the time, doing a master's degree, but she helped Kim and James with the guest list, inviting old friends living in Sydney, like Tim, and new friends I'd made since moving here. They decorated their place with balloons and hung a 'Congratulations' banner. Kim made everyone wear plastic stethoscopes around their necks, but the star of the show was her toddler, my nephew Hugo. He was mesmerised by the stethoscopes. He kept pushing the end into people's legs, pretending to listen to their knees. I joked to Tim that my knowledge of how to use a stethoscope was only marginally better than Hugo's.

Behind the celebratory humour I was nervous – my only experience of med school was the interview to get in, and that had stunned me. I remembered being told our exams would be conducted in the same manner as the interview. That sustained intensity worried me.

I wandered out to the backyard to catch a few minutes on my own. Kim found me.

'What's wrong, brother?' she asked.

'I don't know. I'm a bit freaked out about whether I'm cut out for med school,' I said.

'Are you kidding?' Kim replied. 'You whooped cancer's arse, and did it with a smile on your face – this is going to be way easier than that.'

I smiled at her. Kim could always be counted on for a pithy pep talk. I just hoped she was right.

12

MATURE AGE STUDENT

My first day at medical school felt like walking onto the set of a sexy, yet cerebral, reality show. All the students were smart and good-looking, with clear skin and perfect teeth. Many were the children of doctors, or lawyers, or both. They were confident. The men wore branded t-shirts, the sleeves gripping their large biceps like a blood pressure cuff. The women wore expensive activewear. It was intimidating. During my cancer treatment I had always been the youngest in the room – at thirty-two, I was now one of the oldest. Most of my classmates were in their mid-twenties.

I watched these energetic future doctors file into the lecture theatre. The air seemed to be bristling with excitement, but I felt old and uneasy. Like all good mature age students, I took a seat near the front. Pulling out a pen and paper, I realised that nearly everyone else had laptops – I was surrounded by MacBooks. I hadn't been inside a university lecture theatre in eleven years, and it showed. Suddenly self-conscious, I worried that my height was blocking the view of the students behind me. I wiggled my bum down in my seat and hunched over my notepad.

What the hell had I got myself into?

•

On day three we watched a documentary about people who had donated their bodies to medical schools. This was relevant because we'd be using real bodies to learn anatomy – often a whole body, or just a leg, chest or pelvis. The cadavers were going to be invaluable in allowing us to explore and understand the human body, to feel the liver, to see the path a nerve takes once it leaves the spine, to look at the hairs on a bit of skin overlying a tumour.

The documentary had been added to the curriculum to help us connect to the bodies because other medical schools had had trouble with students taking selfies with the bodies, or posing them in odd ways. Sometimes bits of body were stolen. The documentary was beautiful. One case study was of an older woman, dying of cancer, who had signed her body over to her local medical school. She hoped her death would help future generations of doctors. She was giving back, in the only way she could – by supporting the profession that had supported her.

Her husband sat next to her. She held his hand, explaining her relationship with her body. In a moment of seriousness, she looked off camera.

'Other than cancer, I am really healthy,' she said.

The lecture theatre burst into laughter. I jumped at the sudden noise, almost sliding off my chair. Shock turned to confusion – had I missed the joke?

It took me a few seconds to work it out: they thought this woman's comment was ridiculous. That she could possibly consider the rest of herself, the non-cancerous part, as healthy and whole, was funny to them.

It felt so wrong, so disrespectful. I didn't belong here, with people who couldn't empathise with this woman. My classmates didn't understand what it was to be sick. They had certainly never had the kind of disease this woman was talking about. I had.

How could they so easily laugh at a patient?

No one yet knew about my cancer or why I wanted to be a doctor. When they found out would they only view me as a sick person? Would I be laughed at?

The woman in the documentary and I had the same view of our bodies. A part of us was broken, but that didn't mean all of us was. To everyone else, she had sounded like a patient who didn't understand her illness. But I could feel what she was saying in my bones, and I admired her decision to gift her body to medicine.

The gap between me and my classmates felt enormous.

•

I quickly realised that in medicine, knowledge is like money: the more you have, the more people think of you. But your knowledge is always being tested.

In the few degrees I'd done before medicine, I had never felt nervous attending class. This changed at medical school. Sitting in a lecture theatre often felt like being in a firing line – at any point you could be singled out, and asked to answer a question. What is the normal diameter of the common bile duct? Does gastrointestinal mucosa comprise columnar epithelium or stratified muscularis mucosa? What is a neurological cause of hoarse voice? Which artery most commonly supplies the sinoatrial node? What are the diagnostic criteria for pre-eclampsia and what is a woman's chance of seizure?

Saying 'I don't know' was not an option. As the lecturer glared, and your hundred-odd fellow students stared, you racked your panicked brain for an answer. But neither a correct nor incorrect answer could guarantee safe passage from the spotlight. Answer correctly, and the professor might ask a follow-up question, continuing until you inevitably got an answer wrong. Answer incorrectly on the first instance, and you suffered the embarrassment of 'not knowing your shit' in front of your peers – and if the lecturer really wanted to play with you, they might continue asking ever harder questions, to ensure your ineptitude got full exposure. Frequently, I felt we were expected to know things before they had been taught.

I think this was made worse because many students *did* seem to know things before we'd learnt them as a class. I started to notice similarities about these students. Their blinkers were down and they meant business. Talking to them about anything other than medicine was hard – they just didn't watch, read or listen to much else. They were admirably hard-working but so singularly focused they seemed programmed solely for the mission at hand. I coined a name for them: Med Bots – all medicine and half robot.

'Oh my god, that's a perfect description!' said a friend after class, laughing. I wasn't trying to be mean – truly, I envied the Med Bots' concentration and memory – but I didn't want to turn into one. I felt a more well-rounded approach to medicine would be more sustainable, and effective.

But I was coming to realise the inquisition-style of teaching dominated medical school. This went far beyond Socratic teaching (a question-driven approach to learning), and most of the time it wasn't teaching at all.

In one lecture, a paediatrician fired questions at students, pointing at 'Miss Blue Jumper' or 'Mr Red Shirt'. It was frequently awkward; it was nearly always crushing. At the most extreme, some doctors lectured by starting at the front row and quizzing students in order. It wasn't learning, it was a Mexican wave of dread. As we filed out of the lecture hall we'd whisper 'Man, that was intense!' or 'What an arsehole'.

Despite incredible advancements in medicine, students were still being taught and spoken to in the same way they had been a century ago. At various points during my cancer treatment, I'd felt like the health workers around me had forgotten I was a person. I hadn't expected to feel the same as a medical student. Being called 'Mr Blue T-shirt' in a lecture theatre packed the same punch as being called 'Bed Eleven' in hospital. It seemed the same problem afflicted doctors' interactions with both patients and peers: they'd forgotten they were dealing with actual people.

There were times when I knew the answers of course, but seared in my memory are the times I didn't. One day in an anatomy tutorial a radiologist was firing questions along the rows of students. He reached me mid-lecture. He was an enthusiastic teacher and explained things well, but I wasn't taking in anything he said – I was too preoccupied waiting for my turn. I kept my phone open in case I had time to google an answer. With a CT image of the lumbar spine projected in front of the class he asked me to identify a tissue between two lumbar vertebrae. I paused, my mind going blank.

'This is bone here and here, so what is this dark thing in between?' he asked.

Nope, still blank, I thought.

'Um . . . just space?' My face was burning and my chest was tight.

This was a silly answer, and to his credit he didn't laugh. The dark patch in the CT image was an intervertebral disc, the discs that people with back pain frequently complain about. These discs are large and obvious, but at that moment the panic of being asked a question in front of fifty of my peers overrode my ability to think. It's these moments that my brain laminated and mounted on the wall.

While the teacher in this instance was forgiving, many lectures simply weren't safe places to make mistakes. How could they be? A senior figure, representing a culture that values perfectionism and abhors mistakes, is asking questions without notice in front of an audience of people who value knowing the answer and denigrate anything else. What I needed was trust – in the senior doctors teaching us, in my colleagues and in the culture of medicine. It reminded me of the lack of trust I sometimes felt as a patient, lying in bed at the crack of dawn as a new bunch of doctors approached during the ward round. They knew about my surgery and my latest blood test results, but they didn't really know me, nor I them. There was no rapport. Yet I was expected to answer questions and update them on the most intimate parts of my physiology. The vulnerability I felt in lectures reminded me of the vulnerability I'd felt as a patient – and doctors were in charge in both situations.

I had only just started what would be a long journey in studying medicine but already I could see how this aggressive quizzing in the lecture theatre, and the resulting humiliation, could lead to bullying and harassment. I worried about the years ahead, when we headed out to hospitals to learn on the job.

•

Thank god I had a refuge.

At the start of medical school, we'd been allocated learning groups comprising eight students and one tutor, and my tutorial group was an oasis of warmth and kindness. For ten hours a week, I was bolstered and re-energised by the supportive learning environment I found there.

Our tutor, Fiona, was an experienced emergency paediatric physician who was retraining as a GP. She worked part-time at a domestic violence clinic outside the city, had three children and cared for her unwell father. Despite being stupidly busy, she made us feel important, valued and supported every lesson. I don't care what neuroscientists say about the fallacy of being able to multi-task, Fiona was a pro. In one tutorial, she sat in the corner of the room (her preferred position so the eight of us could 'drive our own learning') sewing gold sequin ballet costumes for her two daughters. The group was discussing inflammation and pain and the way common drugs, like aspirin, help control these.

'They inhibit prostaglandin synthesis,' someone said.

'Yep, via COX 1,' added another.

'I'm really pleased with this discussion, there is great infor-mation flying around the room,' Fiona said, interrupting us. 'But just in case we aren't all on the same page, why don't we take a second to really understand how the non-steroidals work.' She was looking at us now, but her hands were still sewing. 'John, would you like to use the whiteboard and draw up the mechanism of action?'

Fiona played to each of our strengths – John had been a pharmacist before medical school and knew every possible thing about every possible drug. From memory, he scribbled up the chemical pathway that aspirin blocked, and began answering our questions. Once we'd exhausted the topic Fiona stepped in again.

'This is really good stuff. How these medications work is something you'll revise over and over again when you're doctors. Now, let's get back to the patient we were discussing.'

I felt so lucky to have been allocated to Fiona that first year. She was the perfect blend of intelligence, humour and compassion. I wanted to understand everything I could about the human body because I wanted to be like her – not because I feared her.

Fiona reminded us that we were people first, and doctors second. She modelled vulnerability and honesty when it mattered, and she didn't mind taking the piss out of herself. One tutorial, howling with embarrassed laughter, she shared an interaction she'd had at her clinic. A mother had brought her six-month-old baby for a check-up, because a month earlier Fiona had been worried the baby wasn't growing as fast as he should have been. This time around the baby looked plump and healthy. Fiona ended the check-up by measuring the baby's length and weighing him on a set of scales. She was so happy and relieved with his progress that when she lifted him off the scales, she planted a kiss on one of his chubby cheeks.

'Aww, aren't you a healthy little cutie!' she said.

As the mother laughed with glee, Fiona immediately realised her error, her relief turning to horror. It was definitely not okay for doctors to kiss their patients, no matter how young – she'd never done anything like it before. She handed the baby straight back to the mother and apologised profusely, embarrassed she'd let her happiness over the baby's progress get the better of her.

Fiona laughed as she recalled the event, but her cheeks were bright red – she took the patient–doctor relationship very seriously.

After everyone had stopped giggling we had a chat about patient–doctor boundaries. I understood the point Fiona was making by telling us this story, but I didn't see her display of humanity as an error. It felt like a very natural moment, and one that, importantly, the mother had not been concerned about.

'Don't beat yourself up,' I said. 'It happened because you care.'

'One hundred per cent,' one of my classmates added.

Fiona was the kind of doctor who connected with her patients' emotions – her worry and relief over the baby were genuine. Surely, I thought, more harm comes from doctors who are detached and distant than doctors who care deeply?

•

'I'm sixty-five years old and have just been diagnosed with Al-zhei-mer's,' Jane said, punctuating each syllable by knocking herself on the head. 'What the fuck are you going to do about it?' Her voice was loud, carrying anger or panic, maybe both. Even the fingers knocking her head appeared angry, frustrated they couldn't get to the broken bits of her brain. Her kind eyes had become steely and expectant.

I said nothing, I was too shocked – we were at a bookstore, not a hospital. As the crowd milled around us, I struggled to summon a response.

A local doctor had just given a talk about the need to treat older patients with more empathy and dignity. During the Q&A, I asked for practical advice on how to show respect for older patients, identifying myself as a medical student. 'That's easy,' the doctor had said into the microphone, 'treat them like people, and remember that they each have a story.'

Two classmates and I had been chatting afterwards when Jane marched up to me – I'd never met her before. She was lean with short grey hair. A calico bag heavy with books was slung over her bony shoulder.

'Well? It'll be up to you to fix this in the future, so how are you going to help me?'

She continued to stare at me.

'I'm only halfway through my first year of medicine, I have no idea,' I blurted.

My classmates watched, wide-eyed and tight-lipped. I was on my own. My panic gave way to disappointment – I had not shown Jane the slightest bit of empathy, instead I'd said the first defensive thing that popped into my mind *Think*, I said to myself, *this is a person, this could be your patient.*

I didn't feel like a future doctor though – I felt like a dumb student trying to keep my head above the waves of lectures and labs.

But despite how I saw myself, to Jane and her terminal disease, I *was* hope.

In the first week of medical school, we had been lectured that being a doctor is a privilege and a responsibility. We were warned that our words had the power to negatively impact patients. Could Jane see that I was terrified of this conversation?

I asked her to tell me more about her diagnosis. Jane said that she didn't have any family left. Her main fear was having no one to look after her 'when the dementia gets me'.

I was actually listening now. As the heat evaporated from the conversation, we moved on to what she'd been doing to stave off dementia.

We parted with a handshake. 'I truly wish you all the best, Jane,' I said.

She smiled, the creases gathering softly around each eye. She squeezed my hand. 'And the same to you,' she said.

I knew then that many more people were going to look at me like she did, with hope, expectation and sometimes anger. I would need to get better at supporting patients through their fear.

•

Anatomy, physiology, biochemistry, pathology, pharmacology, microbiology, genetics, embryology, immunology, epidemiology, public health, interviewing and examining patients, surgery, obstetrics, paediatrics, neurology, cardiology, primary care, psychiatry, anaesthetics, emergency medicine, medical research, ethics, and medicolegal issues.

The volume of knowledge we needed to acquire as medical students was endless. And with each year the volume of what we understand about medicine, illness and health expands – it's more than one person can ever synthesise.

Most undergraduate medical degrees are six years long, while graduate ones are four years. The content is the same – the graduate programs, like mine, just squeeze it into less time. How? By having fewer breaks and more teaching time.

To 'help' us cope with this, we were often reminded we were the lucky few who made it to med school – thousands had missed out. 'Do you really deserve to be here? Prove it,' was the overarching attitude. 'Work hard, or you've taken the spot of someone more deserving.'

'Don't take breaks – get the degree done in the allotted four years,' was another clear message. 'Okay, only the briefest of gaps if absolutely necessary. But we'll consider you a slacker.'

'Having a baby? Be back within three weeks. That's the maternity policy, take it up with the university if you have a problem.'

'It's really important to eat well and exercise. But memorise this textbook first.'

This was the pressure cooker of med school.

Pressure isn't a bad thing – the stress of medical school just needed to be balanced out, more give-and-take, less take-take-take. I had Sana, interests outside of medicine, and a whole life I'd led before medicine – all of this buffered me from the relentlessness of medical school and gave me perspective. I worried about my classmates though, especially the Med Bots. What was medical school going to cost them, psychologically and personally?

And the costs aren't limited to medical school. Medicine is one giant race – starting at the entrance exam and ending twelve to fifteen years later when you complete training.

You start the race as an applicant to medical school and, if lucky, become a medical student. After graduation you get to call yourself a doctor, but there is years more training to complete before you can call yourself any kind of specialist – be that a GP, paediatrician or haematologist.

Doctors in training attract different labels depending on their level of experience – the hierarchy goes intern, resident, registrar, fellow and (finally) consultant. Consultants have finished training – they're fully qualified independent doctors endorsed by a medical college. Confusingly, they may also be referred to as senior medical officers, specialists, staff specialists and visiting medical officers, depending on where you encounter them. Junior doctors just call them all 'bosses'.

There are a lot of absurd (at best) or perverse (at worst) incentives built into this race to the top.

The problem starts at the beginning of the doctor pipeline: far more people want to become doctors than the universities can accept. This creates an incentive for the universities to demand higher entrance exam scores and enrol more medical students – which they have done, greatly expanding their intakes. In 2020, 3664 new doctors graduated from medical school, up from 2964 in 2010 and three times higher than the 1200 graduates in 2000. While the number of graduating doctors has exploded, training positions have not. The problem is so bad some years that new doctors haven't found jobs as interns, and interns haven't found jobs as residents. It has become normal for residents to miss out on specialty training positions two or three years in a row.

The doctor pipeline gets narrower the further along you get, with the same number of people competing. In fact, the whole business is a pyramid – with a huge base made up of students and junior doctors, and a tiny tip occupied by the top docs.

The top is golden – it's what keeps us in the race. It promises independence, better working hours, power and an impressive income.

From day one, students size each other up. Who do you know in the cardiology department? Have you got a master's? What did you get on the GAMSAT? How much research have you done? Did you ace the anatomy exam? These things matter – it isn't enough to just have a medical degree – the race demands more than ever.

I wasn't really interested in reaching the top of my class but I found the constant competition exhausting, and at times demoralising. It would have been easy to lose sight of why I was studying medicine – to focus only on exam scores and having the best CV. Resisting that way of thinking was hard, especially when important qualities of being a good doctor, like listening, relationship building, compassion and team work, were absent from award ceremonies. Opting out of the competition takes confidence, and while having survived cancer gave me that, it didn't protect me entirely. One Friday night after a long week of class and study I collapsed in bed and called Sana in London.

'I don't think I like this medicine thing very much,' I said.

'Oh no, hard day?'

'Hard month,' I said. My voice was quiet, flat. I didn't really have anything to say, I mainly just wanted to hear her. I rolled onto my stomach, the phone wedged between my ear and the pillow. 'It's just not what I thought it would be.'

'I know. But you're going to be an excellent doctor, you can do this. Maybe try focusing on the good times? The times you ring me up and are super excited about something you've learnt or some feedback you've gotten?'

'But what if to finish a medical degree I end up forgetting who I am and what I value?'

'I mean, yeah . . . that's a risk. It's hard to hold on to yourself in any system . . .' Her voice trailed off for a moment. 'But you know who you are and why you went into this. You're still the same person, you just need to play by their rules for a while.'

'Yeah.' I sighed. 'I better go, I have a couple of hours of study to do. Thanks for letting me whinge.'

I rolled off the bed and dragged my feet to my desk. *You've just got to keep going*, I thought.

The feeling that medical school was a race was hard to avoid, especially since little was being done to ease the extra stress. Instead, the medical school found ways to dial it up – we were made to do endless presentations, projects and reports. These didn't count towards our final marks but there was a constant pressure to perform well because everyone was watching and judging. And in the middle of each year we sat exams that also didn't contribute to our final grade.

The only grade that mattered was derived from a set of all-or-nothing exams at the end of each year. Failing these exams would likely mean repeating the year (which you could do twice before being booted from the program).

I felt that this emphasis on the make-or-break exams at the end of each year devalued all other learning. Many of the skills that a doctor needs – like listening, reflecting and communicating – were ignored by students who were just barrelling towards the exams. I thought the whole thing was a beat-up, and wasn't afraid of telling the faculty.

In the middle of first year, the stress was building as our first mid-year exam approached. More students were staying back after class, laptops and textbooks open. The cram was on – my medical contacts on WhatsApp, Instagram and Facebook went quiet; several students even deleted the apps, self-imposing a social media blackout.

I wasn't cramming. By then I felt more confident and across all of the material we were learning. I'd spent most nights and most weekends for the past six months buried in textbooks, delving deeper into the material we were learning in class. I missed weekends away with friends, gigs, dinner parties and birthdays. It was worth it (mostly) for the privilege of learning medicine. But I didn't want to pour extra energy into cramming for an exam that wasn't marked.

Everyone went to ground the weekend before the exam.

Instead of cramming, I took the weekend off – a rare treat. I scrolled through my contacts, calculating who I had neglected the most. I messaged a friend who I'd first met in China and who now also lived in Sydney.

'Hey! Sorry for being so slack. Catch up this weekend?' I wrote.

The reply came immediately.

'I thought you were dead lol. How the hell are you? Let's do coffee today.'

I put on music and sat next to a pile of laundry on the couch. I folded my favourite jumper and reached for a t-shirt. *Am I being an idiot? Everyone else is studying*, I thought. I folded the t-shirt and then refolded it two more times. *Am I avoiding the exam because I'm burnt out?* The idea of burnout was on my mind because it's common among medical students and doctors. I'd seen signs in other students – snapping at other people, changes in weight, tears in the hallway, yawning in tutorials, unkempt hair, absence from class. Articles on doctor burnout were everywhere in the media, and the problem was worsening, according to experts. I didn't think I was burnt out – but I checked with Sana. Although she was still in London finishing off her master's, we spoke every day. She was the best person to ask if I'd gone off track.

'Do I seem burnt out to you?' I asked.

'I think you're a little tired, and stressed with school,' she said. 'You were probably burnt out towards the end of your last job, but not now.'

I moved to the next possible diagnosis: was I procrastinating? No – it's only procrastination when you avoid a task that's important to you. The unmarked exam was simply not important to me.

Having ruled out burnout and procrastination I slowly settled into the idea that I was doing the right thing. I put the last of the clean clothes away and made a cup of tea. The sun was shining as I went to meet my poor, neglected friend for coffee.

The results dropped a week later and I wasn't surprised to learn that I had failed two sections, but only just. Falling one or two questions short of passing without cramming was a win (for me), but a week after the exam I received an email from the head of department. 'We would like to meet and discuss your recent exam performance' it read. I had been expecting this – the mid-year exam was one of the ways the school identified struggling students and I knew that I hadn't done that well. I sat down and crafted my reply.

> Dear Professor,
>
> Thank you for your email and concern about my result in the recent mid-year exams. I assure you that I'm neither struggling with the course content nor worried about how I will perform at the end-of-year exams. I decided to sit this exam out, so to speak. I didn't deem it the best use of my time, as we are already juggling multiple projects and assessments. I instead opted for work–life balance, and used the opportunity to reflect on the topics of burnout and procrastination – clearing myself of both.
>
> If you would still like to, I am more than happy to meet with you and other members of the faculty.
>
> Yours sincerely, Ben Bravery

I never received a reply, so I never had the meeting. I continued to get emails each year after the mid-year tests, and I replied in a similar way. Part of me hoped that my replies would kick off a discussion between the faculty and us students about the extreme expectations placed on us and the demoralising nature of assessments that didn't count towards our marks, but sadly, they did not. Either way, I did well at the all-or-nothing end-of-year exams, scoring in the top half of the cohort.

•

Medical school wasn't just a shock for me, it was a shock for Sana too.

She returned from London just after my first mid-year exam and we squeezed into a tiny studio apartment within walking distance of the university. In the time I'd had off after leaving my job at the environmental charity and before starting school, she'd had me all to herself. Now, she came second to study.

With all the missed date nights and catch-ups with friends, Sana and I began developing parallel social lives. Or perhaps opposite is the better word – mine didn't exist, while Sana was almost always flying solo. Frequently, she'd go to bed alone while I stayed at my desk studying. Living in a studio apartment meant we still saw lots of each other, but life became more routine for me, and I became more boring for her.

'It's just four years,' I said to make us feel better, even though we both knew that wasn't true.

I saw Mum whenever I flew back to Melbourne for check-ups. After Sana and I had moved out of Graeme's place, our relationship with him had slowly improved and I now stayed with him and Mum again on my visits.

Ian didn't see me as much, and had to make do with phone calls. As my time became less and less my own, I wondered if I'd ever get the opportunity to travel with him again, especially back to China.

Kim and I saw each other most weekends. Kim was pregnant again and, about halfway through her pregnancy, I asked her if a few classmates from my tutorial group could come around and examine Archie inside her belly – she said yes immediately. As her pregnancy progressed she asked if I would be her birth partner – I said yes immediately.

'What! That's so weird,' said Sana.

'He's basically a doctor,' said Kim.

'But he's your brother!'

It wasn't weird to us. Kim and I had always been close – we've felt a sense of safety being around each other since we were little. Plus, this was a win–win. Kim hoped having a student doctor in the room meant she'd get VIP treatment, and for me, what better way to get obstetric experience than helping in the birth of my own nephew?

Towards the end of my first year at medical school, Kim called to tell me she was in labour, while James grabbed the hospital bags.

At the hospital, the nurses told Kim she was three centimetres dilated. Over the next several hours she progressed to nine centimetres, but then stopped. They decided to deliver via Caesarean.

With James and the anaesthetist comforting Kim as she lay on the operating table, there wasn't much for me to do. We'd agreed earlier that if she ended up in surgery, it was okay for me to hang out down the business end. So I did.

As I got into position, far enough from the sterile field but close enough to still see, I imagined Sana's reaction. 'That's your sister, weirdo!'

While the surgeons chatted about real estate prices, I watched them rapidly and elegantly open Kim up. They knew I was studying medicine, so they periodically stopped exchanging investment property tips and explained what they were doing. This was my first time in an operating theatre as an observer rather than a patient (our hospital placements wouldn't start until our third year of medical school). As I watched the surgeons' hands, I wondered if they had been Med Bots at medical school.

Could this level of expertise only be achieved by those with laser focus? Or could I do this too?

The discussion had moved on to interest rates but suddenly stopped. The surgeon lifted Archie out.

'Here he is, a beautiful baby boy,' he said, holding Archie up so Kim and James could see him over the curtain.

As I watched a nurse expertly examine Archie, I was awestruck. *Everyone here, including Archie, is just incredible*, I thought.

The nurse took me over to Kim's placenta on a table and explained how to determine whether it was healthy.

'Put some gloves on and have a good feel of it,' she said.

I felt like one of them.

Back at the operating table the surgeons were suturing the layers of Kim's abdomen together. They'd moved on to discussing the cost of membership at nearby golf clubs.

I could hear Kim kissing her new baby boy on the other side of the screen, but I stayed on the doctor side. *There will be plenty of time for me to kiss him*, I thought, as I continued watching the surgeons – I didn't want to miss a single step.

13

THE PATIENT STUDENT

In the Christmas break between first- and second-year medicine I asked Sana to marry me.

I'd been thinking of proposing for a few months, sneaking around to different jewellers, hunting for the perfect (affordable) antique ring. After hours walking around Sydney pretending I was studying, I narrowed it down to one – a hundred-year-old marquis emerald and diamond ring that I thought would look perfect on Sana's long fingers. It was older, cheaper and had fewer diamonds than the average engagement ring, so I sent a photo to Mum and Kim to make sure I wasn't about to buy something ugly.

'It's beautiful, but it *is* different . . .' said Mum.

'Awesome,' said Kim. 'It's very Sana.'

•

Every year since my cancer treatment had ended, Sana and I headed back to Canada to see her family and friends. This time, I suggested to Sana that we stop in Beijing first. We hadn't been together in Beijing since I'd left to get a visa and have *that* colonoscopy, five years earlier.

I found a trendy boutique hotel in a converted hutong, much nicer than the hutong I had lived in, and hid the ring deep in my suitcase.

For two days in Beijing I carried the ring everywhere. I thought about proposing in the restaurant where we'd had our first date, but it had been bulldozed. I tried her favourite weeping willow, hanging over a small lake in the centre of town, but it had been removed. I walked around the lake looking for somewhere to hire an electric boat like we had done during our last summer there, but they'd closed for the winter.

I gave up finding the right spot.

Unusually for that time of year, the air was clean and the sky was clear. Bright blue skies sparkled during the day and a few stars even twinkled at night. Every now and then, fat white snowflakes fell, and stayed white even after coming to rest in Beijing's busy alleyways.

The clear skies prompted me to think of a swish cocktail bar at the top of one of Beijing's most glamorous buildings. The bar was the city's highest and had incredible views across the capital, with Tiananmen Square and the Forbidden City to the west, the party district (Sanlitun) to the north, and the 'M' shaped headquarters of CCTV, the state broadcaster, to the immediate north-east. The gleaming towers of the business district sparkled all around. It had been a favourite of mine, but Sana had never made it there before her premature departure from Beijing. *Perfect*, I thought.

As the elevator zipped eighty floors up, I unblocked my ears and touched the ring box sitting in my jacket pocket, as if it were going to jump out or disappear any minute.

The doors opened and a wave of music and voices hit us. We were guided through groups of beautiful people sipping cocktails around dimly lit high tables to a seat near the window. The whole city spread out below us, a shadow in the distance marked the Fragrant Hills mountain range, thirty kilometres west of Beijing. Tiananmen Square and the Forbidden City looked tiny.

We ordered drinks and, as Sana marvelled at the view, I took the box from my pocket. I gulped some water, the glass shaking a little in my hand.

'I've been wanting to ask you something, and being back in the city where we first met seems like the perfect place to do it,' I began.

'Oh my god!' yelled Sana, seeing the box, lid still closed.

What followed was a rambling retelling of our relationship, what it meant to me, and how much I loved her. Sana looked from me to the box and from the box back to me. After far too many words from me, she replied with one: 'Yes'.

We spent the next two days in Beijing in a loved-up cocoon, cycling around snow-dusted lanes and snacking on baozi – exactly as we had before I got cancer.

•

In my second year of medicine, I was starting to sound and act more like a doctor – but I was still a cancer patient on the inside.

The threat of cancer returning, or springing up in a new place, is greatest in the first few years after treatment. To catch it early I needed blood tests every twelve weeks, a CT scan and colonoscopy each year, and check-ups with my surgeon every three months back in Melbourne. As demanding as medical school was, I had to remain vigilant. What was the point of all that study if I died before graduating?

But managing medical school and my cancer check-ups was a constant juggle. This had been difficult in first year, but became even harder in second year when our study load increased. Securing time off to attend each appointment involved negotiations with numerous tutors and faculty. If I had too many absences, for any reason, I'd automatically fail. On top of my regular appointments, any new lump or bump anywhere on my body required trips to even more specialists who wanted to do even more tests. No doctor wanted to risk overlooking the return of my cancer.

Through it all, I was learning how to be a better doctor and a better patient, my two halves informing each other constantly. Putting my stethoscope away and donning a hospital gown made me indistinguishable from other patients. Waiting an hour to see a doctor reminded me of the tedium of being a patient. Not being allowed to look at my results until someone smarter had reviewed them brought home the powerlessness of patients. It was all a good antidote to the smugness I felt, now that I had all of this medical knowledge. It was my fifth year post cancer so the high frequency program of scans and blood tests I was on would soon be scaled back.

On the odd occasion when my surgeon wasn't available for our scheduled check-up, someone from his team would run it instead – but even then, he'd usually manage to poke his head in the room and say hello, ensuring some continuity and oversight with my care.

That year though, he happened to miss two of my appointments back to back, with a different doctor conducting each check-up. Doctor one was a tall, no-nonsense, intimidating senior doctor.

'Your five years are nearly up, we'll need to put you on a new monitoring program from next year,' he said. His plan: scaling back the frequency of my check-ups, from once every three months to once every six months. Blood tests would be every six months and no more yearly colonoscopies – although, if I *really* wanted my last scheduled scope, for peace of mind, I could have it.

My mind raced – what if cancer grew in the six months between check-ups? What if we missed the window to act because I was having fewer scans and scopes?

'My surgeon is aware of this change?' I asked.

Doctor one nodded. 'This is how all patients this far from surgery are treated.'

He seemed confident and certain. I had no reason to doubt him.

Three months later, I flew to Melbourne for my final check-up for the year. A new doctor greeted me. Doctor two wore scrubs to signal that she'd just come from the operating theatre. She was a junior doctor, but was only a year or two away from becoming a senior one. She proceeded to outline an entirely different monitoring program. Check-ups once a year (not every six months), same with blood tests, and no more colonoscopies for another five years – and then once every five years after that. Again, my mind raced with questions. What about the optional final scope doctor one had offered? Why had my surgeon changed his mind about the previous plan? What if I noticed a new pain or lump in the year between check-ups? I was confused and anxious – but also a bit relieved. Fewer appointments, tests and colonoscopies meant less disruption to medical school. I wouldn't have to keep pestering the faculty for days off, and I could spend the time studying instead.

Again, I asked if my surgeon was across this new monitoring plan. Again, a nod. I cancelled the upcoming 'optional' colonoscopy and waited a year for the next check-up to roll around.

In the year between check-ups, the hospital upscaled and moved to a shiny new building across town. The development had cost over one billion dollars. But what had previously felt like a cosy one-stop-shop for cancer now felt like an Ikea store. From the outside, dramatic tendrils wrapped around thirteen storeys of glass. A cavernous foyer with neon highlights greeted patients. A letter I received before my appointment had a barcode on it that I scanned at the entrance. A computer told me where to go and a smart lift took me there.

At the clinic I scanned the barcode again and a machine printed a coupon with a number on it. When a doctor was ready for the next patient a screen beeped and displayed which patient number was needed at which room number. I took a seat and waited. The waiting rooms here were larger than at the old hospital. It was shiny, but it was sterile and cold. I had only interacted with computer terminals since arriving. While looking up at the screen that told which anonymous patient to go to which room, I wondered whether a computer would also do my check-up. I got as far as imagining a robot putting on gloves for a rectal exam when my number appeared on the screen.

I found the room and knocked on the door. Mercifully, a human answered – and this time it was one of my favourite humans: my surgeon.

My face broke into a giant smile and we shook hands. He looked grumpy though – cross even.

'Why have you stopped coming for check-ups?' he asked. I stopped smiling. 'Look, you're overdue for a colonoscopy. You didn't have one last year. Why didn't we see you?'

Bewildered, I explained what the last two doctors had told me, how I didn't need as many blood tests and scopes anymore. 'I got a different story each visit,' I added. 'I'm so confused!'

'There is nothing to be confused about. Patients who get cancer at the age you did are seen every twelve weeks for several years. I also do annual colonoscopies and scans,' he said.

'I know that, which is why I was confused when the other doctors changed the plan. I asked several times whether you knew of the changes.'

'If this happens again just tell them you want to see me,' he said. 'I'm always here.'

I was even more puzzled now – if he was always here, always available, why didn't I see him at the check-ups? I'd never been told that I could simply ask for him. And why did doctors one and two – who were on my surgeon's team – give me such differing monitoring plans?

'Which doctors told you this anyway?' he asked.

'Just the other doctors,' I said. I didn't know their names; the consults had been brief, no longer than ten minutes. I'm fairly sure one of them didn't even introduce themselves. 'It's not that easy to challenge a senior doctor. And I'm a medical student now . . . so . . .' I trailed off, defeated.

'It *is* easy. Just tell them you want to see me,' he repeated.

While I appreciated that my surgeon assumed patients would feel so empowered, he was missing the power dynamics at play.

Speaking up is hard. I had gently asked doctor one and doctor two whether my surgeon had made the change to my monitoring program. Stopping the consultation and demanding to see my surgeon never occurred to me – in fact, it seemed preposterous. I didn't know how the clinic was organised – what was and was not possible had never been explained to me.

Even with nearly two years of medical school under my belt, I had found it hard to speak up. The extra knowledge I'd gained about diseases and cures had grown alongside an understanding, and fear, of the medical hierarchy. Ironically, it had become harder for me to speak up now – I was not just a patient questioning a doctor, but a medical student questioning a superior. My surgeon sat at the very top of the hierarchy.

This was the third check-up in a row where I left with a new plan. Except, this time the new plan was the old plan – colonoscopies every year and frequent blood tests and check-ups.

I left the surgeon's room and heard the screen buzz in a new patient. On the way out of the clinic I passed the computer that had first greeted me – the machine that had spat out my anonymous number. I couldn't tell who had been easier to talk to: this computer or my surgeon.

On the drive back to Mum and Graeme's place, I ruminated.

I had been told repeatedly that remaining vigilant, with close monitoring, was key to catching any new cancer early and staying healthy. Missing a lump, or ignoring new pain, could prove fatal. But I'd been made to feel like I had deliberately stopped going to check-ups and tests.

'No one wants me to stay alive more than me!' I yelled. I was alone in the car, but I enjoyed the catharsis of a solitary shout.

Pulling into Mum's driveway, my anger had given way to resigned disappointment. I was disheartened by a health system that expected me to speak up without showing me how. I felt let down by my surgeon, imagining him scribbling *non-compliant patient* next to the note about the missed colonoscopy. I was upset with myself for not doing more to safeguard my health – I had promised I'd never take my body and health for granted after ignoring my symptoms back in Beijing.

While the blood tests and colonoscopy I eventually had came back normal, I couldn't help dwelling on the fallout had they not been. In between daymares that started with cancer coming back and ended with me losing various organs and limbs, I tried to focus on what I could learn from this lapse in my check-up regime. My experience reminded me how easily patients can get confused, which isn't surprising given how opaque and foreign the medical world is. *When I'm a doctor, I'll* always *make sure patients understand me*, I told myself, as daymares continued dancing at the back of my frazzled brain.

•

The check-up mix-up occurred because of sloppy communication from my treatment team, but at least they'd talked to me. At my next colonoscopy, I had *zero* communication.

Lying on the operating table waiting to be put to sleep, I realised I had no idea who was going to be putting the camera up my bum. Normally a surgeon would introduce themselves before I was wheeled into the operating theatre. *Maybe they would speak to me afterwards?* I was mistaken – not even a quick hello then either. I went to hospital, was put to sleep, had the colonoscopy, woke up in recovery, was told by a nurse that the scope had been clear, and went home without ever speaking to the doctor who worked on me. It was baffling, upsetting and, frankly, insulting. It would have been out of character for my regular surgeon not to talk to me before the scope. *Someone else must have done it*, I thought. But I wasn't sure. Raising this with him felt too awkward. I didn't want to sound like I was whingeing. After all, I'd woken up from the scope without any problems and it had been all clear – wasn't that the most important thing?

•

My Fiona in second year of med school was Faisal, a hospital physician who had done high school in the US, medical school in Pakistan and worked as a doctor in the UK. He was half relaxed bohemian and half serious doctor. He had long dark hair, played the guitar and sung in a band, and in addition to tutoring us he was one of the school's main anatomy instructors. As a teacher, he was patient, practical and passionate.

Faisal had been born in Pakistan and had loads of insight about Sana's family and culture, so I asked him for lots of tips.

Her family had been nagging us to get married for years, and now that we were finally engaged it had become more intense. There were numerous marriage and religious customs to get my head around, so after class one day Faisal took me for biryani so he could walk me through the different ceremonies from start to finish.

'There're many pre-wedding parties, like the mehndi or dholki, but the main events start with the nikah – that's the religious ceremony. Then there's the wedding party, which is thrown by the bride's side, then, traditionally, there's a walima, which is a reception thrown by the groom's side – though I suppose that won't be happening with you . . .'

I scribbled on a notepad. *No walima, unless the Sydney version of our wedding counts.*

'You're not just marrying Sana,' he continued. 'You're marrying her family *and* their religion.'

'Jesus!' I said.

'Wrong religion,' he joked. 'But if you love Sana it's worth it – it's always worth it.'

Faisal was a man of many talents, skilled in anatomy *and* matrimony.

●

Towards the end of second year I was required back in Melbourne for a routine CT scan. In the waiting room it struck me that cancer hospitals are strange places. We patients sit side by side during deeply private moments, stripped to our underwear, wearing gowns that never conceal enough flesh, mostly in silence. It's never clear whether people want to talk, or what emotional confrontation is playing out behind their eyes. So, as I waited, I wondered. What does he have? Why does she look so sad? What happened to their leg?

At this scan I talked to one of the other patients. The older man with silver hair had rejected *Hello!* And *Marie Claire*, and settled on *National Geographic*. I was reading the only other copy of *National Geographic*, so we had things in common to talk about. Keith told me that he'd been diagnosed with prostate cancer seven years earlier, and had his prostate and its cancer successfully removed.

'But last month a blood test showed that the cancer is back,' he said.

'Oh mate, I'm sorry to hear that,' I replied.

A scan showed that Keith had secondary tumours in his spine and hip. He had just finished a fancy radiation treatment that fired ultra-thin beams of energy specifically at these small tumours.

'I need a scan today to see if the radiation worked,' he said. He looked back down at his magazine, lost in thought.

Early diagnosis. Successful surgery. No cancer, for over seven years.

That's seven years of normal birthdays, playing with grand-children, loving his wife, getting annoyed at the weather, groaning about bills – all the normal things that aren't cancer.

And then more cancer.

He tossed the *National Geographic* back on the pile of magazines.

'Did you notice any new pains?' I asked. 'And has your PSA dropped this time?'

A PSA is a blood test for prostate cancer. This was the medical student in me, trying to work out if Keith had had early symptoms that suggested his cancer was back.

'I've had a bad back for a long time, but it did get a little worse,' he said.

'What does it feel like after all those years to be back here?'

This was the cancer patient in me, trying to understand such a major setback.

'What were those seven years like?' I continued. 'Did you worry about the cancer coming back?' For me, this question was the most important – I fretted over this often.

'Sometimes, sometimes,' he said. 'But I mostly just got on with life.'

The more time I spent living with 'no evidence of disease', the easier it became. I was safer, statistically, the further I got from my diagnosis, and that brought me comfort. But in the days before check-ups I worried about how radically altered my life would be if cancer returned.

Each step closer to physical and psychological normality meant I had further to fall should the cancer ever come back. It's a strange limbo between illness and wellness. The sprint back towards a healthier and happier version of myself after treatment always evaporated during check-ups – forcing me to stop and look back. The distance from my cancer was both reassuring and frightening, but also an illusion. It was reassuring because time and distance meant progress. It was frightening because the thought of ending up back there was almost overwhelming. And it felt illusory because there was no real distance at all – my body was still my body. Only time would tell whether any cancer was still hiding inside.

•

During second year, I had become good friends with Charlotte, a student in my tutorial group. She was from a regional town and had moved to Sydney to study marketing and commerce. Part way through that degree she became cynical about a career in PR and decided to become a doctor – she had a cousin at medical school and had become fascinated by it.

Charlotte was ridiculously smart, but she concealed this super-power through self-deprecation. 'I can't understand scientific graphs, I'm just a commerce grad,' she'd say during tutorials. She also hid behind little quirks, like how she couldn't stop rubbing her hands together when she was excited about a topic, or how she carried a bottle of vinegar everywhere, in case she ordered fries.

Charlotte was as comfortable memorising a long list of cardio-vascular medications as she was listening to a patient talk about their grandchildren. She appeared to never stop reflecting – on how to be a better student, better doctor and better colleague. During medical school she volunteered at a women's health clinic overseas and represented our university at a meeting of the United Nations in New York. Charlotte was ten years younger than me, but this age difference didn't impede us becoming friends – I introduced her to opera, and she taught me how to use Snapchat.

There were dozens of other medical students like Charlotte at my school – focused on patients and desperately trying to preserve their empathy. But even Charlotte, with her big brain and bigger heart, had noticed that she'd grown more distant over the course of our studies. During one trip back home, her dad commented that she didn't give him hugs like she used to, and her mum confessed that she worried constantly about the pressure Charlotte was under at school.

At the end of second year Charlotte won a stack of awards.

'You're incredible,' I said to her, 'but what's really special, is that you achieved so much while remaining genuine with us and compassionate towards patients.'

As we hugged after the award ceremony, I worried about how much medical school was changing her. *Hang in there*, I thought, *we need more doctors like you.*

14

I WAS PROMISED CANCER

Following my diagnosis, cancer struck several of my family members and friends.

In 2011, as I was finishing my cancer treatment, Nan had a tumour removed from her breast. A year after that, Pop died suddenly from undiagnosed lung cancer, which had caused blood clots in his lungs – he woke up one morning feeling short of breath and died in the back of an ambulance three hours later. In 2015, Mum's youngest sister was diagnosed with terminal breast cancer at forty-five years old – she's still undergoing treatment. Over that same time, one of my friends from China got rectal cancer and one from the US died from melanoma, at just twenty-eight.

Other people I met through cancer support groups died too. There was the thirty-something father of three who used his last bit of strength to build a pizza oven for his kids; the science graduate in his early twenties who managed to see some of South

America with his girlfriend before getting sick and having to rush home; the winemaker who blew her life insurance payout on a shopping trip to Singapore; and the young artist whose work touched a thousand lives, but couldn't keep her own.

All this cancer around me resulted in a mix of grief for these people, gratitude that I was alive to have met them, and guilt that I had made it, and they hadn't.

Cancer was everywhere, except the one place where I went looking for it – medical school. By the end of second year I was left wondering: where is cancer? In my degree, there were no units dedicated to cancer – only a smattering of case studies mixed in with other units. This was despite the fact that cancer is a leading cause of death in Australia, accounting for thirty per cent of people who die. One in two people in Australia will get cancer by the age of eighty-five. In 2019, around 145,000 new cases of cancer were diagnosed in Australia – an average of nearly four hundred per day. Was my school the only one not covering cancer in detail?

I started digging around the research literature, and was shocked by what I found. The only major Australian study of what newly graduated doctors understood about cancer had been published back in 2003, and its findings were deeply worrying.

The survey studied interns and found a huge number felt they lacked the knowledge and skills needed to spot the signs of cancer, or the confidence to chat to people living with cancer. Forty per cent said they had little or no skill in discussing death; one in four didn't have the know-how to spot a melanoma; and more than one-third weren't confident doing a pap smear for cervical cancer. The data was grim, but it was old.

To find out if things had changed, I worked with a team of senior radiation oncologists to survey a few hundred final-year medical students across Australia and New Zealand in 2018. The results were similarly scary.

These medical students still didn't feel confident about cancer, and they ranked oncology as one of the two worst taught subjects at medical school (the other was haematology, which includes all the blood cancers). Many students in my survey, just months away from being doctors, mistakenly believed that being zapped by radiation therapy made patients radioactive. This showed an alarming lack of understanding about how a mainstay of cancer treatment actually works. Imagine if one of these new doctors told a patient this and scared them away from life-saving treatment?

When I compared my data to surveys done in 1990 and 2001, I found that students had become even *less* confident managing cancer over time. Worse still, increasing numbers of students were graduating with little or no direct contact with cancer patients or doctors who treated cancer.

My fellow medical students and I often wondered why a disease that half of all people eventually get was taught so poorly at medical school.

Part of the reason is that there is a great deal for medical students to learn – everything from genetics and how the heart works to disability policy and how to conduct medical research. The sheer size of the curriculum means it can be slow to incorporate change. We are, after all, inheriting hundreds of years of medical knowledge.

Along with an overcrowded curriculum, in Australia there is no set cancer textbook for students. Nor is there a standard list of facts, figures and treatments students are required to know, unlike for other illnesses like ischaemic heart disease, where risk factors, pathology and management are drilled into us. This matters because most medical students concentrate on remembering only what they *have* to know.

The biggest reason why junior doctors lack knowledge of cancer is a lack of contact with people affected by cancer. At my university, every medical student was required to rotate through aged care or palliative care wards, where many patients had cancer. But we were one of the few medical schools in Australia to make this a priority.

Even so, in lectures and tutorials at medical school, I didn't once encounter a cancer advocate or person with cancer. Research shows the more contact students have with cancer patients – whether in class, in hospital or in hospices – the more prepared and confident they are when interacting with cancer patients later on. Given how common cancer is, spending time with people with cancer should be a fundamental part of medical students' education.

•

The first time cancer *did* pop up in medical school was halfway through my first year, when we were presented with a case study on breast cancer. Until this point I hadn't properly told my classmates about my cancer. Now felt like the right time to talk about it.

I had mentioned my experience to Fiona, my first-year tutor, and she was keen to include me in the discussion about cancer and its treatment too.

Moving to the whiteboard at the head of the table, I sketched small and large bowels in black. I'd presented to this group of eight people every week since starting medical school, but this topic was personal. Steadying my hand against the board, in red I added a tumour, sprouting from my sigmoid across to my rectum. In green I coloured in the parts of the bowel I'd lost.

I lifted my shirt and showed them my puckered stoma scar and traced the long scar running down the middle of my body for as long as decently possible (it ended in my pubic hair, a bit too revealing for 11 am on a Wednesday). I picked up the black pen again and drew what my large bowel looked like now, with its fancy J-pouch and staples.

I returned to my seat and tucked my shaky hands under the table.

'Ask me anything you want,' I said.

My classmates were silent, half stared at the whiteboard, half stared at me.

'How long did you have the stoma for?'

'Could you actually feel the poo going into the bag?'

'So that's why some stomas are on the right, I get it now.'

Fiona prompted us to move on to chemotherapy and radiation therapy. These treatments had barely been covered by the lectures that week – the group wanted to know everything, and not just the technical details.

'What did each chemo infusion feel like?'

'You don't have to answer this, but did you think you might die?'

We'd lost track of time and ran late for the next class. 'I'm sure we could speak to Ben about this topic for the rest of the day, but sadly you guys need to get moving,' Fiona said. For weeks afterwards, my classmates asked me questions they hadn't had the opportunity to ask tutors or lecturers, or even their own family members with cancer. It ended up being a significant learning opportunity, especially because cancer was not a topic the curriculum returned to frequently, unlike heart disease or bone fractures.

After we'd been split up into different learning groups in second year, I sent my old classmates a survey about whether my talk about my bowel cancer had been useful for them. This wasn't part of an assignment or study, I was just curious – had they been as moved as I had been by our frank discussions? To get as close to the truth as possible, I made the survey anonymous.

'Are you kidding?' wrote one student. 'It was an irreplaceable learning experience.'

'Instead of approaching the case from a problem-solving doctors' perspective, it was an important reminder to address vast differences in patient perspectives,' one comment read.

'I learnt about more than just tumours, like how the diagnosis can impact people,' another wrote.

'I felt so fortunate to be studying cancer alongside someone who had lived it, it made the discussions incredibly real.'

I'm the first to admit that learning about cancer alongside someone who'd had it is unusual – but it shouldn't be. This kind of patient contact is known to help medical students develop skills, knowledge and empathy. Plus, humans learn best via stories – powerful patient accounts of illness, shared with future doctors away from a noisy ward or menacing seniors, is just what medical school needs more of.

In my time at medical school, my fellow students rated cardio-vascular medicine as the best taught subject. This is because we were taught about the heart early and often. Yet heart disease is responsible for ten per cent of deaths while cancer is responsible for thirty per cent.

What students learn at medical school forms the basis of their medical knowledge for the rest of their careers. I know that many of the students in my medical degree did not feel as confident treating cancer as they did heart disease. And, once we graduated, the opportunities to learn about cancer later on were limited, depending on which specialty pathway we took.

It's time for that to change. In the so-called 'war on cancer', we can't afford to send such an unprepared and uninformed army into the battlefield.

15

POOR HISTORIANS

The patient interview was the first thing we learnt at medical school and something we practised hundreds of times thereafter.

'Get this right, and you have eighty per cent of the diagnosis!' said the lecturer. (The rest of the diagnosis came from physically examining the patient and tests.)

The structure of the interview is always the same, but the questions change depending on the main symptom a patient has. When it's pain, we ask: where is it, when did it start, dull or sharp and so on. When someone has a cough – how long have you had it, any mucus, are you also short of breath, is it worse at night, are you a smoker etc.

We practised by interviewing each other. Tutors would give one of us a sheet with the symptoms and relevant medical history, and the other one would interview them. This was often timed to exactly seven minutes, because just like the interview I did to get into medical school, most exams consisted of bouncing between rooms answering questions and performing tasks in about that time.

This model made me fast at interviewing, but it didn't make me good. The other problem is that we were interviewing people who used the same system to communicate. They knew the questions and the 'right' answers. Everything about learning to talk to patients this way felt wrong. In tutorials I would sometimes mutter aloud that I thought it was stupid.

'But it's good training for your exams,' a tutor said.

'You can do it more slowly in the real world, just learn it this way first,' added another.

The idea seemed to be that we would *unlearn* this method once we were actual doctors. That seemed unrealistic – learning these interviews took hundreds of hours and drills. And it was changing the way I communicated with actual patients.

By the time we were rotating through hospital wards in third-year med school, I found myself getting frustrated when patients took too long to answer my questions. When patients started to tell me about their hip replacement instead of their diarrhoea my eyes would glaze over. Even when family members asked me for medical advice and I started interviewing them, I would get frustrated. 'Just answer the question!' I'd yell at Mum. She wanted to go off on a tangent about a new brain scan she'd seen on breakfast television when all I wanted was for her to describe her headache. Of course, I couldn't respond like this when actual patients did the same thing, but I wanted to.

It was no surprise to me that patient–doctor communication often left patients feeling dissatisfied. We speak a different language, organise information in totally disparate ways, and our learning rewarded us for only listening to information that revealed a diagnosis or helped us pass an exam.

When an interview with a patient wasn't going to plan, I was told to label them a 'poor historian' and move on. Doctors use this to label patients who don't tell them what we want to hear. It means someone who doesn't answer questions quickly or in the right order. Or perhaps wanders off or forgets to include details about their health.

I thought that the label was a cop-out, especially when Ian told me a story where I'm sure he'd been labelled a poor historian. He had woken up in the middle of the night with terrible pains in his back. He stayed completely still to try to keep the pain at bay, but he realised that his heart was beating slowly. He counted thirty-four beats per minute, using the alarm clock on his bedside table to keep time. The male heart usually beats between sixty and one hundred times per minute so he knew he was in trouble and dialled triple zero.

When the paramedics arrived they told him that the number he'd reported for his heart rate couldn't possibly be true and when they interviewed him about his pain they told him he was being 'imprecise'. He'd been trying to describe it as accurately as possible but wasn't comfortable with their definition of burning pain and sharp pain. He had just started telling them this, when another wave of pain hit him and he vomited.

The paramedics told him that he might be having a heart attack – but that annoyed him. He knew that he didn't have any of the typical symptoms like chest pain or feeling sweaty.

'No, you're not listening to me,' he said to them.

'Just answer our questions then,' a paramedic replied. The paramedics were expecting to hear about Ian's symptoms one way, but he was describing them another way. He was off script.

After more questions they took him to emergency and doctors there did their own interview and ordered tests. A scan showed that a kidney stone was the culprit, not a heart attack. After a couple of days he was discharged to wait at home for the stone to complete its journey, which it did a few days later.

Poor Ian had felt hugely irritated by the process but, for me, it showed the importance of the patient interview and how expecting patients to explain their symptoms a certain way is not just frustrating for us, but also for them. Collecting a medical history is how doctors and nurses get to meet and know patients. This is why patients find themselves repeating their story over and over. What patients might not realise is that each doctor worries that the one before them has missed something and this is their chance to pick it up.

As a medical student, I learnt that the interview process can become a kind of frenzied dig for information so that you can arrive at your list of possible diagnoses as quickly as possible. This practice of getting the interview done quickly stays with doctors for the rest of their careers. Unlearning something is harder than learning something. Plus, I'll be the first to admit, the fast pace is handy when you need to interview ten patients in a row before settling into paperwork and admin.

But I still feel that this rapid way of interacting with patients isn't conducive to good rapport. Sometimes it can feel like more of an interrogation, like Ian's 1 am ambulance visit.

The relationship between patient and doctor is just that, a relationship. And, as we know, relationships take time. Sometimes, it's best to start by chatting about the weather or which town the patient is from, rather than zoning in on the lump on their leg. A little investment up front in the patient as a person can make the rest of the interview flow more easily. This is true in emergencies, too – even when it is important to get answers quickly there are always small opportunities for connection, like a pat on the shoulder or a nod of the head. Rather than get frustrated by detours, I now use them as an opportunity to note what issues are important to the patient and to demonstrate that I am listening. Listening is necessary to building trust between patient and doctor, and medicine is nothing without trust.

16

ROUND AND ROUND THE WARDS

It was time to go back to hospital, but not as a cancer patient.

After two years of study, I was unleashed into the real world and got to start traipsing the hospital wards, operating theatres and clinics. Now I was a med student wearing a stethoscope, not a patient in a white gown trying to keep my hairy bum covered.

I was nervous about the year ahead, unsure whether I'd be more hindrance than help to the junior and senior doctors. Above all though, I was excited – getting off campus and into the action was a major point in my transition from patient to doctor. For the first time since starting med school, I felt like a true insider – the doors obscuring the world of doctors from patients were about to open. The year ahead consisted of five weeks in each area of psychiatry, surgery, paediatrics, obstetrics and gynaecology, as well as time at a private hospital doing a mix of intensive care, vascular medicine and nephrology.

'I've got psych first!' I said to a Med Bot who I'd bumped into on the walk to hospital.

He rolled his eyes. 'I heard they do a two-hour tutorial just on feelings,' he said. 'Feelings!'

Either he didn't know what feelings were or he didn't think they were important, so I moved on.

'I'm really looking forward to this term,' I said. Then I made an excuse about needing to stop for coffee so I could walk the rest of the way alone.

Psychiatry was interesting, provocative and upsetting – but mostly it was refreshing. I was impressed with the special way psychiatrists interviewed patients – focusing much more on aspects of a patient's childhood, family, work, attitudes and goals. Over my five-week stint, I practised taking this information and then creating a comprehensive understanding of the patient and their illness using past incidents, present symptoms and future recovery. I found most of the senior doctors very supportive, and their enthusiasm for making sense of a patient as a whole person infectious. At the end of the term I wondered, had I found my specialty?

•

The inner glow that psychiatry had given me was quickly extinguished in the cold operating theatres of surgery, where the closeness I'd felt with the psychiatrists was replaced by a surgical silence.

In the operating theatre, students were mostly relegated to the nosebleeds – back of the room, in the dark, squinting at the action. Bright lights illuminated those performing the work, but it was hard to make out any details from where we were standing.

I was usually far enough away that I couldn't even hear what the surgeons were saying. Words muffled by surgical masks and the beeps of machines don't travel well.

In some theatres it was obvious that no one wanted a student there. While the surgeons worked, nurses watched to make sure we didn't move, so we didn't contaminate the sterile field (the area around the incision that is free from bugs). Even so, we were always somehow in the way. Cables running along the floor had a special way of tripping medical students, as if they were in cahoots with grumpy nurses.

Often nothing was explained to us. I found all of this a shame. Since I'd watched Kim's Caesarean, I'd been keen to see more surgery. What happened on the operating table was nothing short of miraculous, but we were removed from it.

Sometimes a surgery would take fifteen minutes, sometimes five hours. For us students, it was a waiting game. Waiting to pee, waiting to blow my nose, waiting to go home. I wasn't always in the shadows, sometimes I was the surgeon's entertainment.

I was watching one surgery to remove an appendix and I wasn't scrubbed. Being 'dirty', I remained far from the sterile field. I could still see though because the procedure was laparoscopic – a camera had been inserted into the abdomen through a small hole next to the patient's belly button, and it beamed images to a large monitor. When the surgeon pointed the camera towards the patient's head I saw liver and bowel. When she pointed it towards the patient's feet I saw her uterus. It was all so beautiful, I thought.

The surgeon was manipulating instruments inserted via other small holes. Little jaws and clamps moved organs around while the surgeon journeyed to the appendix. I watched the screen with the intensity of a Netflix binge, my mouth open in awe behind my mask.

The senior surgeon wasn't speaking, so no one else did. Bowel glistened on the monitor, occasionally contracting to move digested food along its length. Suddenly, the camera stopped at a blood vessel snaking its way across the monitor.

'Where's the student?' the surgeon said. She didn't look away from the screen.

'Here,' I replied, standing well behind her.

'What is this?' she said.

'Um, do you mean the blood vessel?' I asked.

'Yes, I mean the blood vessel. What is it?'

'Um, I think it is the superior mesenteric artery,' I replied.

'It is an artery, but not the superior mesenteric.' Her camera remained fixed on the artery, waiting.

'Is it the inferior mesenteric artery then?' I asked.

'Don't guess and waste my time. If you don't know, say as much,' she quipped.

'Sorry, I don't know,' I said.

'Aren't your exams soon?' she asked. Her assistant chuckled.

'In a month.'

'Well, I'm not sure what's going on with anatomy teaching at your university,' she said, 'but you need to get studying.'

Sweat beaded between my shoulder blades and ran down my back. I tried to swallow but my throat had gone dry and my tongue was stuck to the roof of my mouth. My skin prickled with embarrassment. *I should have known that artery*, I scolded myself. *Now all these people think I'm stupid.*

Five minutes later she asked me to name an organ centred on the monitor. I got it right. She then asked me to name the arteries that supply it, which I also got right. She asked me to name the veins that drain it, which I got wrong. Satisfied, she returned to work.

These quizzes always ended with an incorrect answer – the game was unwinnable. I felt bad for getting something wrong, regardless of how many correct answers preceded it. My feeling of inadequacy was worse because the quizzing unfolded in public. I hadn't just disappointed the senior surgeon – the junior surgeon, nurses and anaesthetic team were also watching me fail.

After the surgery I raced out of there.

On the bus home I replayed the surgeon's questions over and over in my head. With each re-run I felt even sillier. *My classmates would have known those answers*, I thought, *I'm never going to be as smart as them.*

•

My two favourite things about that surgical term took place outside of the operating theatre – chatting to the patients before they went to sleep and the tutorials we had with Dr Williams, a senior surgeon.

Dr Williams had a round bald head, bushy eyebrows and bright green eyes. He was brilliant at explaining surgical concepts and asked questions in a way that made me want to try and answer them – not hide in a ditch. I hadn't seen Dr Williams in theatre because I'd been allocated to a different team, but I really wanted to – especially after the student allocated to him told me about his ritual before every surgery.

'As the patient is going under, he rests his hand on their hand,' she said.

'And?'

'Nothing, he just leaves it there for a moment and nods. He said that he likes to do that before every surgery, as a sign of respect,' she said.

'That's amazing,' I blurted out.

'Really? I think it's weird,' she said.

'What? No way. I could tell that he was kind from the way he treats us in tutorials. What a nice way to honour his patients.'

I thought the act was lovely – a real homage to the heart in healthcare. I never got to see him in theatre, but that Dr Williams was out there operating restored my faith in surgeons.

•

Around halfway through third year, I began hearing students talking about patients as if they were just human bags of symptoms.

Students are encouraged to see as much disease as possible and, like everything in medicine, this too becomes competitive. The patient is secondary, their broken bit is the real treasure.

Medical students roam around the hospital seeking out funny-sounding hearts to listen to, or bloated abdomens to touch. Some students become excellent hunters. In the student lounge they sit around swapping pathology like school kids trading

Pokémon cards. 'Go check out bed seven if you want to see something cool,' they say.

Having spent nearly a month in hospital as a patient I appreciated what it felt like to be stuck in a bed all day long. Drips, blood tests, ward rounds: day in, day out. Feeling increasingly powerless, I assumed that everyone who came near me was either a doctor or a nurse. Most patients will trust anyone with a stethoscope – and medical students benefit from this. When a student rushes up to a hospital bed, mumbles through a line about them being a medical student or some such and begins the interview or examination, a patient usually just sees a nicely dressed healthy person with a stethoscope around their neck. Patients tend to say yes to whatever nicely dressed people with stethoscopes ask them.

One thing my medical school did very well was stress the importance of patients giving doctors proper consent, but I remained uneasy about exploiting the obvious power difference between patients and everyone else. This meant that I didn't tick off as many symptoms or signs of disease as other students, even though we were expected to see a certain range of conditions in order to pass a term. This did not affect my grades at all – by spending more time with each patient I ended up learning just as much as the Med Bots. It was my way of trying to respect the divide between patients and doctors or, in this case, medical students. This divide, I'd noticed, was leading to some students believing they had a right to *use* patients.

One day in the student lounge I was listening to one Med Bot tell another Med Bot about a patient they should go and examine.

'You should check this patient out. Massive distended abdomen. They have all the signs of liver disease,' the first student said.

'Oh wow. Which ward?' their friend asked.

'G2. You should see the veins, straight out of a textbook. They were so cool.'

I couldn't help myself and butted in.

'I'm not sure cool is the right word. It's certainly not cool for the patient. Sounds like they're in liver failure.'

'Well, not *cool* cool. You know what I mean,' the first student said.

I wasn't done.

'Also, I'm not sure the patient wants all these students gawking at them or asking to feel their abdomen. Make sure you check –'

'They're a public patient in a teaching hospital, they know the deal,' the first student cut in. 'We're here to learn.'

I couldn't believe what I was hearing. This medical student was saying that a patient in a hospital that trained doctors was therefore training material. Never mind that they were likely only there because an ambulance had decided to take them to that particular hospital. Even if the patient had chosen that hospital to go to, it didn't mean that they had given up rights like privacy and rest.

'They aren't here for us!' I said. 'They are here to get better.'

This felt like an obvious point, but one that they needed to hear.

These students were just expressing what I had seen developing in many of my classmates as we progressed through medical school. As their knowledge and skills increased, so did the gap between them and the people they were learning to care for.

I probably reacted strongly to my classmates' view of patients because I was still a patient too. The thought that, while lying in hospital worried about a dozen different things, I had a responsibility to teach a student doctor was nauseating. After my surgery, medical students and junior doctors sometimes visited me to practise interviewing or find out more about my medical history, and when I was feeling up to it I always said yes. Having that choice is important. Had I felt that it was expected, or that a student believed I owed them simply because I was stuck in a hospital bed I would have refused. In the first few days after my surgery, and then again when I sprung a leak and sustained the dry retching attacks, the gulf between me and the doctors felt enormous. Not only were they healthier than me, they likely understood more of what was happening to me than I did, or ever would. Differences between patients and doctors will always exist, which is why doctors must compensate for these by making sure their patients are heard.

•

Every now and then, I crossed paths with a doctor doing their best to bridge this gulf between patients and doctors.

Professor Robinson was a neurologist in his seventies who oversaw our clinical training in third year. He styled his thick snow-white hair into a precise side part, and wore jet black suits expertly tailored to his tall lean frame. He had been a doctor for nearly five decades, and carried himself like a physician in an old English period drama – gently and with nobility. It would be safe to say that Prof Robinson was 'old school'.

During class presentations, he always sat in the front row, but during our talks it wasn't unusual for his eyes to slowly lower, and then his head. We'd think he'd dozed off, until he'd suddenly open his eyes, startling us with a highly intelligent question about the topic being presented. In this way, he kept us on our toes.

In his half a century as a doctor he'd seen it all, but he spoke to patients as though it were the first time he was hearing someone describe a headache or that they sometimes tripped over their own feet when walking. He always had a lot to say to patients, but he balanced that by spending the same amount of time listening.

He would individually introduce us to his patients. As one of us interviewed the patient, and another did the relevant examination, he listened and observed with great focus, often while making small talk with the patient or a patient's loved one at the same time.

He concluded every lesson still at the bedside, explaining the patient's medical history and recent symptoms. He would turn to look at the patient at key moments, allowing them to add to his description or nod that he was accurately representing them. He asked their opinion of how we'd performed.

His patients loved him. Prof Robinson's teaching was like his doctoring – warm and kind. He actually taught us, taking the time to explain concepts and immerse us in the patient's world. He would ask questions occasionally, and encouraged us to consult the other students in the group if we weren't sure – he was one of the few to model medicine as a team sport. He was nearly always the smartest person in the room, but he never made his students feel stupid.

•

By the end of third year I'd spent a lot of time talking to patients. Despite advances in drugs, surgery and scans, it was clear that the process of a patient getting better still started with a conversation. Yet this fundamental aspect of our craft was often neglected in our training – I'd only had one communication workshop in three years at medical school.

As medical school got busier, we were so swamped with textbooks and tests that we had little time to hone the art of making conversation. And since communications skills didn't count towards our exam marks in any significant way, there was no immediate incentive to cultivate them.

Some doctors see communication as a soft skill, rather than an essential one. After a year in hospitals and clinics as a student, I could see plenty of barriers preventing doctors from focusing on high-quality communication. There were crowded waiting rooms and wards, budget issues, endless record-keeping and understaffing for a start. Even so, I didn't want to compromise our greatest diagnostic tool – connecting with patients in a meaning-ful way – because the reward was worth it. When done well, patient–doctor communication led to a more accurate version of a patient's medical history, and helped doctors work out what was wrong sooner.

When I talked about communication with my classmates, they often rolled their eyes. The biggest complaints were that 'there's no time' and 'you can't afford to let patients ramble on'. I didn't have good facts to counter this resistance, so I looked it up.

In a 2002 Swiss study, when doctors were told to ask an initial question and then let patients answer it without interruption, the average time a patient talked was a mere ninety-two seconds – not the hours my colleagues feared if they listened more and cut in less.

Despite this, doctors are infamous for muscling in. On average, doctors interrupt patients within eleven to twenty-three seconds into their first answer. This leaves patients confused and feeling like they haven't been fully heard.

A 2005 study done at a hospital in New York City found fewer than half of patients discharged from hospital knew their diagnosis – this is astounding, a complete indictment of medical communication. We know the American medical system is plagued with all kinds of problems, but it is extraordinary that a patient can leave hospital not understanding what illness or injury they have.

I left hospital a month after my surgery with a pretty good understanding of what happened to me, but this isn't always the case. A study at an Australian hospital in 2014 found that some patients being discharged didn't understand any of their diagnoses. Overall, half of the patients in that study understood less than seventy per cent of what had happened to them.

Another Australian study done in 2015 surveyed patients on the day of discharge and found that between ten and twenty per cent of them felt their doctor had missed important information about them and remained confused after a question of theirs had been answered.

While doctors may know their patients back to front, it's not a two-way street. One study in 2009 by the University of Chicago found fewer than one in five hospital patients could name the doctor in charge of their care. While reading this last study I thought back to the anonymous doctor who had done my colonoscopy, and the time I left a check-up with a new doctor who I couldn't name.

•

The most frustrating example of communication between patients and doctors after my year in hospital as a med student was the ward round.

I remembered how rushed and awkward these were when I was a patient, and had hoped that crossing from patient to doctor would help me understand why. But I soon discovered that as a medical student I felt just as impotent during ward rounds as I had as a patient. Because just like a patient, I had no power or influence.

The thing about ward rounds, and most parts of care in a hospital, is that the senior doctor is running the show. They decide how the patient is greeted and who does or doesn't get introduced. They decide what questions get asked and they choose whether to invite the patient to ask questions. As a medical student and then junior doctor I certainly couldn't change the time of the round or slow the pace of the interrogation. I could not hit pause and make sure the patient knew who we were. In fact, students and junior doctors aren't really supposed to speak at all.

So, during ward rounds, I had to choose between staying back and connecting with the patient or racing on to keep up with the team. I lost count of the number of times an intern or resident rushed back to find me chatting with a patient, only to hurry me along.

The moments when I stayed behind and connected with the patient were small, but significant. Is there something I can get for you? How did you sleep? Is that sunlight in your face? Can you reach that glass of water? Would you like the door open or closed? How are you feeling? These exchanges showed me that other patients feel let down by ward rounds too.

Sometimes patients asked me who the person was who had just been talking to them, not because they were delirious, but because the doctor hadn't introduced themselves. Sometimes they told me about a new symptom or asked a question. Once I even had a patient ask which specialty we were from. How often do patients have no idea who they're talking to or why?

I did sometimes see rounds done well, but good examples were dwarfed by bad ones. As a patient I didn't know when or if the doctor was going to do a ward round, and I certainly didn't understand much of what went on during those early morning encounters. I realised then that communication is the most valuable tool in any doctor's bag – a thought that returned to me as a medical student, scurrying around hospitals.

This isn't trivial – research shows critical information communicated during ward rounds is too often lost. A small study on patients aged sixty-five years and older in Taiwan found that fewer than one in five key pieces of information provided by the doctor could be repeated by patients one hour after rounds. Four hours later – less than ten per cent of messages were remembered.

We need a communication revolution.

And the place to begin is the ward round – the first doctor–patient encounter of the day. We can start with small changes like giving patients advance notice of when the team will be bedside, capping the number of staff present, seeking permission to begin the consultation, and providing clear introductions via the senior doctor. During the visit the lead doctor should sit at the patient's level, someone could take notes specifically to give to the patient and their family, and genuine opportunities to ask questions should be cultivated. These seem like small steps. But for the person under the glare of scrutiny – sick, tired, bewildered – they can be critical.

Some aspects of medical training are changing. Doctors specialising in emergency medicine, for example, are increasingly being tested on their communication skills as part of their final exams. And trainee paediatricians are often required to role-play typical explanations for anxious parents, such as what's involved in sampling fluid from the spine of a newborn. All of this is reassuring.

But communication is a two-way street. Patients, too, must come to the table open to dialogue and empowered to talk. I think patients should always have someone supportive with them, where practical. If a family member or good friend can't make it to an appointment, at least have them on the phone so they can listen in and ask questions. It is entirely reasonable to ask a doctor to write key points down, or draw a picture that the patient can take home to go over again later.

In my spare time, I volunteer with an anonymous helpline that connects people newly diagnosed with cancer with someone who has been through it already. To these patients I am 'Ben who had bowel cancer', not a doctor. A lot of the time I end up re-explaining what the doctor has told them or filling in the gaps. Because of this, I suggest to them, and to all my own patients, that they get a notebook just for medical stuff – somewhere they can jot down questions between appointments and the names of doctors who look after them.

Levelling the playing field between patient and doctor is hard to achieve – even for me. I found it difficult to raise my concerns when my monitoring program was changed, and didn't speak up at all when the doctor doing my colonoscopy never introduced themselves. I was an experienced patient and also a student doctor, getting used to working in hospitals, and yet I couldn't muster the courage. What hope do others have of telling doctors what they actually want and feel?

17

BULLIES IN THE
SCHOOL YARD

In the break between third year and fourth year, Sana and I got married.

In a span of two weeks, we held ceremonies in Toronto and Sydney, with family crisscrossing the world to attend both. Ian, Kim, James, Hugo, Archie, Mum and Graeme accompanied us to Toronto; Sana's mum, brother, and her two aunts and their families came to Sydney.

In Toronto we had five or six (I lost count) different ceremonies and parties. Everything Faisal, my tutor in second year, had taught me had been spot on, except for one crucial factor on the day of the actual wedding. The nikah (religious ceremony) took place in a mosque outside of Toronto and only immediate family were present. Sana sat with her mum and aunts, next to Mum and Kim, with their hair covered – Archie was perched in Kim's lap. I sat a few metres away in front of them, cross-legged, next to Sana's father, uncles and the men in my family – Ian, Graeme, James and Hugo. As the ceremony unfolded I wondered when Sana was going to come and join me at the front of the room, but she never did. Before I knew it, I was holding her dad's hands and repeating vows being fed to me by the imam, who I'd only just met. I was utterly confused, and a glance in Sana's direction showed that she shared my surprise. We'd had no idea that her father had wanted this kind of ceremony, something normally reserved for far more devout families. I had no idea where to look, so I just stared into her father's eyes while he recited his vows to me, after which everyone clapped. Then I walked straight over to Sana.

'Did I marry you or your dad?' I whispered.

'I have no clue what just happened there,' she whispered back.

Christmas later that week was a more predictable affair. While a turkey baked in the oven and thick snow fell outside, the Australians gave stuffed koalas and opal necklaces to Sana's family. Kim served fluffy eggnog (minus the alcohol) as the Canadians handed out maple syrup, Tim Hortons coffee and Hudson's Bay beach towels.

Then we all flew to Sydney and got married again! In Sydney, we held two days of events, hosting a cocktail party at an ornamental Chinese garden the night before our ceremony, which was on a boat in Sydney Harbour.

We didn't have a honeymoon as I had to get back to school. A few days into my first rotation at a busy clinic I wished we'd squeezed one in – it would have made the hell I was experiencing easier to cope with.

•

I'd been struggling with imposter syndrome. Despite passing, getting better grades each year, being admitted to the honours program, working on two research projects, winning a small scholarship, and publishing articles on medical education and healthcare for the ABC, I didn't think I was special. My classmates were also doing extra things in their spare time, completing master's degrees at other universities, getting laboratory experience, volunteering.

No matter what I achieved, it didn't feel like enough, and self-doubt took over. *I'm not a good medical student and I don't know enough*, I'd say to myself. I grew less confident. If a student or teacher asked a medical question, I'd wait for someone else to answer. The self-doubt spread beyond my student world and my internal voice kept saying, *I'm going to be a bad doctor and end up hurting a patient.*

For my first term in fourth year, I was the only medical student at a clinic, which was unusual because students normally travel in packs, with several of us in each rotation (surgery, internal medicine, intensive care and so on).

One Monday morning at the clinic, the senior doctor supervising me was in a particularly bad mood. I was sitting with her in her office, getting the answers to a litany of detailed questions wrong. She grew increasingly frustrated. Her sighs became louder, her eye-rolling more exaggerated. I wanted to curl into a ball and hide under the desk.

Suddenly, she slammed her laptop shut and ordered me to sit in with another senior doctor for a while. I left her office, dejected but also relieved. A reprieve, finally.

It was short-lived. Within minutes of meeting me, this senior doctor, let's call him Dr Smith, was on the attack too – only worse. I'd found him in his clinical room, but he was between appointments, so I couldn't just observe him speaking to patients. He adopted the same interrogative style as many of the other senior doctors I'd met by then. What I wasn't prepared for was the way Dr Smith chipped away at what little confidence I still had left at this stage in my studies.

While waiting for his next patient to arrive, he brought up an anatomy diagram on his computer and pointed to an artery. 'What artery is this?' he said.

Oh god, I thought, *this guy is even meaner than my supervisor.* I started to panic. 'It's the inferior phrenic?'

'Wrong. This is the left middle suprarenal artery. What about this one?' he continued, pointing to a new artery.

'Maybe a gonadal artery?' I replied.

'Wrong. Look where it's going and use your brain. This is a lumbar artery.'

He went back to his inbox and a couple of minutes went by. I sat as still as possible, hoping he'd forget I was there.

'I'm going to say the name of an organ and you'll tell me the Latin or Greek name,' he said.

I stifled a laugh, utterly defeated. 'I'm sorry, doctor, I don't think I'll be able to do that, I've never learnt Latin or Greek.'

'Kidney,' he said.

'Sorry, I have no idea,' I responded.

He rolled his eyes, throwing his hands up in the air. '*Nephros* in Greek. *Renes* in Latin.' He spun his chair around to face me directly. 'I'm going to email the dean of your medical school about your lack of medical knowledge.'

I looked down at the ground, unsure how to respond. He swivelled back to his computer.

'Obviously we need to get very basic here,' he continued. 'Name five evolutionary atavisms.'

My brain had completely stopped working – my head was a tangle of self-loathing and embarrassment. My face was burning and my right leg shook. Annoyingly, I actually knew about atavisms – traits from an evolutionary ancestor that can reappear in an organism – because I'd taken evolution and animal development courses during my zoology degree. This had *never* been taught during medical school, highlighting just how mean he was trying to be.

'Ah, um, I'm not sure,' was all I could say.

Dr Smith ordered me to go back to my supervisor.

'You remind me of myself when I *first* started medical school – I knew nothing and I didn't care. But the difference is that you're graduating soon,' he said.

Once I was out of his office, he yelled to several senior doctors standing together down the corridor: 'This guy is final year – can you believe it?'

Dr Smith had decided that I wasn't fit to practise medicine. Sure, I wasn't able to answer his questions that day, but in two weeks I was due to present a review I'd done of research on people with cancer and depression at a large meeting of senior doctors in New Zealand. I'd be the only medical student presenting. Despite this achievement, and others along the way, senior doctors often had a way of dragging us medical students down if we didn't know the exact answer to their question.

He had decided that I didn't care, which was news to me. He knew nothing of my cancer, the conferences I spoke at, the cancer committees I volunteered on, the cancer patients I supported via a helpline, my passion.

From that point on Dr Smith referred to me as 'Tryhard' – I'm not even sure he knew my actual name.

'Hello, Tryhard,' he'd say, passing me in the corridor.

The attacks continued. One day he joked that if I didn't study harder I'd end up being a social worker, insulting me *and* the social worker sitting next to me. Every time I saw him in the corridor my face grew hot and my heart quickened. As he got closer, I dreamt of disappearing.

Another day, he took me to a meeting, where he introduced me to the executive in charge of the clinic by saying, 'This guy knows a couple of things, but needs to do a lot more work. Students sure are different these days.'

The executive either picked up on his tone or saw my face and felt sorry for me, and came to my rescue.

'Medical students don't have it easy,' she said. 'I'm sure he's worked extremely hard to get this far.'

I smiled at her. Dr Smith rolled his eyes.

I warned other students what to expect at this clinic. And I formally reported Dr Smith to the medical school, but I never heard back about whether any action was taken. Two students at the clinic after me actually cut their time short. They were not prepared to learn in that environment and left. *Good for them,* I thought. But I wondered how many other students had left before them and why these doctors were still allowed to teach. Before medical school, I had put doctors on a pedestal. I thought of them as having superhuman intelligence and integrity. But once inside their world, I learnt that many doctors weren't deserving of that pedestal.

Some *future* doctors weren't either – I saw lots of bad behaviour among my classmates, like the time someone used a slur to refer to First Nations people, or when a group of students were caught cheating on exams. One time I pulled a male student off a woman he had pinned against a wall.

My school was unusual in requiring people applying to medical school to submit a portfolio. The notional idea was that a student's character mattered. Even with this extra step, people of dubious character made it through – I worried about all the other medical schools that selected on exam and interview scores only; worse, some didn't even interview candidates anymore.

Badly behaving doctors were increasingly in the news. Vascular surgeon Dr Gabrielle McMullin created headlines when she explicitly called out sexism and harassment of female junior doctors. At the launch of a book on gender equity that she'd contributed to, she described terrible acts of sexual harassment. She detailed the accounts of female junior doctors unable to find work because they'd upset the men's club by rebuffing assaults by male senior doctors. Dr McMullin suggested, cynically, the status quo meant that it was better for female junior doctors to comply with requests for sex than refuse – keeping their career prospects safe.

Bad behaviour seemed rife, and the power and autonomy enjoyed by doctors at the top meant that little was being done to stamp it out. Why were so many senior doctors behaving poorly? Had they always treated their colleagues like this?

I'd watched people change during medical training. Some of my fellow students' egos and arrogance grew. While they were acquiring knowledge and status, they were also becoming colder and less compassionate.

It seemed obvious to me that the system was changing them. We had such a huge study load, and competition was intense. We knew we would be rewarded if we could demonstrate that we were the smartest person in the room, but this did not bring out the best in people. It even turned some of my fellow students into bullies.

Our very job as doctors is to care for society's sick and vulnerable. How can we possibly do that well when so many of us are riddled with fear, guilt and embarrassment as a result of bullying and humiliation?

Patients aren't the only ones who lose. In 2013, a Beyond Blue study found that twenty-one per cent of doctors either had depression or had been diagnosed with it in the past, compared to fifteen per cent of the general population. Twenty-five per cent of doctors had thought about suicide in the year before the survey, compared to thirteen per cent for the rest of Australia. The picture is similar for medical students – they were more likely to have suffered depression than the wider population (eighteen per cent versus fifteen per cent) and contemplated suicide (twenty per cent versus thirteen per cent).

There are many reasons why doctors have poorer mental health than non-doctors, such as heavy workloads, high stress environments, burnout, a fear of talking to their colleagues about mental health because of stigma, but surely the way we treat each other is another reason. More and more, the families of doctors who had committed suicide began demanding change, which culminated in several hospital departments being stripped of their right to train doctors – these teaching environments were just too toxic to continue.

My own experience of bullying is not unusual. A survey of nearly ten thousand junior doctors in 2020 by the Medical Board of Australia, seven years after the Beyond Blue study, found that thirty-four per cent had witnessed bullying or harassment in the last year and fifty per cent of this bullying was done by senior doctors.

One friend was told they had as much medical knowledge as a toddler – she'd had to turn away at the time so no one saw the tears in her eyes. I saw a senior doctor berate a junior doctor in front of a patient for not examining their leg properly, barking, 'Get out of the way!' I saw one doctor rip another to shreds in a WhatsApp group, for the whole team to read. Once, when I didn't find something fast enough in a new storeroom, a senior doctor stomped in front of me and snatched the item. 'You're going to be eaten alive on the wards,' he said, slamming a drawer shut.

These might seem petty grievances, small instances of rudeness or exasperation. But they are overwhelmingly the norm in everyday interactions between senior doctors and the doctors and students below them. Research has shown that behaviour like this can be utterly corrosive. The effects build up, wearing on junior doctors' mental health, crushing their confidence and leaving them questioning whether they should remain in medicine.

I've lost track of the number of times doctors rolled their eyes when a question wasn't answered correctly. 'What do they even teach you these days?' they'd respond.

A colleague of mine failed to hear a heart murmur when examining a patient in an emergency department, something easily missed by novice ears in a noisy environment. The senior doctor suggested that the student had lied and not actually done the examination. 'Can I even trust you now?' the doctor said.

Having experienced radiation, chemotherapy and cancer surgery, I know pain. But my bully caused a new type of injury – one that ate away at my sense of self. I started to excuse Dr Smith, wondering whether he was correct. Perhaps I deserved this kind of treatment?

Mercifully, I was able to leave him behind, as the four-week rotation came to an end. But junior doctors don't always have that luxury, and sometimes the bully is the one making decisions about their career.

Medical students and junior doctors often dream of a better future, when their generation is running the system – but I bet every cohort before them longed for the same thing. We are thrust into positions of status and power, but there are no courses at medical school on leadership, teamwork, mentorship and peer support. For change to happen, doctors need to develop their interpersonal skills just as much as any other part of their work. Like mastering a new procedure or understanding new drug dosing, doctors should be encouraged to evaluate and practise their teaching, interpersonal and leadership skills. Unless we start to address these skills, I'm afraid the cycle of mean and unhappy senior doctors moulding mean and unhappy junior doctors will continue.

•

At my next rotation I wasn't bullied at all, but I often felt invisible.

This was my surgical rotation, and I got the chance to observe a world-renowned surgeon, known for his meticulous technique and speedy surgeries. Patients flocked from all over the country to be treated by him, and he travelled the world speaking at conferences. He'd even invented several surgical devices, each carrying his name.

The surgeon was gently spoken, with kind eyes. He always seemed to know when to reassuringly smile at a patient – whether they were a regular kid or a celebrity. To his colleagues he was curt, and sometimes outright mean. He never spoke during surgery except to ask for things, which he rarely did as the team around him anticipated every instrument or manoeuvre he needed.

The session I was involved in was to be an eight-hour day in theatre, with him performing the same surgery over and over on different patients. Though normally medical students stood back, on this day I'd be helping with small tasks – adjusting the bed height, tilting the bed this way or that, giving the anaesthetist a hand putting the patients to sleep. All day, we fluttered about while the surgeon worked silently. A junior surgeon from overseas joined for one procedure. Towards the end of that surgery, the senior surgeon suddenly spoke, keeping his eyes on the monitor magnifying the body part he was working on. He seemed to be listing the main steps involved in the surgery. I understood only part of what he was saying. 'If what I've said doesn't make sense, you're in the wrong place and should leave,' he said to the junior, concluding the 'lesson'.

After the final surgery I accompanied the last patient out to the recovery bay. I wanted to help the nursing team set up the monitoring gear as the patient slowly woke up. I was standing next to the bed getting a kink out of her IV drip when the surgeon and his team walked in.

As he approached the patient, I looked up, surprised to find him making a beeline for me. He rested his hand on my hand, which was now holding the bed frame. His hand was warm and soft; mine was clammy, my knuckles white from squeezing the bed frame. He stood close, my two-metre frame towering over his. He was looking at me with the same kindness he reserved for his patients, while gently patting my hand. I was so confused.

'She did just fine, you have nothing to worry about,' he said.

'Oh, um –'

'There were no surprises. She'll be in a little bit of pain but should be up and about in no time,' he continued.

Oh god, he thinks I'm the patient's husband.

'Ah, um. Thanks,' I replied.

'Is everything going to be okay at home? You've got some help organised, right?' he asked.

I looked at the other doctors in his team. As an SOS I furrowed my eyebrows for a split second, and then widened my eyes even more discreetly while the surgeon looked down at the patient. One doctor was smiling and then caught himself, the rest were dead pan. I'd had conversations with each of them throughout the day: they knew I was a medical student and not the patient's husband, but no one dared correct the surgeon.

'Yes, everything is fine,' I said eventually.

'Great, come and see me in my rooms in two weeks.'

The group walked off to the next patient.

Alone again, the nurse and I turned to each other, stunned. Her cheeks and lips were smashed tight, trying not to burst out laughing. My face burnt with embarrassment, my mouth dry.

The nurse propped the unconscious patient's head up and I unkinked the drip again.

'So, how long have you and this patient been married?' she asked, before cackling with laughter. My cheeks burnt all over again.

I'd spent all day in this surgeon's operating theatre while he worked for hours. I was still wearing hospital scrubs and my name badge (which would have been directly in his line of sight because of our height difference) that said BEN, MEDICAL STUDENT in large bold letters. All that aside, at nearly two metres tall, I'm hard not to notice. I'd helped wheel in and out half-a-dozen patients, and he'd even asked me to manipulate the bed and monitors a couple of times. This wasn't an organ transplant with fifteen doctors and nurses wearing identical masks and gowns. This was routine surgery with him, an assistant, anaesthetist and a couple of nurses. It was far from crowded. He just didn't see me. I was noise to be filtered out.

As the recovery nurse relayed the incident to another nurse I made an excuse about needing a coffee and left. On my way to the hospital canteen I passed the surgeon's assistant – the one who had let a smile escape when I glared at the group for help. He started laughing. I laughed too. I'd clearly made his day.

'Oh my god, what the hell was that?' I asked. 'Did I do the right thing? Should I have said something?'

'Man, you did the only thing you could do. You played along and rode it out. Nice work.'

'Thanks, I guess,' I said.

He headed off down the corridor. 'Good luck getting the wife home, mate, and don't forget that appointment in two weeks!' he yelled over his shoulder.

The power of the medical hierarchy had been on display that day because no one in the surgeon's team felt comfortable to tap him on the shoulder and say, 'Um, sorry doctor, this is not the patient's husband – he's a medical student.' Instead, they all watched the surgeon pat my hand and inquire whether I'd organised support for my wife once she was home.

In these kinds of situations, speaking up was too risky. The top doc might have a fragile ego or be a bully. And often they had some control over your advancement, perhaps even completing the evaluation needed for your next job.

It isn't that every senior doctor behaves badly, but enough do so that it can feel almost normal. I had become desensitised so quickly to poor behaviour during medical school, as had my colleagues, that it wasn't until the odd friendly and supportive senior doctor came along that I realised just how little I expected from my senior doctors.

•

On my next rotation, the immunology team I was with was asked to go to the intensive care unit to see a 'difficult' patient. This phrase, like a 'poor historian', is all too common on the wards and irks me because it's lazy and judgemental. The junior doctor who ran the immunology team was a Dr Mohammadi. She had black, tightly curled hair that she wore half up, half down. Red thick-framed glasses hinted that she had a quirky side.

Dr Mohammadi was known for her warmth and learnt the names of each of her students on day one.

The patient in the intensive care unit was Audrey. She was in her mid-thirties, spoke with a French accent and taught modern history at a local university. Three days earlier, Audrey had felt pain in her pelvic area and was overcome with nausea. She had gone straight to her GP.

She was given medicine for the nausea and told to return if things got worse, which they did over the weekend. On Monday the pain had spread down both legs and her left leg had ballooned in size. The GP directed her straight to hospital.

A scan of Audrey's body showed that the large vein that collects blood from the legs and pelvis and delivers it to the heart was full of blood clots.

Audrey was getting treatment for the blood clots in the intensive care unit, but she was unhappy. She had been openly discussed by the overnight intensive care doctors as being 'difficult' and needing a review by our team.

Intensive care on this day was noisy. A rowdy conversation between a few nurses was taking place two beds away from Audrey's. Across the room a doctor was loudly questioning a confused patient. And from every direction, beeping. Relentless beeping in every tone imaginable – an alarming chorus bouncing off sterile walls.

Among this noisy jungle was our patient. Audrey's bed was walled off by disposable curtains, all hospital blue. She was surrounded by stands and pumps pushing different fluids into different cannulas. She had a large cannula in her right thigh, one in her left thigh, one in each arm, and one entering her neck.

Potent clot-busting medicines were being fed into her body. This treatment is so risky that it has to be done in the intensive care unit in case things go wrong.

Audrey glared at us. Dr Mohammadi asked her what had happened in the few days before coming to hospital. She carefully asked about the usual risk factors for blood clots. Was she a smoker? Did she have diabetes? Was she on the contraceptive pill? Did she have high blood pressure? Had she recently had surgery, been sick or been on a long-haul flight? Audrey's responses were all no, and all curt.

Dr Mohammadi started explaining where the different clots were located in Audrey's body and how they were being treated. She listed the names of the veins involved. Why Audrey had developed so many large blood clots remained a mystery, but Dr Mohammadi mentioned a few possible causes and then waited patiently while Audrey typed each of these into her phone, to look up later.

Audrey put the phone down and burst into tears. She tried to raise her hands to cover her face but was restricted by all the tubes. She looked away as tears rolled off her cheeks and onto her hospital gown.

'I'm not sad,' she said, turning back to Dr Mohammadi. 'I'm just relieved to finally understand what is happening to me.'

Up until that point, no one had taken the time to explain to her what was going on and why. Perhaps the patient's direct manner, or maybe her need to know the small details of her treatment had landed her the label 'difficult', but it appeared to me that she had just wanted to understand her problem and the treatment plan, like anyone else in her situation would have.

That night, instead of revising the anatomy of the major blood vessels, I searched medical journals for articles about 'difficult' patients. I was shocked to learn that being labelled difficult affects the quality of the care and follow-up you receive. Many patients actually fear being labelled difficult and so will just say and do things to please doctors and nurses, something researchers called 'acquiescence bias'. One study I read explained how some patients who feel afraid, uncertain and powerless in hospital can develop patterns of thinking similar to people who have been kidnapped. They censor any questions they have, minimise their own concerns and agree to things even when they are against values they hold. Psychologists term this Hostage Bargaining Syndrome.

This was not just a matter of semantics, it affected patient care.

I shared all of this with Dr Mohammadi the next day. She didn't know about those studies, but she wasn't surprised.

'I always form my own assessment of a patient,' she said. 'Most of the time there is some unresolved issue that means they get labelled like that. I approached her gently and tried to explain everything I could simply. She was angry with me at the beginning, but she needed time to trust that I was going to help her. I didn't change the treatment plan, I just went in with an open mind and answered her questions.'

The simple parts of medicine are often the first to fall under stress and time pressure. Yet, it is the simple things that matter. Audrey will not remember the name of the thrombolytics that dissolved her blood clots, or the emergency physician who admitted her – but she will remember her anger at being dismissed, her hurt at feeling abandoned, and then her relief at finally meeting Dr Mohammadi.

•

My next rotation was on a general medical ward at a small hospital. Every doctor on the ward was just like Dr Mohammadi – I couldn't believe my luck.

The first thing I noticed was that the doctors, nurses and patients were all happy. At least once each ward round, a patient would describe their time in the hospital as one of their 'best experiences in hospital', or even 'amazing'. When it came time to leave, patients went out of their way to thank everyone from the cleaner to the doctor.

I couldn't believe what I was seeing. After ward rounds I chatted to patients – I was desperate to know if they really were this comfortable in hospital. I spoke to a patient who had fallen sick on a cruise ship docked nearby, a retired doctor with a leg infection, and a woman with a rare disorder who had spent her fair share of time sick – they all described feeling welcome, cared for and validated.

I was in my final year of medical school, and I'd become disappointed in the health system and unsure of my place in it. I had been going from rotation to rotation, developing an increasingly pessimistic view of medicine.

But this happy little ward proved that it was possible to deliver care with kindness and joy. How? Well, we started with a thorough ward round – no racing from patient to patient. We did this by splitting into smaller teams, which also created an intimacy between the doctor and patients, even though the ward was busy. Either a junior doctor or I worked the computer, while another led the consultation. All the doctors consistently and clearly introduced themselves and anyone else present to the patient. The lead doctor often pulled up a chair or squatted beside the bed to get down to the patient's level.

Patients were encouraged to update us about their symptoms and worries. The doctors then provided honest, authentic updates about what was happening with a patient's treatment. A plan was discussed at the end of each consultation.

The whole ward adopted the same caring culture. The hospital itself didn't have the best reputation – this ward was an island of kindness in the middle of a hostile sea. Interactions between nurses, allied health professionals, technicians and doctors were respectful and professional – this was the first place I'd seen that functioned like a true team, reminding me of places where I had worked before medicine. Despite sickness and pain, positivity and kindness flourished.

Alongside a patient's frustration or sadness was friendliness and compassion. The effect was contagious – I even saw patients share phone numbers so they could keep in contact. And we regularly had to interrupt conversations between patients in order to perform a test or ask a question. Nurses were jovial with each other, and I overheard several using their own experience of illness to comfort particular patients

I could see the positive effects of such a supportive environment on patient wellbeing and it was clear that it wasn't costly or cumbersome to create. For the first time in years, I was reminded that a future where doctors and patients come together in kindness was possible.

•

I met Geoff while on placement at a general practice towards the end of fourth year. His face twitched and he'd often catch his breath mid-sentence as rivers of fiery pain, invisible to us, flowed up and down his body. He had chronic pain because of a medical error and was at the surgery for a refill of his prescription painkillers.

Up until that error, Geoff had been a tiler. One warm summer morning, he was helping manoeuvre a large block of granite into a new kitchen, when it fell. Geoff twisted under its weight and immediately felt pain. It burnt his lower back, stinging its way up and down his spine, and shooting hot waves down both legs.

Geoff had damaged a couple of vertebrae in his lower spine, but had his back surgically repaired using a set of plates and screws. He made a full recovery and the pain disappeared.

About a year later, however, a painful left shoulder sent Geoff back to the doctor, and surgery to repair his shoulder soon followed. It was during this surgery that Geoff fell off the operating table.

Patients aren't supposed to fall off operating tables.

An operating table is about a metre and a half off the ground. This isn't very high, but an unconscious person falls like a sack of potatoes – hard and fast, with no control. Among the drugs used in general anaesthetics are ones that paralyse muscles and the nerves that control them, the same nerves that signal to the brain that a body is in free fall and the same muscles that hold an arm out to soften the landing. Geoff hit the ground with a dull thud.

The worst was confirmed when he woke up some hours later – the screws and plates holding his back together had been damaged.

Then, pain returned. Since the fall, Geoff had had three further surgeries on his back, but he remained in pain.

What made him fall was never clearly explained to him – for Geoff, the mistake remained a mystery, leading to a mistrust of doctors, and surgeons in particular. His mistrust of doctors impacted his ability to return to his old life – he delayed surgeries and sought second, third and fourth opinions, even though each doctor gave him identical advice.

Geoff taught me that each time we touch patients, cut and poke them or knock them out with powerful drugs – we have their trust. We become guardians and protectors of their right to be safe, comfortable and respected.

At medical school we memorised the risks associated with tests, surgeries and drugs, but we spent next to no time learning from people who have been harmed by healthcare. Before meeting Geoff, these risks were abstract for me, but now, each and every time I enter a patient's space, mind or body I think of how even the most simple and routine things, like making sure a sleeping patient doesn't fall, need to be conducted with care and concern for our patients.

18

BEING SICK

As I was approaching the end of medical school, I reflected on how I got in – someone who started life like I did doesn't typically make it to medical school.

I was born to a teen mum and had no father figure in my life. Once, when I was about a year old, Mum returned home from work to find my baby bottle full of cola; another time she left me with Wayne 2.0's parents and returned to find me sipping beer, while they joked about how I kept falling over. I was three. Most of my family smoked cigarettes, and they all drank, sometimes to excess. I was only the second member of my extended family to finish high school, and the very first to go to university.

This is not your classic doctor origin story.

I'm not a disadvantaged minority by any means. The fact that I did make it to medical school is a sign of the privilege I carry; social mobility was possible because I'm a man, white and tall.

Even in a society that rewards these traits, I felt out of place in medical school, an outsider among the mostly privately educated children of Sydney's upper-middle classes. These were the progeny of 'good' families peppered with professionals. They mostly lived in nice houses in wealthy suburbs. Achievement breeds achievement, status follows status.

Not only are most medical students fit and healthy, but they also inhabit family trees full of fit and healthy people too. One study started in the 1960s among male civil servants in the UK famously showed that, even within a similar group of people, in this case public service employees in London, those of higher status enjoyed better health. Decades later, the study was repeated to include women, and the pattern held.

In Australia your postcode also determines your health. Wealthier, prettier suburbs have less disease. When disease does occur in these postcodes, it is picked up earlier and people tend not to develop the same long-term consequences as people in poorer postcodes. This pattern has been shown for cancer, heart disease and chronic diseases like diabetes.

With greater wealth comes the capability of affording specialists and private health insurance, allowing for rapid diagnosis and access to fitness clubs, physiotherapists and psychologists. The pathway to medical school for kids in the wealthy postcodes is also different. By different, I mean easier.

All of this is reinforced by the idea drilled into medical students that they have *earnt* their spot at medical school, that luck had nothing to do with it. Someone may indeed deserve to be a doctor, but to ignore the social determinants of success, such as birthplace, parental income, housing status and so on, is illogical when medical students spend so much time memorising the effect of those same factors on illness.

That's not to say these students don't deserve to be doctors, of course they do. Many are brimming with intelligence and compassion – they will be excellent healers. But for others from diverse backgrounds with different health experiences, also brilliant and empathic, structural barriers in our unequal society make medical school a more difficult, improbable prospect. If the majority of medical students are entering medical school from privileged backgrounds with good health and easy access to doctors, it follows that some (if I'm being generous) or many (if I'm not) will struggle to empathise with the homeless patient with uncontrolled diabetes, the sex worker with depression who uses amphetamines to feel happy or the person with brittle asthma who won't stop smoking.

I've seen this play out countless times – throwaway comments about how many sexual partners a female patient has had or how an overweight patient 'doesn't want to help themselves'.

Properly addressing this issue would require vast changes to address inequality in schooling and access to university – this is a society-wide issue. As we await a more equal and just society, there is at least one small thing medical school can do to help remedy the skewed class representation: involve patients in teaching students about the disease experience.

Medical students see a lot of sick people, but mostly they don't learn what it's like to be sick. And while they don't need to have been sick themselves to be a good doctor, they need to understand sickness. Developing the ability for a future doctor to imagine walking in patients' shoes, or more appropriately, their gowns, should be a core goal of medical schools. Patients and future doctors should sit side by side, informing each other and fusing as the equal halves of healthcare that they unmistakably are. This is an uncomfortable conversation for medicine, and one that largely remains left out of lectures.

•

The contact I had with patients at med school was mostly passive. In surgery, I spoke to patients before they were anaesthetised; on the wards we rounded on patients with the team; and in clinics I was given a chair in the corner to watch patient consultations.

While learning on the job, I also interviewed patients to find out their medical history, examined patients and collected blood. I was expected to do these tasks quickly, like a doctor would – there was no time for extra questions. How have you coped since getting this diagnosis? How much do all your medications cost? What was your last time in hospital like? Even if I did find time for these questions, very few senior doctors would have been interested in the answers.

I can recall the only three times patients were invited to lecture us with more clarity than I can for most other lectures I had – because I was able to marry the medicine I was learning to a story. I wasn't the only one connecting the dots – the questions my classmates asked these patients showed that they were as curious about the human side of medicine as I was. But sadly, these sessions weren't part of the core curriculum – the content wouldn't appear on any exam – and many students skipped the sessions altogether, dismissing them as 'fluff'. For those of us who did bother to turn up, the effect was palpable.

I'll never forget the mother of a man with schizophrenia who cried in our lecture theatre as she recounted watching police stuff her son in the back of a police van after a psychotic relapse. 'I didn't want to call the police, but he was getting worse and I worried he may hurt himself,' she said.

Later that year, a neurologist arranged for a man with Parkinson's disease to speak to us. Lifting his shirt, he showed us a pump that fed medicine into his body 24/7 – these drugs allowed him to continue walking. Afterwards, his wife spoke about the depressive episodes she developed after her husband had become ill five years prior.

In one lecture, a psychiatrist invited a mother and her daughter to speak to us – both had an eating disorder. The mum spoke about the guilt she felt that her illness contributed to her daughter's. One student asked about the strategies they used to minimise how much they ate; another asked what it felt like when they talked to doctors about their eating disorder.

These opportunities to hear from patients – and my classmates' thoughtful questions – inspired me to start an evening lecture series. A small group of us organised patients with diseases like cystic fibrosis and diabetes to come and talk to us. We threw in free pizza to attract as many students as possible.

These talks opened up parts of the patient world hidden from us in our regular teaching. A young woman with cystic fibrosis talked about the costs of her medication and showed us the bowl of pills she took three times a day. An athlete with type one diabetes explained that he was tired of having to explain to the people he worked with the difference between types one and two, especially when his colleagues accused him of 'not being fat enough' to have the disease.

It was a shame that we had to organise these learning experiences ourselves after regular classes had finished for the day. They were easy to pull together and well attended – what was stopping my medical school from putting patients at the heart of our learning? I entered medicine with an intimate knowledge of where the system can let you down, and an awareness that patients often suffer unnecessarily. Most of my classmates had no experience with this. In fact, for many doctors this insight doesn't come until much later – long after medical school.

A growing number of doctors have spoken about their experiences crossing the patient–doctor divide and becoming patients themselves. Most famously, Dr Oliver Sacks, in an interview with the *Harvard Business Review* in 2010, revealed that he could more easily talk to patients with illness after his own diagnosis of ocular melanoma. 'I can speak as one of them,' he said. 'We're all patients.' In *When Breath Becomes Air*, Dr Paul Kalanithi described his shock at realising what a hospital felt like from a patient's perspective, after his diagnosis of metastatic lung cancer. Melbourne-based neurosurgeon Dr Michael Wong wrote for the ABC about finally understanding how it felt to be a patient – 'the loss of control, the fear and pain' – as he lay in hospital after being stabbed fourteen times.

For doctors who become sick or seriously injured, these experiences often push them into patient advocacy and force them to recalibrate their approach to medicine, to consider more than just the test result, the malady, or the wound at hand. They begin to see and treat a multidimensional *person*, rather than a one-dimensional *patient*.

Their words have impact: the discussion afterwards among the medical community shows that doctor accounts of illness really do impact other doctors and nurses.

I saw this first-hand when, during one of my surgical rotations, the patient was a nurse.

I met Samantha in the anaesthetic bay while she was waiting for surgery to remove a clot in her right leg that was affecting blood flow to her foot. There was a risk that the clot would eventually block off the blood supply altogether and leave her lower leg without any oxygen. A leg will die without oxygen.

As we talked she lay quietly, eyes fixed on a fluorescent light above. Despite working in an operating theatre every day, she was scared. Samantha had become a patient, lying under a standard blanket and wearing a standard gown. All she could do was wait.

When we settled her onto the operating table she burst into tears. The nurses in the room recognised one of their own in distress and, like a pride of lions, they formed a protective ring around her.

'You'll be fine, love, I know it feels strange on this side of things,' one said.

'You'll be done in no time. We'll see you on the other side, okay?' reassured another.

Once she was asleep they opened up.

'You forget how scary this is for patients, don't you?' the anaesthetic nurse commented.

'I'd be terrified under these lights,' said the scout nurse, as she gathered surgical tools needed for the operation.

'We really do take all of this for granted. I wonder if the more you know, the more scared you are . . .' added the scrub nurse.

These normally no-nonsense surgical nurses had clearly been moved by seeing themselves on the operating table. It was striking to witness this mix of empathy and sympathy. The acknowledgement of feelings in a space where they are often ignored was refreshing.

Regardless of how empathic nurses and doctors are when they enter medical school, the system does its best to replace it with detachment, efficiency and objectivity. Empathy is a skill that requires time and energy; neglect it, and it atrophies like a wasting muscle.

The challenge is to cultivate empathy in doctors before the point when they, or someone they know, becomes the patient. Engaging patients and connecting with their words and experiences should begin on day one of our training, not decades later when doctors themselves become ill.

As students and doctors we are surrounded by resources better than any textbook on how to empathise and connect with patients – the patients themselves. We need look no further than the end of a stethoscope to find out what it feels like to be on the other side.

19

THE END OF THE BEGINNING

Over the course of my four years at medical school I became more and more anxious about attending lectures, tutorials, ward rounds and surgeries. I worried about looking and sounding like an idiot, especially after my experiences with bullying senior doctors. Each night I dreaded the next day. I lay in bed awake, long after I needed to be asleep, my heart racing while I imagined freezing on the spot again, or giving a wrong answer.

Deep breathing helped calm my mind, but it didn't bring sleep. I started taking sleeping pills in third year to make the nights better, and overeating to make the days better. I gained five kilos, then ten. I didn't recognise who I'd become.

By my final year, it was time to see a psychologist again – not about cancer, but for anxiety.

Studying medicine is a seven-day-a-week job and as a student I had no control over my timetable, so trying to find time to see a counsellor during business hours was nearly impossible. During haphazard, last-minute appointments, the psychologist taught me about cognitive behavioural therapy. This therapy is based on understanding the differences between thoughts, feelings and actions and how to stop a negative thought, say, leading directly to a negative feeling. I learnt cognitive tricks to help me regain control over the kind of runaway thoughts and emotions I had in situations where my knowledge was being evaluated publicly. I was able to take the edge off my anxiety, but it didn't cure it – the techniques were just too hard to implement while I was being quizzed or mocked by a senior doctor.

Sadly, the only way I could cure this anxiety was by graduating from medical school.

•

As graduation approached, I had to acknowledge that medical school had changed me.

I wasn't just anxious; I was struggling to hold on to my humanity. The nature and intensity of medical training meant I had to be vigilant to preserve it. It had to be cultivated, just like MRI interpretation skills or suture knots.

Occasionally, Kim pointed out that I had become a little colder and more detached. Sana lamented my loss of patience when discussing a new symptom she'd developed. Mum complained that I had become closed off to other views, especially when she would try to tell me about the latest cure she'd bought online to solve a problem she didn't have. Ian told me that he missed our regular, long phone calls – there was always just a bit of extra study I had to do instead. The friends I had before medical school fell away entirely. Kim had to stop asking me for updates about them. 'I have no idea,' I'd say. 'I only see you now.'

Lots of things about medical school left me questioning my decision to ever sit that entrance exam. I was gaining knowledge, but not the specific knowledge I wanted that would actually contribute to patient care on the wards. Misidentifying anatomy, missing a blood draw and misdiagnosing illness were common – all while missing my free time, and the freedom of the life I had left behind. I wanted to be a doctor badly, but there was little point in becoming one if I lost myself in the process. I knew it was my humanity that made me special, and it was my humanity that would enable me to influence the art of medicine. If not for the patients and people like Fiona, Faisal, Prof Robinson, Dr Mohammadi and Charlotte – doctors and colleagues who reminded me it was possible to be a person first – I'd have called it a day.

Patients need doctors, despite access to Dr Google. They need diagnosticians of course, but they need advocates and guides more. When machines and software eventually become as competent as us at collecting histories and conducting examinations, our role will still be crucial to the health system. Healers always have been, and always will be, people. Our shared humanity is what underpins our compassion and the drive to ease suffering in others.

But losing that humanity is a real risk in healthcare.

Studies of medical students, and other healthcare workers such as nurses, show that as they progress from year to year they change, and not for the better. Some change is good, like knowledge about medications and how to help someone in an emergency. Some change is bad. Empathy and compassion decline during doctor training, replaced by cynicism and something called compassion fatigue. Something is wrong with a model that takes people who (mostly) want to help others and, while giving them the knowledge and skills to do that, removes the empathy and compassion that motivated them in the first place.

Instead of triggering a radical overhaul of the training and education system, this fact appears to have been accepted as a cost of becoming a doctor. This makes me angry: as a medical student and as a junior doctor – but mostly, as a patient.

Becoming a doctor should not come at the cost of our humanity – that is too high a price to pay.

If not for facing death as a cancer patient and struggling with treatment, I'm sure I would have emerged from medical school a very different person – a much more cutthroat, less compassionate person. And even with my experience as a patient keeping me grounded, I didn't escape its tentacles fully.

After medical school I focused on identifying ways that I had changed for the worse and worked to undo this damage. I wondered if my colleagues were doing the same.

Too often, I hear people describe doctors as being 'like a computer' or 'stand-offish' or 'very smart, but not big on talking'. Obviously these aren't good attributes for a doctor and we need to start making changes to how doctors' minds are moulded in medical school.

Medical schools shouldn't just be based on other doctors determining whether someone will be a good doctor – patients and other people with experience of sickness need to have input too. Doctors can evaluate a student's knowledge and skills, but patients need to tell us whether the doctor-to-be is warm, engaging and understanding. Doctors train to be of service to the public – it's time patients had a proper say on how that service is delivered.

These skills matter because patients and their families consistently complain about poor communication. In any given year, grievances about communication make up between eleven and twenty-one percent of all complaints handled by the Health Care Complaints Commission in New South Wales. That may not sound like much, but this puts communication as one of the top most complained about aspects of healthcare each year, jostling with 'professionalism' for second place behind 'treatment'.

•

I went to medical school because I wanted to make healthcare better, more compassionate and patient focused – but a part of me also wanted to figure out what had happened to me, to regain control over my body and cancer.

I think I was looking for secret knowledge only doctors possessed, or maybe I hoped to understand why I got cancer in the first place. I finished medical school without any secret knowledge, nor am I any closer to understanding what caused my cancer. But what I did gain was a medical perspective through which to process my cancer experience.

By the end of medical school I could describe how tumours grow and the genetic errors that lead to cells becoming cancerous. But I also understood how life-changing that is, how the diagnosis distorts you. I could tell you how tumours cause certain signs and symptoms on an anatomical and pathological level – but I also understood the horror of seeing blood in the toilet bowl, and the confusing mix of panic and denial that follows.

I hoped to bring this experience of illness and medicine into my work as a doctor. It is a feeling inside me, both everywhere and nowhere in particular. It allows me to feel and connect. It allows me to notice things other doctors may not – a patient's hidden question, the need to clarify something or re-explain it.

Above all, it gives me a familiarity with distress, a comfort with being uncomfortable.

I'd gone to medical school to become an oncologist. Over time, I crossed off surgical oncology (too much anatomy, and I like my patients awake) and radiation oncology (too much physics, and I wanted lots of contact with my patients), which left medical oncology – the chemo doctors. As a patient I hadn't developed a particularly strong rapport with my medical oncologist, I knew my surgical oncologist a great deal better, but I liked that medical oncologists got to treat patients throughout the whole course of chemotherapy, and the science of matching the right chemo drug to different tumour types was an exciting research field. Despite not getting the chance to spend time in a cancer clinic as a medical student, at the end of the four years medical oncology remained on my list.

Senior doctors love asking medical students 'what they want to be', but many tried to dissuade me from entering oncology – not because they knew about my past, but because it was 'too depressing'.

I didn't see it that way – I was alive because of cancer surgery, chemotherapy and radiation therapy. Yes, I had scars, and my body (and mind) had been affected, but I was alive and happy – the furthest thing from depressing.

•

Four years after starting medical school, and eight years after that fateful colonoscopy in Melbourne, I became a doctor. On top of class or clinic five days a week and study almost every evening and weekend, I'd been writing about the medical system for the ABC (the lack of cancer education; problems with patient–doctor communication), and I'd managed to publish results from various research projects in medical journals and present at a couple of conferences. For a little while I'd also run a club for medical students interested in general practice. I was excited about the finish line, but utterly exhausted.

Our graduation was held at the old Mint in the city, towards the end of 2018. Tickets were strictly limited – only Sana and Mum were able to attend. They cheered loudly when I was awarded a prize for my honours research, and even louder when I was given a special award for 'contributing to the medical community'. I was shocked, and grinned goofily while shaking the dean's hand. So, the school had been reading my articles after all.

'My son's a doctor!' Mum shouted as we strolled from the Mint to a restaurant downtown.

I tried to shush her.

'No way. I'm so proud of you,' she said, 'you're an inspiration. To have gone through what you did, and with such grace – and now you get to help others . . . it's amazing.'

'It really is, Benny,' said Sana.

'Well, I couldn't have done it without you two.' I let go of Sana's hand and gave her a hug, then hugged Mum. 'C'mon,' I said, 'Kim and the boys are waiting for us.'

Hugo, now five years old, was the first to spot us in the restaurant and came running over. He carried a present under each arm. 'Here you go, Doctor Uncle Ben!' he said.

Kim, James and Archie jumped up from the table.

'Congratulations, brother!' said Kim, grabbing me around my waist.

Between sips of champagne, I watched the boys take turns playing with the stethoscope the school had given me as a graduation gift. Hugo put it in his ears and then held it to Archie's chest. I thought back to the surprise party Kim had thrown me when I first got into medical school, and Hugo using it to listen to people's knees. He now knew exactly where it went, and so did I.

During dinner, Sana surprised me with a gift. On a box wrapped in shiny silver paper she'd cut out letters and spelt 'Doctor's Survival Kit'. In it I found chewing gum, chocolate, a jar of pill capsules containing tiny motivational messages, moisturiser, and a book on writing. She always knew exactly what I needed, and when. The book on writing seemed slightly out of place at the time – but perhaps Sana had known I would end up writing a book before I did.

My thoughts turned to Ian. I had forgotten to tell him about my graduation, only realising while ironing my shirt before the ceremony. I'd put down the iron and messaged: 'My graduation is today! I'm so sorry I forgot to tell you, I've been slammed lately.'

I got his reply as we were leaving the Mint, hours after he'd received my text.

'Congratulations, Benj, but I'd really liked to have come down for this.'

Ouch, he was pissed off. But he was right to be disappointed, I'd missed so many birthdays, weddings and holidays because of medical school. My communication with my family had been really poor at times, especially with Ian and Mum. At least Mum and Graeme got to see me when I was back in Melbourne for check-ups, but poor Ian often had to wait a year, or more, before I either found time to visit him or could make time for him to visit me.

I wasn't alone among my classmates in having to sacrifice family time for medicine, and with my first internship only four weeks away I worried that it was only going to get worse.

Happiness wasn't the dominant feeling I experienced when I finished medical school – it was relief. I was just glad it was over and that I could begin to put a lot of the experience behind me: the teaching style, constant questioning, bullying, bad behaviour and cynicism. I'd miss the friends I'd made, as we'd all been allocated to different hospitals, and I'd miss certain teachers – but I was ready to move on.

After my relief, I felt apprehension. Getting through medical school was just the first step in my training. Now I had to learn the actual job of being a doctor and compete for sought-after jobs. Many of my classmates had scheduled extra work – extra research, laboratory time, workshops at other universities or clinics in other countries – in the four weeks before their own internships. I hadn't planned a damn thing before mine, except lying in the sun and swimming in the harbour. Part of me wanted to stand up at graduation and shout, 'Relax!', but part of me was feeling worried about the competition too. Would I get a good job in Sydney? Which specialty would I choose? When would be the best time to start studying for the next round of exams?

The race was far from over.

PART 4

BEING A DOCTOR

20

READY, SET ... DOCTOR

My first rotation as a freshly graduated doctor was in oncology. This was not a happy accident – I'd requested the cancer ward. This moment had been years in the making. Finally, I could put my new knowledge and old experience to use, giving patients the kind of compassionate, attentive care they deserved.

But I was terrified. Everything on the ward was intimidating, even Panadol.

My first task was to prescribe it for a patient.

'Prescribe it?' I asked the nurse. 'You can buy it from Coles, can't you just give the patient some?'

The nurse explained that every medicine had to be formally prescribed, no matter how common. I had a lot to learn.

So did everyone else: that first Monday was also the first day for every junior doctor in the hospital, everyone from interns with no experience, to residents, registrars and fellows with years of experience. It's an unusual quirk of the New South Wales health system that all junior doctors start the new working year on the same day in late January, each of them landing on a new ward, many for the first time. This system, no doubt dreamt up by administrators to make administration easier, is a recipe for total chaos on the wards.

Thousands of junior doctors across the state leave a set of patients on one Friday in January and get a new set of patients on Monday morning. The only doctors who stay in place are the senior doctors (the consultants) but they're not on the wards as much, spending time at other hospitals, clinics, teaching and seeing their private patients. It means junior doctors, who make up the bulk of the workforce, are operating blind. This shuffle is especially daunting for us interns – we're not just new to hospital, we're new to doctoring.

The nurses and patients don't rotate – thank god – but so much knowledge accumulated about patients and their treatments still evaporates overnight. Relationships between junior doctors and nurses, physiotherapists and social workers disappear too.

Anxious junior doctors keen to do a good job and impress consultants scramble to learn as much as possible about patients as quickly as possible. Anxious nurses watch on, picking up their rushed mistakes and frenzied errors. I hadn't anticipated that my first day as a doctor would be such a stark display of everything that healthcare fails at.

On the oncology ward I worked under a registrar who was seven years out of medical school and training in general medicine. Let's call him John. Despite years of clinical experience, John still carried the title of junior doctor, and so it was his first day on the oncology ward too. He had done his medical degree outside Australia, but arrived two years earlier, and so found himself having to redo years of medical training. He wasn't sure what kind of specialist he wanted to be, but he didn't want to work in cancer.

'I don't like oncology, everyone dies,' he said, a few minutes into our first ward round.

He didn't know about my bowel cancer; no one did. The fact that I had been on an oncology ward and was still very much alive may have surprised him.

John's clinical knowledge was impressive. He could recall medical facts quickly and seemed to have entire textbooks organised in his mind. Unfortunately, this was the only thing organised about John. His ward rounds were frazzled. I had to chase him after each patient just to make sure I could document the treatment plan correctly. If I was uncertain, the patients must have been even more confused. Our first day together was a long, slow slog. Neither of us knew any of the patients, or how the ward worked, but on top of that John kept disappearing. To where, I had no idea. By noon, we'd only seen a quarter of our patients.

This worried me, because time is an extra precious commodity on a cancer ward – after all, most patients are on borrowed time. The vast majority of cancer patients only come to hospital as outpatients for treatments like chemotherapy or radiation – for someone with cancer to be in hospital means they have either had surgery (like I did), developed a serious side effect or illness (like my blood clots), or because their illness is quite advanced.

Francisca was one of the patients we still hadn't seen by noon. She was in her early sixties and had liver cancer. She had immigrated to Australia from Spain with her husband in the 1980s and started a family. Francisca seemed whip smart, knew everything about her cancer and 'ran' her room like I imagined she ran her house – with total control. A notepad, pen, mobile phone and reading glasses were lined up on her bedside table, exactly equidistant from each other and the edge of the table. I watched her order her daughter around, who sat beside her hospital bed. Francisca was very much a matriarch, and liked things done her way.

Francisca's cancer was being treated at another hospital, but she had developed a fever at home the previous Friday night and our hospital was the closest so the ambulance had brought her here.

In the emergency department a blood test had showed that her white blood cells, the ones that fight infection, were low. This isn't uncommon in cancer patients undergoing treatment – white blood cells are made in bone marrow, which is extra sensitive to chemotherapy. The bone marrow usually bounces back after a few days, but without her full army of white blood cells, even a simple infection could have been deadly for Francisca. Her fever may have been a sign that an infection had already set in, so she was sent to the oncology ward and given antibiotics through a drip.

Her fever resolved over Saturday and Sunday, the white blood cells started to increase on their own, and by Monday, when I saw her, she felt much better.

But her next chemotherapy was due in two days, and she was panicking that she would miss the treatment at the other hospital if her white cells didn't return to normal and she had to stay with us longer. Francisca was desperate for every drop of chemo – the cancer had already spread beyond her liver, it was stage four. Her chemotherapy wasn't shrinking the tumours, but it had stopped them getting bigger, and she worried she'd lose control over the tumours if she missed the infusion. Whenever she imagined her death, her chest pounded and set off the alarm on the heart rate monitor. Hearing the warning beeps, and knowing that Francisca was at risk of major infection, nurses checked on her regularly.

On that Monday, my first day on the ward, she'd woken before the sun was up. Her daughter had arrived before visiting hours. All day Francisca had watched the clock while her daughter watched the corridor for signs of a doctor. By noon they were furious. Both of their mobile phones rang constantly, each conversation with worried family getting louder.

After lunch, their patience had run out and Francisca's daughter asked to see a doctor.

John had disappeared off the ward, so I went to see Francisca. On the way to her room I practised what I was going to say.

I smiled as I entered. Francisca and her daughter glared at me with their arms crossed in front of them. Three other family members sat squished together on a small couch near the window – they looked angry too.

Before I could say hello, my pager beeped. I ignored it.

'I'm so sorry we haven't seen you yet,' I said. 'I'm not sure if the nurses explained this already, but today is an interesting day because all the doctors are new.' I left out exactly *how* new.

Francisca's daughter went to speak but Francisca shot a finger at me.

'It may be *interesting* for you, but I am not *interested* one bit!'

'I'm sorry, I didn't mean it like that. I . . . uh . . . just wanted to explain why things are a bit slow today,' I said.

My pager beeped again, the same number.

'I want to know if I am okay to have chemotherapy on Wednesday,' Francisca said.

'The registrar isn't on the ward at the moment, but I will ask them about this as soon as possible.' I turned towards the door as my pager beeped, yet again.

I used a phone at the nurse's station and dialled the number that had paged me three times.

'Hello doctor, we have one of your patients here and she is not supposed to have her blood sugar measured but a new nurse did this in front of the family and the reading was very high and they are now concerned so please come down and fix the sugar and talk to the family,' the nurse said in one breath.

'I'm sorry but I don't know what patient you're talking about or where you're calling from,' I said. 'It's my first day.'

'Yes sorry doctor, this is about Mrs Lee she is a patient under the palliative care team the sugar was twenty-something and her children are here,' she said in a rush.

'I'm the oncology intern, but the switchboard has been mixing me and the palliative care doctor up all day,' I told the nurse. 'I'll let the palliative care doctor know.'

I sent the palliative care doctor a message and sat back down at a computer to wait for John. The stethoscope around my neck felt heavy. Thirty minutes later, Francisca's daughter found me at the computer ordering blood tests for a patient we'd seen earlier – John still hadn't returned. She stood close to me with her arms crossed and her eyebrows gathered in the middle, forming a scowl. I assured her I wouldn't leave the hospital that night without an answer for Francisca. Fifteen minutes later John returned to the ward. I rushed up to him and said that we should see Francisca first and why. He agreed.

Her room had the same number of people in it, but the three people on the couch near the window were not the same three who had been sitting there earlier.

John introduced himself and apologised for the wait.

'I've been waiting all day!' Francisca said, finger raised again.

'I know, but we had other patients to see. Some people on this ward are very sick,' John said, 'more sick than you.'

Francisca's daughter stood up from her post beside the bed. 'You are lucky that my mother isn't *more sick* or she would be dead!'

John explained that Francisca was doing well and if anything had changed he would have come to see her earlier. One of the people near the window, an older man in a large coat that didn't quite cover his belly, took out his mobile phone and started filming.

John didn't notice. He continued to explain that Francisca's white blood cells were improving and that she had not spiked a temperature in thirty-six hours. John explained that her chemo-therapy could go ahead, but he had to check with the senior oncologist. The man in the corner holding the camera coughed. John noticed that he was filming.

'Sorry, sir, you can't record this,' John said.

'I make video for us, to show family,' said the cameraman.

'He is doing it for us,' Francisca's daughter added. 'So we can explain why my mother is in hospital to family who cannot visit.'

'Even so, you can't film here,' John repeated. 'Please put the phone away.'

The cameraman and Francisca looked at each other. Francisca nodded and the man lowered the phone, tucking it into a coat pocket.

I expected John to ask to look at the footage that had been recorded, but instead he continued explaining that the blood tests Francisca needed had been ordered, and that we would start the paperwork for her to go home in time for chemotherapy.

While John examined Francisca, listening to her lungs and checking for any swelling in her legs, I did my best to type up a record of this review in Francisca's file. As the intern, my main job during ward rounds was to operate the computer and update patients' medical records. The computers sat on top of small standing desks with wheels. We could update records, review results and order new tests while on the ward round. When they were first introduced in public hospitals they were called COWs – computers on wheels – but we weren't supposed to call them that because apparently patients had overheard doctors talking about cows and assumed they were referring to them. The replacement name, WOWs – workstations on wheels – felt silly to say so everyone still called them (and some of the patients) cows.

John came over and we clicked through the results of the daily blood tests Francisca had been having.

'Everything looks good, I'll talk to the boss and let you know the plan,' he said.

I wheeled the computer out the door. 'That was a bit intense, hey?' I said to John. 'They were so angry.'

John had his head down, doing something on his phone. 'I guess . . .' he muttered, not looking up.

I was desperate to learn from Francisca and whether I could have done something earlier to make her less angry at us. I had wanted to make sense of all that emotion in the room and to get John's take on the situation, but my attempt to start a conversation had fallen flat. *I'll bring it up next time we see an irritated patient,* I thought.

I didn't need to wait long. Our very next patient was Roger, a local businessman in his fifties with a history of prostate cancer. He had thick dark hair, combed neatly to one side, was clean-shaven and wore a collared shirt *under* his hospital gown. Two mobile phones sat on top of several books stacked next to his bed, and he had the TV set to the rolling news channel. This was a man not used to being idle.

He'd fallen at home over the weekend and been admitted to the cancer ward. He was meeting us for the first time. Roger's oncologist also worked at another hospital.

I wheeled the COW – I mean, WOW – into his room. John took the mouse from me and clicked through Roger's file. He introduced himself quickly and then went back to looking at the screen.

'Hi, doctor,' Roger said, 'I'm feeling much better. I have an appointment with my oncologist next week.'

John replied, not looking up from the computer, 'Yes, but you are at this hospital now and I need to check everything is okay. Where is your primary cancer?'

'Does that mean where do I have cancer?' Roger asked. I noticed his jaw go tight, his hands were clasped in his lap.

'Yes,' John said, still looking at the computer.

'I had prostate cancer, but it was cut out. I'm nearing the end of chemotherapy, only a few more left. Like I said, I am supposed to see my oncologist next week and have a scan.'

'You had a scan here when you came in,' John said.

'Yes, I was hoping you could tell me whether I still need the other scan next week?' Roger replied.

'I am reading your notes, please wait,' John responded.

'Look, I've been asking this same question all weekend.' Roger's jaw was tightening again. 'But I've seen a different doctor each day and no one can tell me if the scan I had here is the same one I need for my appointment next week.'

John continued reading the report of Roger's scan, which had been done in our emergency department. It showed a couple of tumours in his lungs that hadn't been there when Roger was last scanned at our hospital for a different problem. He'd been having his cancer scans done at another facility and we couldn't see those records.

While reading, John was mumbling to himself. Words escaped here and there, '. . . tumour . . . tissue . . . invasion . . .' Then he turned to Roger. 'Your cancer has spread to your lungs. Sorry if you are only hearing this for the first time.'

John looked at Roger for several seconds – it felt deliberate, forced. He was doing what the medical textbooks told him to do: 'make eye contact with the patient'.

My heart dropped and my face went hot. I looked from John to Roger and back again. John had just delivered the potentially devastating news that Roger's cancer had spread with less emotion, or warning, than a weather forecast. Roger's cheeks were flushed and his eyes narrowed. He turned to stare out the window.

When Roger didn't say anything, John returned to the computer and continued mumbling through another report. I stood frozen next to John, stunned.

After two more minutes of this Roger had had enough.

'Look, I'm quite upset with you. I already know about the tumours in my lung. I just want to know if I need to get another scan when I get out,' Roger pleaded. 'And then you can leave please.'

'I'll need to check and get back to you,' John said as he headed for the door.

That a doctor would tell a patient their cancer had spread like John had just done was unbelievable to me. Roger was furious, and I was pissed off too. My mind went straight back to finding out about my own cancer and how carefully the gastroenterologist had allowed the bad news to unfold, how he had made sure that Mum was in the room. I would have been crushed if he had told me as bluntly and unexpectedly as John had just told Roger. I was relieved that Roger had already known about the lung tumours because this had at least prevented a distressing encounter from becoming a devastating one.

I spun the WOW around and headed for the door, racing to keep up with John. But first I turned to Roger.

'I'm so sorry for that, mate. I'll pop back once we've seen a few more patients, okay?'

My pager beeped as I caught up with John. In between Francisca's angry family filming us and Roger kicking us out, the mystery palliative care patient with the high blood sugar had died.

'Yes hello doctor, your patient Mrs Lee has died can you come and certify the death please and also explain to the family?' the nurse asked, again breathless.

'She died? Just now?' I replied.

'Yes, doctor, the family are here waiting and quite shocked, can you come and explain to them?'

'Um, remember Mrs Lee is under the palliative care doctors?' I reminded her. 'I will let them know what has happened. I haven't had anything to do with her and I think it is best that they talk to the family.'

'Thank you, doctor, the family are here and waiting.' The nurse hung up.

I shot the resident on the palliative care team a text: 'High sugar patient Mrs Lee has died. Can you verify death and speak to family?'

She replied: 'Yep. Family deluded.'

Mrs Lee hadn't died because of her high sugar level, she'd died because of her advanced cancer. Still, I felt terrible. The family wouldn't have recognised any of the new doctors, and the palliative care resident wouldn't have known much, if anything, about that patient yet.

I would need to mull over this later. Right now, there was a stack of paperwork to start and patient notes to update. The sun was getting low in the sky and John had disappeared again.

Sana messaged: 'Hi hot doctor. How's your first day? What time will you be home for dinner?'

'It's fucking chaos! I have no idea what I'm doing. Won't be home for dinner. Sorry.'

Welcome to medicine, I thought.

My stethoscope felt like a shackle around my neck.

•

In New South Wales, which hospital you get sent to as a new graduate is a kind of lottery. When we were graduating we were all asked to rank the hospitals in the state from most to least preferred, and then a secret computer decided where we ended up. The system is silly, but every intern needs a hospital to work at (in order to qualify as a 'real' doctor) and every hospital needs a certain number of cheap doctors to stay afloat (as an intern I earnt thirty-four dollars per hour). More interns want to be at hospitals near the city than those hospitals need; and some hospitals aren't preferred by anyone, but they still need interns to keep running.

The secret computer didn't care that I lived a fifteen-minute walk from a major hospital, instead it allocated me to one two hours away. Sana's career was really gaining momentum, she'd just wrapped up two years on TV at SBS and was now writing articles for the ABC from their city studio – moving was not an option for her. Plus, since I'd finished med school, we'd begun talking about starting a family. To have a baby we needed to ship my sperm from Melbourne and use IVF. We'd read that IVF costs tens of thousands of dollars, but we'd only had the one salary, Sana's, for five years so our savings were meagre. I'd found a public clinic that provided free IVF, but their only clinic was in the city – another reason to stay put.

I managed to swap into a hospital only an hour or so from home. For fifteen dollars, I could use the expressway and get to the hospital in forty minutes on a good day or an hour on a bad day. Avoiding the tolls could take up to an hour and a half – each way. One benefit of all the driving to work was that I had a lot of time to think before and after each shift.

•

I left the hospital that day a couple of hours after Sana had called. Poor Sana had cooked (something she only did on special occasions), but she'd had to eat alone. I dropped into the driver's seat and put my stethoscope on the passenger seat, then realised that I hadn't used it all day. I thought back to packing it carefully in my bag for my first day of med school and then putting it on as I entered hospital for the first time as a student. This universal symbol of medicine had sat impotently around my neck all day. Medical school hadn't been totally honest with me about being an intern: it was mostly about paperwork and chasing more-experienced doctors around.

I put the key in the ignition and got ready for the long drive home in Kim's old hatchback, which Mum had bought off her and given to me as a graduation gift. As I turned onto the expressway towards home I thought about the events of my first day as a doctor: freaking out over Panadol, John disappearing, Francisca pointing her finger at me, being filmed, Roger kicking us out of his room, Mrs Lee dying.

Roger and Francisca had received what was considered good medical care. The emergency department had been thorough, the appropriate tests and scans done. They had been moved to the cancer ward soon after admission and hadn't spent days in the emergency department like some patients had to. They'd received the correct medication and plenty of food. They slept in clean sheets and had nurses keeping an eye on them twenty-four hours a day. And doctors had seen them, albeit briefly, over the weekend.

The financial cost of all this care to them was zero, but the personal cost seemed high.

The system had put them in hospitals they weren't familiar with on a weekend, when hospitals run on a skeleton staff and other services like scans and tests shut down altogether. They'd had ID bands secured to their arms and been asked to take off all their personal items and wear a white hospital gown – the uniform that denotes patients from everyone else. They'd been seen briefly by a doctor, but that doctor was stretched, responsible for half the hospital over the weekend. Plus, they weren't the doctor who would be making decisions about them on Monday morning.

Roger and Francisca had questions, but no one was able to, or wanted to, answer them. 'Wait for your team on Monday,' they'd been told. On top of this, the infection Francisca had developed had left her exhausted, and Roger remained a bit shaky after his fall.

When I'd approached Francisca, I made the mistake of blaming 'the system'. Francisca didn't care that the system forced nearly all doctors in the state to start new jobs on new wards on the same day. After all, had the system cared about what was important to her? The system hadn't known that Francisca was consumed with fear over missing chemotherapy. It isn't designed to collect this kind of information. It likes simple sets of symptoms and quick tests. All the touchy-feely stuff is noise to most doctors – a distraction from the tasks of diagnosing, treating and discharging patients home. Nurses are much better at responding to patients' feelings, but they too are pulled in different directions and usually understaffed.

Francisca's infection had been treated and she'd been kept safe while her white blood cells recovered. The system had looked after the physical part of her health. But these were things done *to* Francisca. When it came to doing things *with* Francisca, the system wasn't so great. Inside the hospital she was powerless.

The system makes many patients and their families feel like this. At times, patients just want their doctor to listen to their experience and feel as though they've been heard.

And Roger? The system had done its job addressing Roger's physical needs – his heart had been checked, his head scanned, ruling out any serious, life-threatening reasons for his fall. But the system had ignored his mind. It was clear when we arrived in his room what mattered to him – the scan he needed for the appointment with his oncologist. While John wasted time mumbling through the report, Roger had grown more and more angry. The system had allocated Roger a bed number and then allocated him a doctor who gave the impression that Roger's bed number was the most interesting thing about him.

If Roger or Francisca had made an official complaint I wouldn't have been surprised. It is not that a mistake happened or that they were put in any danger. Medical mistakes happen all the time. The wrong medication is given or too much medication is given; patients fall and hurt themselves on hospital wards regularly; surgeries don't always achieve what they were supposed to achieve. Patients appear to be mostly okay about this, accepting that medicine is complex and that no one is perfect.

What irritates patients enough to complain are things like being treated rudely, being dismissed, having concerns minimised, having news delivered poorly, and feeling shut out of decisions made about their bodies.

This means that it is not a lack of knowledge about diseases and treatments that will most likely get a doctor into trouble, it's their interpersonal skills. I wondered if patients got most upset about the interpersonal side of their doctors (the soft skills) because technical medical details (the hard skills) are mostly a mystery. The human side of the doctor is the one that the patient best understands. Patients know what it is like to have to explain something to someone. Patients have had to break bad news. Patients have had to build rapport with someone before. This is all part of life, of being a person.

Because this aspect of the doctor–patient relationship isn't foreign to people in the same way the medical mumbo jumbo can be, they know pretty quickly when things don't feel right.

As I crossed the Harbour Bridge into the city, I thought back to John and how his bedside manner was interfering with his role as a doctor. Having the biggest brain in the world seemed irrelevant if your patient no longer listened to you.

Roger had clearly decided he wanted nothing to do with John. For Francisca, it wasn't as personal. She didn't seem to get annoyed at John's bedside manner, in fact I think she probably responded well to his bluntness. Francisca, her daughter and the guy collecting video evidence were upset with the system, not us.

As I trolled my street for a place to park, it hit me: I *am* the system now.

•

On the drive into the hospital on my second day, I decided to start keeping a list of patients to revisit after our ward round. If a patient looked confused when John or a senior doctor explained something I would write their name down. When a patient got cross with John or sad about a new scan result I would make sure I popped by later to see if I could help. If a patient seemed lonely, I would add them to my list so that I didn't forget to spend a few minutes with them in the afternoon. I decided new patients should automatically go on the list as well because they almost always had extra questions about what was wrong with them.

This became my own secret ward round. It reminded me of trying to stay back and talk to patients during ward rounds when I was a medical student. It was more difficult now as I had an already busy job, but I needed it as much as the patients seemed to. I don't think John ever noticed that I was doing this, but the nurses did. They started approaching me regularly with requests for more than just Panadol or to order a scan.

'I've printed the CT report for Mr Jones in bed fifteen, would you be able to walk him through the results when you have time?'

'Between you and me, Khan in bed four isn't happy with John, can you have a chat to her?'

'Mrs Ping in bed twenty-two has lots of questions after the consultant saw her this morning. I told her you could pop back when her son comes in at three o'clock.'

If I saw that a patient had visitors, I stuck my head in the room to meet them and find out if they had questions. They always had questions, so I started carrying a whiteboard marker around with me. Each patient's room had a small whiteboard, handy for drawing pictures of tumours or writing down the names of the medications people were being given.

I realised that most patients and families just wanted to understand. They were so appreciative for a few minutes of my time, they often fell over themselves with gratitude. I was not solving diagnostic dilemmas or performing breakthrough surgeries, I was just talking. Plus, spending time with families now made it easier to have difficult conversations when a patient later deteriorated. And spending extra time with patients meant they would tell me things, sometimes critical things, about their health or home life that I would then communicate to John.

As the weeks went by, I started asking patients about their mood and feelings. I treated finding out about their emotions as normal, in the same way I asked about a headache or checking their inflammatory markers on the WOW. I wanted them to be able to share their emotions as routinely as their physical symptoms. This didn't just seem to make the patients more comfortable, it revealed their inner world in ways that helped us better care for their bodies.

I remember one patient with lung cancer who lived in a caravan and was under threat of eviction. The council required him to repair the roof of the caravan as part of it had caved in. He was itching to get out of hospital – the deadline to have the repairs completed was approaching. Quite sensibly, he didn't like the idea of being homeless with lung cancer. When I told John this he was able to take this into account when deciding which antibiotics to use, getting the man out of hospital a couple of days earlier than first planned so he could close the hole in his roof.

•

Zipping home along the expressway one night after about eight weeks on the cancer ward, I thought back to my first job in the hairdressing salon and how Bernard liked to make clients feel special from the moment they walked in the door. In a way, making myself truly available for patients – my secret ward rounds, staying back late to talk to family, re-explaining results and drawing pictures on their walls – was my attempt to better serve them. I then thought about my time in the Science Circus and how I'd learnt to provide information in as many forms as possible. I knew from the reading I'd done on ward rounds as a medical student that patients forgot a lot of what doctors told them. I certainly had as a patient.

Several times when I was being treated for my cancer, Sana had arrived at the hospital and asked me: 'So what did the surgeons say this morning?'

On days where different doctors had seen me, or if I'd been visited by the physio or had bad sleep the night before, I'd look at her blankly, having forgotten what the surgeons had said earlier that morning 'I dunno, something about the stoma,' I'd say.

As I entered the tunnel under Sydney Harbour, now only a few minutes from home, I decided to design a one-page sheet for patients that I could hand out the next day. The sheet was divided into three sections. It had space for patient questions and another where I filled in the name of the condition that we were treating and how. In the last section we recorded what our goals were. I messaged one of the senior doctors to ask if this was okay, bypassing John as he just wouldn't have got it. The senior doctor replied straight away: 'Go for it!'

I stuck the sheets to the whiteboard in each room and updated them during ward rounds.

Some patients weren't fussed with them. But I noticed when we approached others on our rounds they had already removed the sheet and held it tightly, ready to fill it in themselves. Sometimes a spouse would point to the sheet on the wall and ask us how 'goal one' was going today. I noticed visitors reading the sheets too. As one patient joked, 'It means everyone is literally on the same page.' Another told me that it meant they didn't have to explain the same thing over and over again throughout the day.

My secret ward rounds and my information sheets were helpful, but they didn't address the core reasons that patients don't receive the care that matters most to them. It would be unkind to blame John for the fragile doctor–patient dynamics I saw play out every day on our ward – John was not a bad person, I actually liked him a great deal.

It was no surprise, to me, that John didn't have good touchy-feely skills. The problem wasn't John. He was as smart and focused as they come. The problem was that the teaching he'd received while becoming a doctor, the training he'd received once a doctor, and the time the system allocated him to care for patients didn't focus on or reward the skills that his patients needed from him.

And this was letting him, and the patients, down.

21

RACING TO SOMEONE ELSE'S CLOCK

All the small steps I'd adopted to help improve patient communication during my twelve-week stint on the oncology ward were thrown out the window on the surgical wards. There was just no time.

The surgical department was ridiculously busy. It comprised at least fifteen consultant surgeons, nine surgical registrars, two residents and ten interns. We were arranged into six teams. When it was a team's turn to accept all the new patients, the surgeons worked through the night on emergency cases. Us interns started at 6.30 am so the surgeons could see all their patients on the wards before heading back to the operating theatres at 7.30 am to start operating again. With up to forty patients to see, and only a couple of minutes to see each patient, the ward round was a sprint.

The wheels on the WOWs failed to keep up, so we ditched them and just scrawled something on paper that we could type up later.

Everyone working on the ward cared, but there was only enough time to deliver the basics. My main job as an intern was to keep patients progressing, as fast as possible. I made sure antibiotics and fluids were running, prescribed pain medications, got any scans organised urgently and flagged any issues with the registrar – while she was down in theatre performing back-to-back miracles.

The scores of patients coming and going blurred – recalling exactly who had had their appendix out and who had had their knee operated on became hard. And then I met a patient who stopped me in my tracks.

Semir was a 36-year-old accountant with bowel cancer. He had immigrated to Australia from Azerbaijan after university and, while renewing his qualifications in Sydney, he met his wife and fathered two children.

Like many younger people with bowel cancer, Semir was diagnosed late, after the cancer had already spread beyond the bowel. Despite tumours in his liver and lungs he managed to still work part-time. In the weeks leading up to his admission to hospital Semir had started to feel weaker. He worried that the chemotherapy holding his tumours at bay was no longer working.

He was right. His cancer was on the move and the tumours had become resistant to chemo. This had happened twice before – he was running out of drug options.

Semir was in hospital because he'd fractured his arm while picking up a bottle of orange juice. He had been clearing the breakfast table, and while carrying the juice back to the fridge he felt an explosion of pain in his upper arm. He called an ambulance and was taken to emergency.

In the emergency department they got on top of his pain and X-rayed his right arm. It showed a fracture in the humerus – the long bone between the shoulder and elbow. Semir's fracture was up near the shoulder and the bone was completely broken in two. The bone below the break had dropped away from where it was supposed to be.

The humerus is a strong bone and normally only breaks under heavy duty force like a car accident or when a person playing a contact sport gets tackled and falls the wrong way. Carrying a bottle of juice back to the fridge is not an extreme force. Evidence for why Semir's arm had broken doing something so simple was clear on the X-ray: the bone around the break looked weak. It was more translucent than the rest of the humerus. Instead of bright white areas of bone, this part looked mottled and dark, as if moths had been eating away at it.

The radiologist analysing the X-ray thought the pattern in Semir's humerus looked suspiciously like bone cancer.

Bowel cancer is one of several cancers that likes to spread to bone. Sadly for Semir, it looked as though his bowel cancer had metastasised, or spread, to his arm. A sample would need to be collected from the bone to determine if it was cancer, but the possibility devastated Semir and his wife. When I met Semir his right arm was in a sling, a Quran lay open in his lap. He looked up and greeted us with a smile. I made eye contact from behind the WOW while the registrar did the doctor stuff.

Semir had been in hospital for three days, but his arm still hadn't been fixed. His left arm cradled his head, his eyes looked at the ground. His voice cracked slightly, the strain of the last few days evident. He asked us why his arm had not been operated on, and the registrar explained that he was on a waiting list.

At medical school, surgeons had taught us to always indicate whether the dominant arm was the one dislocated or fractured. They liked to fix the dominant arm quickly so as to get the patient back to normal function as soon as possible. Semir had fractured his right arm, his dominant arm. This was the arm he used to hug his kids. Attached to that arm was the hand he used to bathe, to eat and to work on his computer and manipulate a mousepad. Losing use of his arm prevented Semir from working. When Semir didn't work, his family didn't eat.

The accountancy firm that employed him had accommodated his diagnosis a year earlier, and his gradual decline since. He could only manage a few days of work each week, and his company allowed him to work these from home. This once proud family man, strong in spirit and earning a good salary, was now huddled in a hospital bed without a pay cheque. Semir was too ashamed to apply for welfare – so his wife and I worked on the paperwork out of his sight.

The team explained to me that Semir was a low category case. Low category cases get added to the bottom of the list of patients requiring operations. Worse, they get bumped off the list as new cases are brought into the emergency department. Each night since he'd arrived in hospital Semir fasted from midnight, just in case surgery happened the next day. The hunger didn't bother Semir, he was used to fasting each Ramadan. What upset him was the daily cycle of hope and disappointment. He grew frustrated – each day his arm remained broken delayed his recovery and ability to work. I called the surgical team again and pleaded Semir's case, to no avail.

The surgeons justified his low priority because they deemed the surgery to be 'palliative'. Many doctors use the term palliative to describe treatments that don't cure – it is a dirty word to many doctors and patients. It was true, Semir's cancer wasn't curable, but he was very much still alive and wanted his arm back. He belonged at home with his young children, not in a shared hospital room, lying rigid with pain. The fact he possibly only had a few more months to live gave Semir's case a sense of urgency for me; to the surgeons, it meant he could wait another day or two. Doctors had written him off, and that broke my heart.

I would often stop by his bed to say hello or update him on scans or tests, even when I didn't have the time or had nothing new to say.

Sometimes Semir got angry. He and his wife didn't understand why a hospital was letting someone's broken body go unfixed. He knew that he was running out of time, and was confused about why that didn't motivate the surgeons. I didn't think it helpful to tell him that they weren't rushing to fix his arm because he was dying.

A week went by before Semir's humerus was repaired. Analysis of a sample of bone near the fracture confirmed that it was a tumour and that it had spread from the one in his bowel. He started physiotherapy and returned home. I learnt later that further chemotherapy was withheld: his cancer had stopped responding to a variety of drugs and he'd grown too frail to try more. He died a few months later, at home with his wife and kids.

Semir's story highlights major problems with the health system. His experience wasn't patient-centred. The way patients were prioritised for surgery failed to take into account the person attached to Semir's arm: his desire to work and provide for his family, his young children, his volunteer work at his mosque, the cancer clock counting down to his death.

This prioritisation system exists because more people need healthcare than the system can manage. There are only twenty-four hours in a day, and surgeons need sleep and rest. A few of the junior surgeons I nagged about Semir lacked compassion, but just as many really wanted to help him. They had empathy, but were nearly always running behind on their work, and exhausted. Junior surgeons aren't the ones deciding who gets surgery anyway, senior surgeons do.

Most senior surgeons who work in a public hospital also work in private facilities. For orthopaedic surgery in particular, a great deal occurs in private hospitals, funded by private health insurance. In the private system patients often tell stories of being able to call their surgeon and schedule surgery in two days' time. Twice, Semir asked me to transfer him to a private hospital for the surgery, but to organise that would have taken longer than he was likely going to have to wait at our hospital. Instead, Semir had to stay put, and was made to wait and fast, fast and wait, again and again, for more than a week. Caring for Semir made me reflect on myself as a patient doctor. Semir and I both knew he was dying, but only I knew that we both had bowel cancer. I never told him that I'd also had his disease – I wanted our interactions to remain about him. Even though I intimately understood some of what he was experiencing and badly wanted to tell Semir that I could feel his turmoil in *my* bones, I dared not put myself in his story as anything more than just another doctor involved in his care.

I also felt guilty: Semir literally did feel cancer in his bones, as the tumours rendered them soft and fragile. My disease had been caught before it had spread; *just* before. I was lucky; I was alive. I'd felt survivor's guilt a few times since my treatment ended, but never as intensely as during my time with Semir. There was no justification for why I survived and Semir didn't. It seemed unfair.

As a medical student I had learnt about the social determinants of health – factors about a person that predict and affect their health. Semir had a few of these working against his desire to remain alive: he was a man of colour, an immigrant and probably lived in a postcode with unfavourable health outcomes. That some forces of society were stacked against him just made me feel guiltier.

•

During my time in the surgical wards, it was clear that everyone in the surgical team was stretched. Working in that environment put me in survival mode: I just needed to get through each day and keep as many patients safe as possible. I thought back to my time as a patient on a surgical ward – the rushed ward rounds and doctors who seemed to be itching to be somewhere else made more sense. I remembered being a medical student, when I had been ignored by surgeons who were obviously totally focused on the body in front of them, aware that lots more bodies were waiting. Did that also explain some of the times senior surgeons pounced on me? I wondered if they were trying to get in as much 'teaching' as quickly as possible once they remembered I was standing there, waiting to learn from them. Taking a day off during my surgical rotation was only possible if another intern agreed to cover my work, plus their own work. We were all exhausted, but we tried our best to help each other take a day off here and there. When I needed to accompany Sana to the IVF clinic, two other interns put their hands up straight away.

I'd been injecting Sana with combinations of hormones for a few weeks. When the nurse tried to show her how to do it, she screwed up her face – exactly as she had when she'd been asked to inject me with the clot-busting drugs during the end of chemo.

'God, no. Show him, he's the doctor,' she said.

Her ovaries were now full of eggs. She sat beside me in the clinic's waiting room, feeling bloated and uncomfortable. The eggs were going to be collected while Sana was under general anaesthetic.

'You'll love it. It's the best sleep ever,' I said.

'You're such a weirdo.'

When the nurse arrived to take her to theatre I totally forgot about her sore tummy and, mid-hug, picked her up off the ground.

'Ow! Put me down,' she said.

'I'm so sorry! I just got excited,' I said.

'Of course you're excited, you're not the one putting your body through this crap.'

'Love you,' I said, kissing her goodbye.

While waiting in the recovery area, I thought about all the patients back on the surgical wards. I felt bad that I'd given up trying to make things a little clearer for them. No extra visits, diagrams, information sheets or chats with family.

I was seeing first-hand what effect being busy had on good doctoring. Time was critical. I wondered if the good doctors I worked with were that way because they were better at freeing up time to really connect with patients. If all doctors had more time, could they all be great?

I closed the *National Geographic* I'd been staring at but not reading and picked up a patient feedback survey and pen from the coffee table. I flipped the survey over and scribbled an equation: Good teaching + good training + ample time = good doctor.

I flicked the pen in the air. I couldn't wait to share this with Sana – once she'd had time to properly wake up and eat something, of course.

The need for good teaching – like the teaching I'd received from Fiona, Prof Robinson and the few patients who had lectured us, and had *not* received from others – became obvious during med school. All the training we did after med school was a key factor too – John had gone through seven years of training and was still blind to how to connect with patients.

Now that I was being slammed on the surgical wards I realised that the best teaching and training in the world was useless without adequate time. But how could we fix this? Creating time for junior doctors could be achieved by reducing their patient load, and that would require hiring more doctors. Other strategies could include using medical scribes (people trained in medical record-keeping) to update patient notes, and fostering better dialogue between hospitals and training colleges so as to evenly distribute the demands placed on junior doctors. Even more flexibility and control over their roster would reduce background stress on junior doctors, allowing them to focus more fully on the patient in front of them.

But change will never occur as long as power rests with the top doctors, colleges and hospitals only. Junior doctors are expected to just do what they're told, even when it is unreasonable, unjust and sometimes illegal. Acknowledging that they are people, and not just tools to be moved around where the work is, is the first step in restoring their power as people. I wrote the word 'power' down on my bit of paper and circled it angrily.

'Ben? Ben?' called a nurse from a door across the waiting room.

'Sorry, coming,' I said, throwing the feedback form with my notes on it in my bag.

'You can come through and see Sana now, everything went perfectly.'

22

FRIENDS WITHOUT BENEFITS

Several months into being a doctor I rotated off the surgical wards and on to the geriatrics ward. It was beginning to feel like just as I got comfortable working with one team and one group of patients, it was time to move on to another.

With first-day nerves, I quietly walked into the doctors' office on the geriatrics ward. Three of the four computers were occupied.

'Hi,' I said. 'I'm the new intern.'

Two of the doctors glanced in my direction and returned to their screens. *Gee*, I thought, *some doctors really aren't people people.*

The third doctor introduced himself though, and we quickly became friends.

This doctor was a resident – meaning he'd already been a doctor for a year longer than me. Let's call him David. David was clean-shaven and had perfectly spiked hair, as though he'd just come from the barber. He wore tailored pants and a crisp collared shirt every day. He had a warm smile and liked to talk. He helped me log in to the computer system and explained who was who on the ward. He spoke fast and worked even faster – he had shortcuts for everything. He was helpful and friendly for the entire three months we worked together.

David was a thorough doctor, but he had stopped caring. He had gone into medicine because of status and job security – his family had pushed him into it. He'd been a physiotherapist before medicine and frequently questioned his decision to become a doctor. What started off as exciting had quickly become a chore. David's cynicism bubbled up frequently. He'd roll his eyes when a patient requested extra painkillers. He'd tap his foot and scroll Facebook while a consultant talked to a patient. He tried to complete all his work quickly so he could spend the afternoon focused on his own life. He really enjoyed reading about cars online.

He was less than two years into his career as a doctor and was already bored. He was aware of the change in his behaviour but seemed powerless to combat it. As a doctor in his second year of training, he was under pressure to apply for a specialty training program. He was thinking of becoming either a general practitioner or hospital physician. Each of the programs were competitive to get into. He'd already become a member in each of the medical colleges that oversaw general practice training and physician training, costing him hundreds of dollars. As an intern the year before, he'd used his spare time to study for the entrance exam to become a general practice trainee. Then, he'd taken holiday leave to sit the exam – a necessity because there were no allowances for extra time off in his roster. He was now focused on the physician program – he was hedging his bets.

All of this struck me as a distraction from his day job.

Getting on a training program has become hyper-competitive for junior doctors. Many miss out on their first, second and third attempts – creating a class of doctors with general qualifications unable to advance their career. No doctor wants to get caught in this limbo.

To look attractive to training program recruiters, junior doctors need to do much more than their actual job of being a doctor. Research work at night and on weekends is common. Many juniors are doing master's level programs on public health, anatomy or medical science on weekends. There are countless extra courses and workshops targeted to junior doctors, and all cost a small fortune.

This extra work chips away at precious downtime and occurs outside the main job of being an actual doctor. The hospitals that employ junior doctors don't care about this strain, it's not their problem. In this way, junior doctors are caught between the hospitals that employ them and the training colleges that control their career – they are beholden to both systems. This extra stress outside the hospital adds to the stress inside the hospital, further chipping away at the patient–doctor relationship.

The health system I trained in was stretched. There were never enough beds to accommodate all the patients who needed help. As an intern I did overtime nearly every day. Had I stayed at the hospital each night to get absolutely everything done I would never have left. This volume of work meant that I was able to see a large number of patients, but it allowed little time for reflection or connection. I began to feel the drain straight away. David had had eighteen months working like this – it was no surprise that he was showing signs of burnout.

•

While training and exams weigh on the minds of junior doctors, life inside the hospital continues to grind them down. The way hospitals sometimes treat junior doctors is outrageous, and I've often felt it would not be tolerated in most other industries. My friends working in sectors like business and non-profit are gobsmacked when they learn what junior doctors have to put up with. Hostility is built into every part of the life of a junior doctor.

Junior doctors are paid by the hour and work according to a roster, but until recently they were expected to work overtime and not be paid for it. In some departments there are two rosters. One roster looks okay, with regular start and finish times and lunch breaks. The second roster is what the hospital actually expects you to work, and can include starting much earlier and finishing much later. Forget lunch breaks; allocated days off are often ignored too. Having two rosters gets around the rules governing how many hours doctors can work and the amount of rest time needed between shifts.

To top it off, many hospitals still don't pay for this extra work. Even though governments have stepped in and ruled that junior doctors should be paid overtime, there are several class actions underway in New South Wales and Victoria to pay junior doctors what they are owed. This problem isn't isolated to one or two hospitals.

It's no wonder that some doctors realise they are heading for burnout in one specialty, and so switch to another, even when it hurts.

Amy and I became friends when she rotated to my hospital. I'd called her to see if she could examine a geriatrics patient who had come in with abdominal pain and who I thought had appendicitis, and we hit it off. Amy, like everyone in general surgery, spent a lot of time thinking about and managing patients' bowels. She loved making poo jokes and I loved laughing at them.

Amy was short and lean. For some reason I didn't understand, she felt compelled to compete in triathlons and most of her time outside the hospital was spent training. She had dark blonde hair that fell to her shoulders, and her soft blue eyes had a way of becoming piercing when she was thinking hard about what was wrong with her patients.

She'd gone to medical school to become a surgeon. From the moment she stepped into an operating theatre her dream was confirmed – the place just felt right. She had a surgical way of thinking and loved the physicality of operating with her hands. To beef up her CV she did research in surgery, helping to develop materials for non-surgical doctors to manage common problems after a patient had an operation.

A year before Amy started at my hospital, the department had lost the right to train junior doctors wanting to be surgeons. This was the first time a surgical department anywhere in the country had lost the right to teach doctors. So Amy's job involved rotating through a bunch of surgical departments in crisis.

She had hoped that things might have changed after the department lost the right to teach, but they hadn't.

As the most junior doctor on the team, she was expected to prepare notes on each patient before the ward round, which started at 7 am. Amy is a thorough doctor, if I were in hospital I would want her looking over my results – her ability to spot patterns and problems is unparalleled. But Amy was never going to thrive in that surgical department. She worked up to eighty hours per week, yet was rostered, and therefore paid for, only forty. When Amy got the courage to ask human resources for help, they allocated an extra junior doctor to her team – for a total of one day only.

Towards the end of her time with the department, Amy nervously submitted a claim for just one fortnight's overtime. She meticulously filled out the form, entering every patient's medical record number, the exact time she had spent helping them, and the problem that required her to stay back.

She received an email from human resources two days later – they were not happy. They had audited her usage of the electronic medical record system and found that her entries on the claim form did not perfectly align with the electronic records. In one example, they provided screenshots of a patient note she had electronically signed off at 7.10 pm, on a day where Amy said she'd worked until 8 pm.

Amy was baffled, surely human resources knew that being a doctor didn't only happen inside a computer? Junior doctors check results, review paperwork received from other hospitals, call family members, speak to patients' general practitioners, read through reports, replace IV drips, chart medications and discuss issues with nurses, among other things. Human resources thought Amy was trying to cheat the system. This came as a kick in the guts at the end of the hardest year of her life. Amy was dejected – this hospital was still toxic and didn't want to change – and, soon after I met her, she told me she was planning to abandon her dream of a career in surgery.

'I'm over it, these aren't my people,' she said.

The final straw had occurred during an interview for a new surgical job. The interview panel comprised several male senior surgeons with world-renowned reputations. At one point in the interview, they asked her to identify suture knots and choose which best suited certain surgeries. She was confused – she had applied for a training position, but they were testing her *before* they'd taught her. She had assisted in loads of surgeries, even leading some under supervision – unusual for such a junior doctor. But she hadn't seen these particular types of knots used.

Part way through her answer one of the senior surgeons started chuckling. Two others exchanged smirks and rolled their eyes. The lead interviewer finally cut her off.

'You clearly do not know, so stop there,' he said. 'Thanks for coming in today.'

After that interview, Amy started looking into other specialties.

I knew that she'd do well in any field she chose, but I couldn't help feeling heartbroken – for her, and the system training junior doctors. Amy was focused and she cared, a rare combination in medicine. She was the kind of doctor who always got down to the patient's level, sitting naturally at the bedside while she worked, holding a hand when a patient was overwhelmed. Instead of nurturing Amy, the system had broken her.

It's not just surgery's loss, Amy would have been one of those surgeons patients love.

•

I met many more doctors during my internship who had been pushed around by the system.

One friend was moved for six months to a hospital a couple of hundred kilometres from home. He was so grateful for a training position that he was prepared to make the move, but was upset when the hospital informed him he wouldn't be allowed to have visitors at the run-down share house the hospital rented for junior doctors. This meant that his wife could not easily visit him there.

On the psychiatry ward where I had been rostered for a few weeks after their intern had become ill, I met another doctor whose life was disrupted by how unaccommodating the hospital could be with a similarly long-distance move. Kerry was one of the hardest working doctors I'd ever met, but working hard does not shield junior doctors from the bitter aspects of the system.

She was a registrar; she was the last to leave each night and knew everything about her patients. Patients and nurses all loved her. She had wavy brown hair and wore thin glasses that perfectly framed her big brown eyes. She chewed on her pen when she was thinking, and had the world's largest collection of glamorous skirts – in the month we worked together I didn't see the same skirt twice. She was generous with her time and more generous with her knowledge – telling me medical facts and observations of her patients all day long.

Her next rotation was approaching, and she was worried. She was rostered at our hospital up until the last Friday of the current term and then at a hospital eight hundred kilometres away on the following Monday. She begged the hospital for a few days off to organise her life, load the car and make the trip. They granted her leave, but there was a catch – the days would be deducted from her annual holidays and she had to organise someone to care for her patients, they weren't allocating a doctor to cover the ward.

Most other industries have people who can stand in or back-fill for this kind of thing – but not medicine, there is just no one available. This is also the reason why, at many hospitals, junior doctors have to indicate when they want holidays right at the start of the year and take their holidays in four-week blocks. The hospitals can't have too many people away at the same time because there is no slack in the system, so holidays were staggered across the year. There is also little coordination to make it easier for junior doctors to transition between hospitals over vast distances – even when those hospitals are in the same network and the move is compulsory.

The hospital system survives with no backup because it knows us junior doctors lean on each other. Kerry sheepishly asked if I could cover her patients. 'Of course I will,' I said, even though it meant that my patient load doubled and I was even later getting home each night – this was just what was expected of us.

23

PUTTING PATIENTS FIRST

Back on the geriatrics ward, I was still as busy as ever.

My team was led by an exceptional registrar with many years of clinical experience. The resident on the team, with two years of medicine under her belt, was one of the friendliest doctors I'd ever met. All three of us liked talking to patients, but the pressure to quickly move from patient to patient was ever present. On a good day we only had twenty patients; on a bad day we had forty. Geriatric patients are complicated to treat – one in five people over the age of sixty-five have at least two chronic medical conditions; over the age of eighty-five it jumps to three. Patients' medication lists are long, and someone in their seventies can have a medical history as thick as an encyclopaedia.

One such patient was Leslie. We met Leslie after she'd been admitted from her nursing home with a cough and fever. In the nursing home, she shared a room with her husband of fifty years,

Frank, who had been admitted to our hospital on a different ward and under a separate team a week earlier due to shortness of breath.

Leslie had also been having trouble breathing. Hers was because of pneumonia; Frank had been struggling because of lung cancer. He was admitted under the respiratory team, but he was frail and the cancer was advanced – there was little they could do except make him comfortable.

Leslie was hard of hearing and her dentures had been left behind at the nursing home, so communicating with her was challenging. Between coughs she told us about Frank's admission.

We reviewed her antibiotics and made sure she was getting soft meals because of the missing dentures. Her regular medications were all being correctly administered. Physically she was frail, but nothing major, except the pneumonia, seemed to ail her.

I thought that it would be really nice for Leslie and Frank to have some time together. I shared my idea with the team. Their response was crushing: 'Good luck,' they both said. These were two of the kindest doctors I'd had the privilege of learning from, but even their compassion had limits. The system had worn them down.

Undeterred, I messaged a colleague working on Frank's ward, who told me that Frank was probably close to death. When a small gap in my day opened up, I went to speak to the nurse in charge of our ward. I was told there were too many impediments to my idea. No spare rooms with two beds. No porters available to move either Leslie or Frank.

It never happened.

A week later, Frank died without Leslie nearby. Despite their physical proximity within the same hospital, Leslie and Frank may as well have been in different countries. The system is rigid, hard borders are everywhere – blocking holistic patient care and preventing human connection.

The irony is that our ward was covered in posters espousing patient-centred care. The Australian Commission on Safety and Quality in Health Care defines patient-centred care as care that is 'respectful of, and responsive to, the preferences, needs and values of the patient'. True patient-centred care, they say, should attempt to understand what is important to the patient and then make decisions with patients, and not for patients.

The idea of patient-centred care is great marketing, and has been rapidly adopted by hospitals all over the world. Sadly, though, it more often than not gets reduced to making sure a patient has consented to having a test, taking a medicine or being operated on. To most doctors, if a patient says yes to something, it has been a patient-centred decision. But patients say yes to nearly everything doctors ask of them regardless of whether they fully understand it or believe it is necessary. This is partly because of power differences, confusing medical jargon or because the patient is distracted by pain.

As a patient I rarely felt at the centre of my care, adding to my ever-present uneasiness that I didn't really have a grasp on what was happening inside me. Sometimes I actually couldn't be at the centre – like during surgery when I was asleep or when nurses switched over bags of chemotherapy containing drugs with long names I could never remember. It was unrealistic to expect me to have fully understood the chemotherapies, surgeries or radiation therapy needed to cure my cancer.

For a great deal of my care, I felt like a bystander watching things happen around me. Other times, I felt like a passenger in someone else's people mover, a bit closer to the action and moving along with everyone else, but with no idea where we were going or how long it was going to take. If I had been given more information about the planning session before my radiation, I might not have been left feeling so exposed for so long. And if I had been warned about blood clots during *all* of my treatment, not just after surgery, I may not have found them so shocking. But, often, I just had to trust that the people around me knew what they were doing, that they had my back.

My experience showed me that patient-centred care needs to be about more than ensuring patients properly agree to what is being done to them. To achieve this, the system has to acknowledge that patients are more than their illness or symptoms. Even though patients all look the same in their matching gowns and in identical beds, we need to remember that they have a whole life outside the hospital. They don't stop being a person when we re-label them a patient.

Leslie was more than her pneumonia. She was an accomplished teacher, spending her last years in a nursing home with her husband of five decades. We could have treated her pneumonia *and* safely allowed her to be close to Frank before cancer consumed him. Had the system wanted to fully care for Leslie, time with Frank could have been organised.

Healthcare remains system-centred. Acts of kindness attempting to treat the whole person are possible, but only when they fall within current ways of doing things. A wall less than three metres from Leslie's bed carried a sign promoting patient-centred care, but the reality on the ward was far different.

●

Unsurprisingly, trying to take a day off in geriatrics was as hard as it had been in surgery. It was always hard – on every rotation, in every ward. Sana was having to attend more and more IVF appointments alone, even big ones.

Eggs collected from Sana earlier in the year had been mixed with the sperm I'd frozen eight years earlier, and we now had three embryos in the freezer. I'd been by her side and held her hand when the first embryo had been implanted, and again when we found out that it had not been successful. But the next embryo was due for implantation and I just couldn't get away from the hospital. She went alone. I asked her to snap a photo of the embryo as they displayed it on the large screen above her bed, but the doctor had told her it wasn't allowed. Instead, she messaged me afterwards.

'All done. The doctor was grumpy. I wish you could have been there.' Her message came while I was rounding with the registrar.

'Everything okay?' the registrar asked.

'Yep. How much potassium did you want for Mrs Yao?' I replied.

I thought back to some wisdom a senior doctor had shared with me during my psychiatry term as a medical student: 'If you let it, medicine will take everything from you – and then some.'

24

BABY STEPS ARE NOT EASY STEPS

Small things can improve patient satisfaction, but in a complex environment like a hospital, even tweaking small things can be hard.

On the wards, I was reminded of just how many doctors a patient meets during a hospital stay. Within a patient's own treatment team, there might be multiple doctors of differing seniority. A patient might also be seen by other teams (an endocrinologist might review an oncology patient, for example, or a surgeon may review a geriatric patient). One team of doctors may not even know the names of the members of the other team. So what hope do patients have?

It gets worse – nurses, physiotherapists, occupational therapists and social workers walk in and out of patients' rooms all day, and there's a new batch of junior doctors every ten to twelve weeks.

Nursing staff are flat out keeping track of doctors' names, let alone the patients.

In our rapid surgical ward rounds we sometimes didn't introduce ourselves to the patients. But this bothered me because people meeting and exchanging names is as human as it gets. We like to know who we are talking to and are less comfortable around strangers – names matter, that's why everyone gets one when they're born.

At the start of the year, Linh, a fellow intern, had lobbied the hospital to give us all name badges. I had enthusiastically embraced the name badge rollout because I found them helpful. Other doctors would glance at mine to learn my name, patients would look at it when I introduced myself. Nurses seemed to find it easier to use my name, ditching the generic 'doctor'. And I lost track of how many times I spotted a doctor on the ward, glanced at their badge and thought, *Ohhh, so* that *is who I've been speaking to on the phone.* It made approaching other doctors so much easier.

I figured that name badges were also a small way to address the power imbalance between patients and doctors. When I was a patient, I had no idea that patients' names were recorded and communicated everywhere from the moment we arrived at hospital. Patients' names are printed on sticky labels, tied around their wrists and sometimes written above their bed. They're on meal trays, medical files and projected during meetings for all to see. In contrast, doctors' names appeared on faded identification swipe cards attached at the hip or on crowded lanyards around the neck (both awkward spots to stare at).

The information gulf separating patients and their doctors starts with names.

Once name badges had been rolled out, I did some reading about them and learnt that studies consistently showed that patients want doctors to wear name badges – and that they preferred them on the doctor's breast pocket.

Linh and I happened to be working together on the same ward a few months after the badges were first launched. We were bummed to learn that many of our colleagues seemed uninterested in donning their badges. We began counting how many juniors wore them – that proved easy: only one in four.

Linh and I wanted to find out why such a simple measure was meeting so much resistance, so we pitched a small research project to our bosses and distributed a survey to the one hundred interns and residents at the hospital.

Around twenty per cent of junior doctors told us that they just didn't see any value in wearing a name badge. The same proportion didn't want to because senior doctors didn't. Of most concern, sixteen per cent of the junior doctors did not want their patients to know their name! That last reason made Linh and me uncomfortable. Our badges had our given name only, but some doctors still didn't feel safe with patients knowing their names.

Doctors have full access to a patient's most personal pieces of health information and perform invasive and sensitive examinations and procedures on patients every day – yet the trust patients placed in them was simply not reciprocated.

We wondered if this was just a quirk of the culture at our hospital. I informally surveyed a second group of junior doctors, representing every hospital in New South Wales. I reported back to Linh that about a third of hospitals had name badges, but few doctors wore them. Another third of hospitals had name badges and junior doctors liked wearing them. The last third of hospitals didn't have name badges at all.

Despite campaigns to improve the way doctors greet patients, and the use of communication aids like name badges, uptake remained poor and easy opportunities for human connection were being missed.

•

No matter which ward I found myself working on, all patients loved talking about how much they hated hospital food.

I tried not to laugh when they talked about this, because it was a serious issue, but sometimes they were just too funny.

'I might only have a few months left. I'm not spending it eating this shit,' said a woman on a cancer ward.

'It's a good thing I'm too nauseous to eat. This looks, and smells, like something my cat has dragged in from the garden,' said a man on a surgical ward.

Lukewarm, flavourless, sloppy – served in plastic, wrapped in plastic, and eaten using a plastic knife and fork. Many hospitals offer a choice of meals, but why risk the fish stew? Better to stick with the devil you know and re-order the chicken surprise for lunch. At least, that was my strategy when I was a patient in hospital.

Meals in hospital are like meals on a long-haul flight – they break up the boredom and give you something to do, even if for just ten minutes. Food is also incredibly important when recovering from illness, when the demand for nutritious and satisfying food is greatest.

Food unites us. Those who run the hospital system and work in it also eat – they know good from bad. So why has hospital food been allowed to get so bad? The answer is multi-layered – though cost and efficiency are the major factors.

Even if we could magically fix hospital food overnight, there's a bigger problem: making sure patients can actually eat it.

Undernourishment is an issue for many patients. Hospital wards buzz with constant bustle and all this activity can interfere with patients eating their meals. Patients don't always get the help they need to peel off a plastic cover, or to lift a spoon to their mouths. They may not like the taste of the food, or be able to chew it safely. Sometimes a patient is wheeled off for a scan and returns to find their tray has been cleared away before they've had a chance to eat their meal. Doctors – who understand how important regular food is to recovery and mood, and who also eat themselves – sometimes decide to do the ward round during a mealtime. While the patient waits, not wanting to eat in front of an audience, a pretty average lukewarm meal turns into a below average cold one.

One way to fix this is to leave patients alone during mealtimes – no doctor visits, no tests, no physiotherapy, no forms to fill in.

This idea of a *protected* mealtime for patients has been circulating around hospitals for a while – but few have managed to implement it. A team of dietitians and occupational therapists at my hospital decided to give it a go.

Ensuring patients were left alone for a half-hour once meals arrived sounded simple, but the planning team had experienced pushback. I naïvely thought that if the idea was expanded to include junior doctors that there would be more support.

Eating lunch and having downtime is good for doctors. These two activities improve thinking and mood. If we expanded the meal breaks to include patients and doctors, I told the team, both would benefit.

Resistance to the idea of leaving patients alone to eat in peace for thirty minutes grew to outrage at having to do the same for doctors. Some nurses were uncomfortable with the idea of not being able to ask junior doctors to complete small tasks. Ward managers worried that it would delay patient discharges and the paperwork required before each patient left hospital. Some senior doctors didn't like the idea of having ward rounds interrupted by a meal break, or moving their preferred start and finish times.

Eventually, the hospital agreed to trial the meal break, but only for patients and only on a few wards. When I spoke to a junior doctor on one of the trial wards, he said that the senior doctors had told him that they had no intention of honouring the patient meal break. 'The patients can eat later,' they'd said, 'we're too busy to worry about their lunch.'

This made me angry. It was like the doctors who didn't want to wear name badges. It was as if patients simply didn't matter. Getting a lunch break for doctors was always going to be difficult – I could count on one hand the number of times I'd had a full lunch break as an intern – but surely making sure patients were able to eat was something the hospital could get behind.

In the first couple of weeks I'd spent in hospital recovering from my surgery I had been unable to eat, dry retching before the first mouthful. Once the leak in my colon had been found and my appetite returned, I eagerly awaited the meal tray and its plastic treats three times a day. Eating made me feel better, and although the food wasn't at all like the food I ate out of hospital, just the act of eating helped me feel a little more normal. It was also nice to eat at the same time as everyone else in my room, pretending for a moment that a group of friends had gathered for lunch somewhere, rather than four sick strangers sharing a hospital room.

•

Name badges and lunch breaks are not rocket science. Not all changes to the health system need to be large (although some will have to be), but the failure with the name badge rollout and the resistance to getting patients and their doctors a lunch break shows how difficult change will be. To set up initiatives for success, they must be designed to improve the experiences of patients *and* doctors, not one or the other. A name badge is useless to patients if a doctor doesn't wear it because senior doctors in the team aren't wearing theirs; leaving patients alone to eat lunch won't work if the doctors don't understand the benefits to patients (and themselves too). There are hundreds of small aspects of a hospital that can be improved for patients and doctors, but getting them on the same page will only be possible if we begin to level the playing field between them.

25

NIGHT-TIME CONFESSIONS

After my experience looking after Semir on the surgical ward, I often wondered what would happen if I let patients know that I was secretly one of them.

It is natural, I think, to want to reassure someone that you understand their pain and sadness because you've lived it. I felt a strong pull to disclose with Semir, but I managed to keep our relationship about him. I'd like to be able to say that I never slipped up, but one time I did – three-quarters of my way through my internship.

I was in the middle of a term they called 'relief' but that should have been called 'overnights', because that's what we mostly worked. My slip-up happened at 1.30 am during a run of night shifts – I blame fatigue.

I'd been called to see Andrew because he couldn't sleep. This is a very common complaint in hospital and one I understood intimately – my month in a four-bed hospital room recovering from surgery had made me realise that every aspect of a hospital has been unintentionally designed to keep you awake. Fluorescent lighting, beeping IV poles, frequent blood pressure and temperature measurements, delirious people yelling, blaring TVs, narrow beds – the list goes on.

Andrew wanted medicine to knock him out. He was a carpenter in his early forties and suffered from ulcerative colitis (long-term inflammation of the large bowel). The medicine to treat it had stopped working a few months earlier and his condition forced him to go to the toilet up to twenty times a day. On construction sites this meant spending a considerable part of each day in a portaloo, which he described as a 'living hell'. His ulcerated colon was getting worse and he had chosen to have it removed. He ended up with a temporary stoma – one of those diversions for faeces that I'd had after my surgery.

Andrew was in hospital that night because his stoma had been reversed three days earlier and he was still recovering. Having the stoma reversed is great in the long-term, but messy in the short-term because the bowel downstream of the stoma (which has basically been asleep for a few months) suddenly finds itself full of faeces again.

Since the reversal he'd been going to the bathroom every forty-five minutes. Memories from the peak of his colitis returned: rushing between portaloos, packing spare underwear each day, blood and mucus in the bowl. He was terrified that this would be his life again, that the bowel left behind wouldn't function normally. No wonder he couldn't sleep.

I remembered my own similar panic well. After my stoma had been reversed, learning to live with my new bum took months. It was uncomfortable, smelly and messy – but the hardest part was trusting that it would get better. My mind went back to when I first had to buy nappies. I was in a pharmacy, looking up and down the 'incontinence' section. 'If I'd known how hard this was going to be, I'd have kept the stoma,' I mumbled to myself.

Andrew seemed to be regretting his decision too. I knew his feelings would pass, but I understood his current fear intimately.

I started by asking about his sleep, but all he wanted to talk about was his bowels. I reassured him that the diarrhoea and endless bathroom visits would likely improve with time. I helped him understand that the bowel would warm back up, remember its role in life, and cooperate.

Andrew was charming. He was also disarming – it's not often men admit they are scared. This may explain why I suddenly told him that I'd had a stoma reversed too.

'I've been exactly where you are now,' I said. Then, before I knew it, I was telling him about my cancer.

'Bowel cancer! Jeez,' he said.

Oh shit, I thought. He waited for me to say more.

'Yep . . .' I said, buying time.

'And when was your stoma reversed?'

'Um . . . ah . . . seven years ago,' I said. *Why aren't you stopping?*

'When did it get better for you? How are you now? Do you, you know, have many accidents?' Andrew was off and running, he'd clearly recovered from hearing the c-word.

This is why you don't talk about yourself at 1.30 am on a crowded ward and with eight patients still to see.

'Well, um . . . like I said everything should get better soon.' I was keen to get back to why I was actually there. 'Now, about this sleep of yours, mindfulness may help . . .'

I gave him some advice about sleep while he downloaded an app to help him meditate. I saw him a couple of nights later, but I felt awkward and embarrassed that I'd talked about myself with him. I also felt exposed, like he knew my secret. I worried that I had crossed an invisible professional boundary. Would Andrew now see me as something other than a doctor? I also felt bad because I hadn't handled my slip-up well, and probably left him with more questions than reassurance. Part of me wanted to correct this and have a proper chat, but I worried that I'd already given too much of myself away.

I vowed to be more careful during night shifts, when I'd more likely be tired and drop my guard. After getting home from that shift, I made myself some breakfast for 'dinner' and googled whether people had studied this part of the patient–doctor relationship. I learnt that many doctors do disclose information about their health to patients and, while this may help build rapport initially, patients can feel like the relationship has become a little less about them. That sounds selfish, but patients should be selfish.

My heart sank as I pulled down a blind to block out the morning sun and climbed into bed: Andrew's experience was his alone, and my role in it was as a doctor, not a fellow patient. It felt wrong to have inserted myself into his story, when my only job was to support him and provide the best possible care.

•

I missed another embryo transfer. This time I was asleep after a night shift. Getting out of the overnight roster had proved impossible, there was simply no one to take my place – I had to let Sana down again.

That morning, I arrived home just as she was leaving for work. I'd bought flowers as a 'sorry I can't be there' gesture. They were a poor substitute for my presence, but she resisted the temptation to make me feel guiltier than I already did.

'Thanks, Benny, these are beautiful,' she said.

I woke up at 6 pm and checked my phone.

'All done. The doctor was okay. Hope this one sticks, I do *not* want to go through a harvest again,' her message read.

This was our last embryo. The thought of another egg collection cycle – with its needles, bloating, blood tests and ultrasounds – was unappealing to both of us. Plus, having embryos put in and then fail had hit us both harder than we'd expected. Urine sticks and initial blood tests after the first two embryo transfers had come back positive, meaning that the embryos had attached to the uterus. By the second blood tests, the results were negative. The embryos had disappeared.

I knew that the normal rate of miscarriage was usually around one in five, but nothing about this process was normal – we knew the exact moment an embryo was hanging out in her uterus. Had we been trying to make a baby the traditional way, we would have always been kind of guessing – did my sperm find your egg? Is there a little ball of cells growing? Will the next period be late?

With IVF, every single step was precisely measured and controlled. Waiting, tests, hugs and kisses, waiting, tests, disappointment. The pressure was intense. It was like riding a roller coaster again and finding ourselves upside down on a loop-the-loop – except this time we'd chosen to hop on.

We were used to big emotional swings. The high of falling in love had been smashed by cancer. Settling into Melbourne had been hijacked by needing to move out of Graeme's place. Radiation, tight finances, infertility, surgery, losing my business in Beijing, leaks, welfare, chemotherapy, clots, starting over in Sydney, med school, anxiety and the sacrifice of spending less time together – we'd survived it all, and we knew we could get through IVF, together.

I left for work at 9 pm. The drive in was a blur because my mind was on a loop, hoping that our last embryo was indeed our lucky last.

26

THE PATIENT HEALTH SYSTEM

I rounded off my intern year working in the emergency department. It was so busy that I'd have to see a patient in a consulting room (if I could find an empty one), put in a drip, order antibiotics, give pain medication and send them back to the waiting room. Only the sickest of people got a bed, there just weren't enough – not in the emergency department, not in the whole hospital. Patients who should have been in a ward would get stuck in the emergency department for an extra day, or three, before moving upstairs.

That summer, massive fires burnt across greater Sydney in the worst fire season on record. The air became thick with smoke, and the haze that settled over the city reminded me of the air in Beijing.

If the wind blew from a certain direction, smoke filled the emergency department and overwhelmed the air conditioning. We handed out masks so already sick patients wouldn't get worse. And then news broke of a new virus in China and the masks served another purpose. Patients kept coming. I watched as the pandemic stripped a lot of the humanity that remained in healthcare – now we had to speak to patients behind layers of plastic; families couldn't visit sick loved ones; people waiting for surgeries had them cancelled; women had to give birth alone; and people had to die alone. Already burnt-out junior doctors had their training interrupted and exams cancelled – causing worse backlogs in a clogged doctor pipeline. Stressed senior doctors and nurses, with too many patients and not enough time, had to make tough, sometimes life or death decisions about who got the most care.

By the end of my internship, the frustrations I'd had as a patient were now accompanied by frustrations I faced as a doctor.

As a patient I had spent a lot of time thinking of ways to make healthcare and the patient–doctor relationship better, but I had only understood half the equation – the patient side. Back then, it had been easy to quickly judge aspects of the health system that were failing patients. The simple way I had viewed the hospitals and doctors was still valid, and important – some things done in healthcare are just stupid, and patients are often the first to realise – but I was missing the other half of the equation.

At medical school I expected to learn more about cancer, though mostly I wanted to learn about why our healthcare system is the way it is. I had wanted to understand patients and hospitals the way doctors did. But studying medicine didn't answer the questions I had about healthcare, it just brought up bigger ones.

Fellow medical students who managed to hold on to their humanity – their empathy, communication and compassion – became junior doctors in a health system that doesn't value these traits as much as patients do. Wonderful and caring junior doctors wanting to practise with compassion found little support – everyone in the system was strained.

Throughout my internship I saw that patients *and* junior doctors both felt powerless and frustrated.

With many patients and doctors being ground down by the system, it is no wonder the patient–doctor relationship is so easily shattered. I grew shocked at how much the relationship was being ignored – especially when the wellbeing of one is dependent on the wellbeing of the other. When doctors hurt, patients suffer; and when patients are hurt, doctors suffer.

This relationship between doctor and patient is a relationship between two humans, and it doesn't occur in a vacuum. Each patient–doctor encounter takes place in a broader environment – a kind of ecosystem. Maybe the motivation to understand the interconnectedness of life from my earlier zoology training never left me. To truly understand an animal, you need to study its environment.

In hospitals, patients were reduced to numbers, organs or burdens. Junior doctors were reduced to labour to be manipulated in spreadsheets.

This may sound depressing, but there is hope. Accepting the idea that good patient care requires good doctors, and that cared-for doctors provide the best care, leads to a different way of thinking.

But we can't look at only half of the equation. An idea can be patient-centred, but may further strain doctors, leading to poorer care. Likewise, solutions for doctor-centred problems may make things worse for patients.

We've got to dig deeper – and embrace *human*-centred healthcare.

Human-centred healthcare recognises that the system can disappoint both sides of the patient–doctor relationship. It's about prioritising the values that make us human – communication, respect, empathy, compassion, kindness and balance.

This idea isn't new, and it's not tricky – mealtimes, name badges and a ward round information sheet are simple things to try to change.

Every day in all hospitals, multiple things unfold that ignore the fact that people inhabit the space. Doctors compete for limited computers and equipment is broken – making it harder for them to do their job. Patients get poor-quality food wrapped in plastic. Doctors don't eat. Nurses discuss patients within earshot of other patients. A senior doctor scolds a junior doctor. Visitors have nowhere to sit. Medical teams come and go, unknown to nurses or each other. Patients are given two minutes of attention on ward rounds. The junior doctor works late for free. Another makes a mistake after working thirty hours straight. Few people say hello. Applying a human-centred approach to healthcare would mean looking at the system and asking: why is it done this way? Who is this helping?

But I'm the first to admit – as an experienced patient and now a doctor with growing experience – that injecting humanity back into healthcare is easier said than done. In my short career as a doctor I've already seen multiple hospital initiatives struggle to achieve change, which is why I think we need to start before doctors get to hospital.

The focus on humanity must be fostered among the medical students who will one day be senior doctors, starting with how we select those for medical school. Lots of people who would make fantastic human-centred doctors miss out because the current hyper-competitive system favours grades. It's time to focus on people's human qualities instead.

At medical school, patients and people with direct experience of illness should form a critical part of the students' education. Integrating patients into medical school education is easy – patients and patient support groups are everywhere!

Graduating from medical school should never come at a cost to someone's humanity. Instead, medical schools should focus on protecting students' passion for people and cultivating clear communication skills, compassion and warmth. The system needs to do a better job of assessing how students are treated by senior doctors and other healthcare staff while on the job. So much of the attitude you hear from senior doctors about how harsh medical training is boils down to 'That's how it was when we did it.' They seem to treat 'pay it forward' as a medical mantra, in the worst way.

The mental health of medical students remains dire, and negative experiences during these most vulnerable learning periods can ripple forward for years, altering the kind of doctor they become. This is bad for them and bad for patients.

Pumping out compassionate doctors who treat patients as equals would have a tremendous impact on the system, but only if the system enables them to act on that compassion. The system for training junior doctors is currently outdated. It is a system of punishing rosters, unpaid overtime, inappropriate behaviour from senior doctors, excessive competition for training positions, overwhelming patient volumes, and moving between hospitals and regions every few months with no support. We need to appreciate that junior doctors are human and treat them as such.

Human-centred care extends to the patients' environment too. Being sick is inherently stressful, but the system can be rethought in ways that don't *add* to patients' stress, from how patients communicate with their healthcare team (an antiquated space that has resisted all technological progress) to the way patients are (and aren't) staggered to arrive at appointments. Giving patient liaisons or advocates – allies who help to bridge the patient–doctor divide – the same status as doctors and nurses, using plain language for clear documentation (something GPs have been seeking for years, too) and making waiting times reasonable and transparent, perhaps with real-time tracking – all these could be possibilities with a human-centred rethink.

Within wards, patients should be given the same courtesy that the rest of society affords them. This means creating predictable times when senior doctors will be on the ward, or providing other ways for the senior doctor to be contacted. Being left to wonder when the doctor is coming is a major source of angst for patients and their families. Taking a human-centred approach would help protect basic human needs, as well. For privacy, new hospitals should have as many single rooms as possible. Special spaces for patients to mingle could be created, so that natural social contact can occur. Hospitals should have dedicated spaces where doctors and nurses can discuss patients in private – this is an essential part of care, yet commonly takes place in busy hallways or crowded storerooms.

While lots of great programs exist – some hospitals have musicians, many hang art on the walls, some new hospitals only have single rooms, and some wards have fixed doctor hours and times for families to ask questions – these changes are piecemeal and insufficient on their own. A big look at the whole of healthcare is needed.

At my most idealistic, I daydream about rebuilding the healthcare system from the ground up. But I know this isn't possible because the machine is too big. Accepting the status quo isn't possible either – too many patients, and too many doctors are dissatisfied.

Only once we accept that healthcare depends on humans can we refocus on the core values of the patient–doctor relationship. We all know what these values are, because we all know what it is to be human. Perhaps we just need a reminder, so we can get about fixing the system – one patient and one doctor at a time.

27

THE FINAL
LOOP-THE-LOOP

I went to medical school to become a cancer doctor – an oncologist. After stints as a medical student in intensive care, psychiatry, obstetrics and gynaecology, pathology, paediatrics, general practice, anaesthetics, general medicine, vascular medicine, sports medicine, orthopaedic surgery, neurosurgery, vascular surgery, general surgery and emergency, I worried that not enough attention was being given to the human side of caring for patients – but some specialties seemed to do this better than others. By the end of medical school, I'd added a few more options to my specialty shortlist – which was now oncology, general practice, psychiatry and rehabilitation medicine.

Then, as my internship drew to a close – having worked in oncology, geriatrics, surgery, emergency, and covering other wards like gynaecology, dialysis, endocrinology, gastroenterology and respiratory medicine on night shifts and weekends – my specialty list was narrowed to just one option: psychiatry.

When it came to taking medical histories from patients, I was always most interested in what we call the 'social history'. This is the part that allows us to learn more about the patient as a person. Sadly, many doctors tend to reduce this to asking about exercise and whether a patient smokes cigarettes. It can be so much more than this. What about the patient's home life? Did they live pay cheque to pay cheque? Had they had any prior bad experiences in hospital? These were the things that interested me, and helped me understand the person in my care.

I also felt the other specialties I rotated through tended to focus only on the problem or bit of anatomy they were concerned with, at the expense of the whole person. Cardiologists were rightly focused on the heart, gastroenterologists on the gut and ortho-paedic surgeons on bones. Why the cardiologist's patient wasn't taking their cholesterol medication, why the gastroenterologist's patient drank to excess, or why the orthopaedic surgeon's patient refused to use a walking frame seemed less important to other specialists.

Any doctor can memorise anatomy and diagnostic tests, but it takes a special kind of doctor to combine this expertise with good communication, empathy and compassion. I generally found these doctors in psychiatry.

Psychiatrists begin their training learning the same medicine as every other doctor, but their specialty training allows for a much richer connection with patients. In addition to understanding, mapping and treating our most complex organ – the brain – psychiatrists are directly concerned about how a patient feels, what their home life is like, what bothers them and what makes them tick. I was also struck by how attentive psychiatrists were to the patient–doctor relationship. At their best, not only do they value the relationship, but they also place patients on the same level as themselves – referring to the relationship as an 'alliance'.

Psychiatrists don't separate patients from their environment. They know that someone's home, workplace and hospital room affect and reflect them. They also don't rush patients or expect that they will reveal everything about themselves straight away – they haven't forgotten that trust takes time. In psychiatry, patient interviews and ward rounds are long.

I was confused when I heard other specialties openly mocking this approach – how could they not see that more time with patients resulted in a strong patient–doctor relationship? I eventually had to stop telling other doctors I wanted to specialise in psychiatry, because the backlash was too intense. One senior doctor told me, 'Why did you bother studying all of this medicine then?' and another commented, 'What a waste.' A resident, when learning that I wanted to be a psychiatrist, was positive, but not because of any respect for the field or its patients – 'Good work–life balance,' was all he could muster.

Psychiatry services are among the busiest and most stretched in our public hospital system. Despite this constant, and growing, pressure, psychiatrists have held on to their holistic approach to illness. This isn't always possible, of course. During psychiatric emergencies and severe illness (think mania, suicidal behaviour or dangerous hallucinations), the traditional medical training of a psychiatrist dominates: getting to the root of symptoms and initiating treatment. That may mean rapid medication, sedation and keeping the patient safe. But as soon as a patient is able to sit down and talk, that same psychiatrist will be there too.

For these reasons, psychiatry struck me as the specialty that could best address my ideas about patient care, medical education, and the hospital ecosystem. Oncology would have been as rewarding in the long term – but I'd have to wait until I was a fully qualified consultant before I could be in charge of my own time. I worried about becoming cynical like David, the resident I'd met on the geriatrics ward, or disillusioned like Amy, the senior resident being slowly ground down by her specialty. I didn't want to lose any more of myself during training. Psychiatry and its focus on spending quality time with patients would be rewarding immediately, even as a junior. Psychiatry isn't perfect, but it was the best chance I had at being the doctor I wanted to be now *and* in the future.

As I prepared to tell my family my decision, I braced for the inevitable shrink jokes.

They didn't disappoint.

'Everything is always the mother's fault with you lot! You don't need more study to know that,' said Mum.

'Will you still talk to me when you're a fancy shrink?' said Nan.

'Excellent. Psychiatry needs more people like you,' said Ian.

'Awesome,' said Kim. 'Does this mean I get free therapy?'

•

As I was preparing to enter psychiatry – applying for jobs, mapping out the best time to sit exams, researching different hospitals – I was also preparing to become a father. Our third and final embryo, transferred near the end of my internship, had hung on – Sana was pregnant.

As the due date neared, Sana half-jokingly, half-seriously worried the baby would be too big for her slim five-foot frame.

'What if I can't push him out? My husband is two metres tall,' she told the doctors. An ultrasound was arranged to assuage her concerns.

Due to the Covid-19 pandemic, I wasn't allowed to attend any of the antenatal appointments. Sana was alone when she got the results. Our baby wasn't too big, he was far too small.

'It could just be that he's small, like you,' the doctor told her. 'But we'll do another ultrasound in two weeks to see if he's still growing.'

I wasn't supposed to be at the second ultrasound either, but I'd flashed my doctor badge at the hospital's entrance and they'd let me through. I only made it as far as the waiting room though because the doctor insisted on following policy and taking Sana in alone.

I didn't need to wait long before my phone rang.

'Hi . . . speaker . . . doctor says . . . baby,' Sana said.

Is the line bad or is Sana crying? I thought. My heart dropped.

'Hello . . . the scan . . . that the baby . . . gained any weight . . .' the doctor said.

'I'm sorry, I didn't catch that at all. Can you please repeat it?' I asked.

'Why . . . he come . . . only . . . outside.' Sana was definitely crying.

The call went dead and the doctor appeared. She gestured me over.

'Quick, come with me. It's stupid to use the phone when you're only ten metres away.'

Inside the room I sat next to Sana and held her right hand; her left hand held a ball of tissues.

The doctor told us that the baby was the same weight he'd been two weeks ago.

'What does that mean? Is he going to be okay?' Sana asked, panic rising in her voice.

'What we have now is something called intrauterine growth retardation,' the doctor explained. 'Because you're thirty-seven weeks we need to induce the baby soon. Like, tonight.'

Back out in the foyer, we game-planned. Sana needed to return home to pack for the hospital stay, and I, frustratingly, needed to return to work. I was now in the first year of my five-year psychiatry training program, and I'd only been given a few hours leave to attend the appointment.

'I'll try to be back by the time they start the induction,' I told Sana.

'Okay. Go do what you need to do.'

We parted in the hospital entryway, her Uber heading north to our flat, mine heading south to work.

With ward rounds to finish, patient discharge files to write, and my own leave request to process, I missed the induction. Sana had been alone, again – but I couldn't blame my absence on the pandemic this time.

Sana's contractions began early the next morning. In the birthing suite, I placed a tiny pair of baby shoes on the table next to her bed – a reminder of the prize that would follow all her pain.

Her birth plan was characteristically unsentimental, just one sentence long: 'Epidural please.'

Labour progressed slowly. Normally, this wouldn't be an issue, except our baby was underweight, and small babies don't cope well with long labours. A drug that is identical to the hormone oxytocin was administered, to help the uterus contract more regularly, and Sana got her epidural. Soon after, her blood pressure dropped dangerously low. The midwife hit the emergency button, beckoning a crush of doctors and midwives from across the ward.

With fluid through a drip, Sana's blood pressure improved, but now the doctors and midwives were worried about something else – the baby's heart. His heart rate kept dropping, setting off an alarm. It would bounce back, then fall away again. As labour dragged on, it stayed lower for longer. He wasn't coping. We were on another roller coaster, crashing through a terrifying loop-the-loop.

The senior obstetrician on shift, Dr Jain, had a perfect brown bob and wore an elegant pearl necklace with her scrubs. She held Sana's hand and spoke softly and clearly, avoiding medical mumbo jumbo. She was keen to continue with labour, rather than a Caesarean, as Sana's cervix was still dilating a little each hour. But she wanted to monitor the baby more closely. A special heart rate monitor was attached directly on his head and Dr Jain started sampling blood from his scalp every couple of hours – this would tell us whether he was getting enough oxygen. Before every procedure, Dr Jain and her junior doctors talked to Sana about what to expect. At each step they asked for permission to touch her, then explained what they were doing. 'Okay, so I am feeling the baby's head now . . .'

Our baby's heart rate continued to struggle, reflected in the blood tests that showed he was going longer without the full amount of oxygen his little body needed. A new alarm sounded. His heart was critically low. Again, the midwife hit the emergency button. Again, staff raced into the room.

'We're going to move to the operating theatre,' Dr Jain said. The plan was still for Sana to birth the baby, her cervix was now fully dilated. 'But we need a backup plan – which is why we are going to theatre. If it ends up that we have to get your baby out quickly, we'll need to do a Caesar.'

More doctors and nurses arrived – I counted fifteen all up – as Sana was rushed away.

Inside the operating room I sat eye level with Sana, holding her one free hand with both of mine. Midwives, an anaesthetist, the obstetrician and others crowded around us. A paediatrician hovered nearby, waiting to assess the baby as soon as he was out.

'Okay, we need you to push!' Dr Jain said, once a clamp around the baby's head was in place.

Sana's face contorted as she squeezed, her head lifting off the wet pillow. She'd been crying, not from pain – the epidural had taken care of that – but from fear and panic. Several rounds of pushing and pulling went by. Machines beeped from all corners of the room.

'Dr Jain, I don't have a signal,' said the midwife. She'd been monitoring the baby's heart rate, using a probe held against Sana's abdomen. She looked from her monitor to the probe, and back again. 'This baby needs to come out now.'

'Okay, Sana, this one is going to be it,' said Dr Jain. 'You've done so well, really amazing. This is going to be our last push, okay?'

Dr Jain's junior gripped the baby with a second device.

Sana groaned, her eyes shut tight. She pushed, the doctors pulled, I cried.

And then he came out. He was silent as they carried him to the paediatrician. I didn't look – my focus was Sana. The baby was in the best hands possible, and Sana needed to be in mine. I hugged her head while we waited.

And then he cried.

A final blood test indicated that he had indeed been dangerously stressed, but he was free now, pink, and had ten fingers and ten toes. In the end, medicine had saved his life just like it had saved mine nine years earlier.

We spent the next few days in a cocoon in hospital, as a series of lovely, kind, patient midwives showed us how to feed, bathe and hold our baby. Because of the pandemic we weren't allowed visitors – but this wasn't a huge blow for us – Sana's family were stuck in Canada, my mum was in Melbourne and Ian in Queensland. Kim was desperate to meet her nephew though, and so on the third day I carried him to the front of the hospital so Kim, wearing gloves and a mask, could cuddle him.

On the fourth day we named him Evren, a Turkish word meaning 'universe'.

And a day later, on the exact ten-year anniversary of our first date – where we'd rode our bikes carefree through Beijing, sipped rosé over lunch and partied all night at a rooftop bar – we brought our two-kilogram baby boy home, and fell in love all over again.

EPILOGUE

At the end of my first year of psychiatry training I took a year off to be a stay-at-home dad. As Sana and I had learnt, medicine was a hungry beast.

'Evren has a whole childhood ahead of him competing with my patients and work,' I said to Sana. 'The least I can do is give him my undivided attention now. Plus, it'll mean that I can look after you for once.'

I often ask myself whether I'd be happy doing what I'm doing if cancer came back. Getting sick gave me a new way of deciding how I wanted to live – it's why I was able to leave my old career and start medical school in my thirties. Later, it made the decision to take a year off and care for Evren an easy one.

Evren was six months old when I took over from Sana. Impressively (for him and Sana), he'd gained a whole kilogram each month since his birth.

'He's a good feeder,' I boast to strangers. 'I think he's going to be tall like me.'

He is our whole world – a world ten years in the making and one that almost didn't happen, twice.

One day, we'll start talking to him about my cancer. The genetic mutation that caused it was never identified, so I have no idea whether it's something I might have passed on to him. Every colonoscopy I've had since that very first one in Melbourne has been clear, and ten years after my diagnosis, my risk of developing more cancer was starting to feel theoretical.

That changed at my most recent colonoscopy.

Polyps (a bit of bowel jutting out from the wall) were found, and one of them was pre-cancerous. Not all polyps become bowel cancer, but all bowel cancers start off as polyps. My colon had sprouted two new polyps since the last colonoscopy a year prior, and one of them was on its way to becoming cancer.

'What?' I blurted at the doctor.

'To be on the safe side, you need to keep having regular colonoscopies,' she said.

Because my cancer was diagnosed at twenty-eight, the advice from doctors is that Evren starts having colonoscopies at eighteen years old. I've told Sana that for his eighteenth birthday I'm wrapping a box of laxatives in fancy paper and mocking up a gift voucher for a colonoscopy.

'Yes, I could have given you a car, buddy, but this is more important,' I imagine myself saying. 'You may end up thanking me, just like I thank your nanna.'

As I watch his little body learn to navigate the world and his little bowel learn to navigate food, I worry – I want him to access a health system that cares, one that sees him as more than a (potentially) faulty colon. I hope the doctors looking after him appreciate that he will likely be scared. At the very least I hope they introduce themselves before inserting a camera up his bum!

If my son one day becomes a patient, I want him to experience the health system the same way he entered it that day in the operating theatre – surrounded by smart as hell doctors practising with kindness and humanity. To make this experience, and all the positive ones I've had, universal, an overhaul of the health system is needed, but both doctors and patients must be seated at the table.

ENDNOTES

Chapter 5: What goes up must come down

'While bowel cancer is increasing . . .' Australian Institute of Health and
Welfare. (2021). *Cancer.* https://www.aihw.gov.au/reports-data/health-
conditions-disability-deaths/cancer/overview

Chapter 7: The pointy end

'Getting a hole in the large bowel . . .' Daams, F., Luyer, M. & Lange, J. F.
(2013). Colorectal anastomotic leakage: Aspects of prevention, detec-
tion and treatment. *World Journal of Gastroenterology*, *19*(15), 2293–7.
https://doi.org/10.3748/wjg.v19.i15.2293

Chapter 8: The blunt end

'Clots are a common side effect . . .' Donnellan, E. & Khorana, A. A. (2017).
Cancer and venous thromboembolic disease: A review. *The
Oncologist*, *22*(2), 199–207. https://doi.org/10.1634/
theoncologist.2016-0214

Chapter 12: Mature age student

'In 2020, 3664 new doctors . . .' Medical Deans Australia and New Zealand. (2021). *Student statistics report 2021: Snapshot of findings.* https://medicaldeans.org.au/md/2021/11/MDANZ-Student-Statistics-Report-2021.pdf

'The problem is so bad . . .' Scully, R. P. (2016, January 19). *Internship crisis escalating.* The Medical Republic. https://medicalrepublic.com.au/internship-crisis-escalating-with-40-grads-expected-to-miss-out/1558

Chapter 14: I was promised cancer

'In my degree, there were no units . . .' Australian Institute of Health and Welfare. (2021). *Cancer.* https://www.aihw.gov.au/reports-data/health-conditions-disability-deaths/cancer/overview

'In 2019, around 145,000 new cases of cancer . . .' I've used information for 2019 here because in 2020 disruptions from the Covid-19 pandemic caused a drop in new cancers being diagnosed. Australian Institute of Health and Welfare. (2021). *Cancer.* https://www.aihw.gov.au/reports-data/health-conditions-disability-deaths/cancer/overview

'I started digging around the research literature . . .' Barton, M. B., Miles, S. E., Tattersall, M. H., Butow, P. N., Crossing, S., Jamrozik, K. . . . Atkinson, C. H. (2003). Cancer knowledge and skills of interns in Australia and New Zealand in 2001: Comparison with 1990, and between course types. *Medical Journal of Australia, 178*(6), 285–9. https://doi.org/10.5694/j.1326-5377.2003.tb05198.x

'To find out if things had changed . . .' Bravery, B. D., Shi, K., Nicholls, L., Chelvarajah, R., Tieu, M. T., Turner, S. & Windsor, A. (2020). Oncology and radiation oncology awareness in final year medical students in Australia and New Zealand. *Journal of Cancer Education, 35*(6), 1227–36. https://doi.org/10.1007/s13187-019-01586-3

'Research shows the more contact students . . .' Cave, J., Woolf, K., Dacre, J., Potts, H. W. W. & Jones, A. (2007). Medical student teaching in the UK: How well are newly qualified doctors prepared for their role caring for patients with cancer in hospital? *British Journal of Cancer, 97*, 472–8. https://doi.org/10.1038/sj.bjc.6603888

'This kind of patient contact . . .' Granek, L., Lazarev, I., Birenstock-Cohen, S., Geffen, D. B., Riesenberg, K. & Ariad, S. (2015). Early exposure to a clinical oncology course during the preclinical second year of medical school. *Academic Medicine, 90*(4), 454–7. https://doi.org/10.1097/ACM.0000000000000521

Chapter 16: Round and round the wards

'In a 2002 Swiss study . . .' Langewitz, W., Denz, M., Keller, A., Kiss, A., Rüttimann, S. & Wössmer, B. (2002). Spontaneous talking time at start of consultation in outpatient clinic: Cohort study. *BMJ, 325*(7366), 682–3. https://doi.org/10.1136/bmj.325.7366.682

'On average, doctors interrupt patients . . .' Singh Ospina, N., Phillips, K. A., Rodriguez-Gutierrez, R., Castaneda-Guarderas, A., Gionfriddo, M. R., Branda, M. E. & Montori, V. M. (2019). Eliciting the patient's agenda-secondary analysis of recorded clinical encounters. *Journal of General Internal Medicine, 34*(1), 36–40. https://doi.org/10.1007/s11606-018-4540-5

'A 2005 study done at a hospital in New York City . . .' Makaryus, A. N. & Friedman, E. A. (2005). Patients' understanding of their treatment plans and diagnosis at discharge. *Mayo Clinic Proceedings, 80*(8), 991–4. https://doi.org/10.4065/80.8.991

'A study at an Australian hospital in 2014 . . .' Lin, R., Gallagher, R., Spinaze, M., Najoumian, H., Dennis, C., Clifton-Bligh, R. & Tofler, G. (2014). Effect of a patient-directed discharge letter on patient understanding of their hospitalisation. *Internal Medicine Journal, 44*(9), 851–7. https://doi.org/10.1111/imj.12482

'Another Australian study done in 2015 . . .' Chia, Y. Y. P. & Ekladious, A. (2021). Australian public hospital inpatient satisfaction related to early patient involvement and shared decision-making in discharge plan-ning. *Internal Medicine Journal, 51*(6), 891–5. https://doi.org/10.1111/imj.14872

'One study in 2009 by the University of Chicago . . .' Arora, V., Gangireddy, S., Mehrotra, A., Ginde, R., Tormey, M. & Meltzer, D. (2009). Research letters. *Archives of Internal Medicine, 169*(2), 199–205. https://doi.org/10.1001/archinternmed.2008.565

'Four hours later – less than ten per cent . . .' Chen, K. L., Chang, C. M., Chen, C. H. & Huang, M. C. (2018). Information reception and expectations among hospitalized elderly patients in Taiwan: A pilot study. *Journal of Nursing Research*, 26(3), 199–206. https://doi.org/10.1097/jnr.0000000000000228

Chapter 17: Bullies in the school yard

'Vascular surgeon Dr Gabrielle McMullin . . .' Matthews, A. (2015, March 7). *Sexual harassment rife in medical profession, senior surgeon Dr Gabrielle McMullin says*. ABC News. https://www.abc.net.au/news/2015-03-07/sexual-harassment-rife-in-medical-profession-surgeon-says/6287994

'The picture is similar for medical students . . .' Beyond Blue. (2013). *National mental health survey of doctors and medical students*. https://litfl.com/wp-content/uploads/2019/06/bl1132-report-nmhdmss-full-report_web.pdf

'A survey of nearly ten thousand junior doctors in 2020 . . .' Willis, O. (2020, February 10). *Culture of bullying, harassment and discrimination in medicine still widespread, survey suggests*. ABC News. https://www.abc.net.au/news/health/2020-02-10/bullying-harassment-medicine-doctors/11949748

'Research has shown that behaviour . . .' Rosenstein, A. H. & O'Daniel, M. (2008). A survey of the impact of disruptive behaviors and communication defects on patient safety. *Joint Commission Journal on Quality and Patient Safety*, 34(8), 464–71. https://doi.org/10.1016/S1553-7250(08)34058-6; Grissinger M. (2017). Disrespectful behavior in health care: Its impact, why it arises and persists, and how to address it – part 2. *P & T*, 42(2), 74–7. https://www.ncbi.nlm.nih.gov/pmc/articles/PMC5265230/

'One study I read explained how some patients . . .' Berry, L. L., Danaher, T. S., Beckham, D., Awdish, R. L. A. & Mate, K. S. (2017). When patients and their families feel like hostages to health care. *Mayo Clinic Proceedings*, 92(9), 1373–81. https://doi.org/10.1016/j.mayocp.2017.05.015

Chapter 18: Being sick

'One study started in the 1960s . . .' Kalsi, T. (2021). *Whitehall II.* Institute of
    Epidemiology & Health Care, UCL. https://www.ucl.ac.uk/
    epidemiology-health-care/research/epidemiology-and-public-health/
    research/whitehall-ii

'In Australia your postcode also determines your health . . .' Dunlevy, S.
    (2014, August 20). *Good health comes down to your postcode, your
    education and your income.* News.com.au. https://www.news.com.au/
    lifestyle/health/health-problems/good-health-comes-down-to-your-
    postcode-your-education-and-your-income/news-story/cdb172de7335d
    401c668c475fc0c1e49

'Most famously, Dr Oliver Sacks . . .' Burrell, L. (2010, November). Oliver
    Sacks on empathy as a path to insight. *Harvard Business Review.*
    https://hbr.org/2010/11/lifes-work-oliver-sacks

'In *When Breath Becomes Air* . . .' Kalanithi, P. (2016). *When breath becomes
    air.* Random House, New York.

'Melbourne-based neurosurgeon Dr Michael Wong . . .' Wong, M. (2017,
    August 23). *I was stabbed 14 times at the hospital where I work.
    I survived, but not everyone is so lucky.* The Conversation. https://
    theconversation.com/i-was-stabbed-14-times-at-the-hospital-where-i-
    work-i-survived-but-not-everyone-is-so-lucky-82824

Chapter 19: The end of the beginning

'Empathy and compassion decline during doctor training . . .' Neumann, M.,
    Edelhäuser, F., Tauschel, D., Fischer, M. R., Wirtz, M., Woopen, C. . . .
    Scheffer, C. (2011). Empathy decline and its reasons: A systematic
    review of studies with medical students and residents. *Academic
    Medicine, 86*(8), 996–1009. https://doi.org/10.1097/
    ACM.0b013e318221e615

'In any given year, grievances about communication . . .' Health Care
    Complaints Commission annual reports for 2013–14 to 2020–21,
    available at https://www.hccc.nsw.gov.au/Publications/Annual-Reports

Chapter 23: Putting patients first

'The Australian Commission on Safety and Quality in Health Care . . .'
Person-centred care. (2022). Australian Commission on Safety and
Quality in Health Care. https://www.safetyandquality.gov.au/our-work/
partnering-consumers/person-centred-care

Chapter 24: Baby steps are not easy steps

'Once name badges had been rolled out . . .' Lill, L., Wilkinson, T. (2005).
Judging a book by its cover: descriptive survey of patients' preferences
for doctors' appearance. *BMJ, 331,* 1524–7. https://doi.org/10.1136/
bmj.331.7531.1524

Chapter 25: Night-time confessions

'I learnt that many doctors . . .' Otri, D. (2017). *What patients say, what
doctors hear.* Beacon Press, Boston.

ACKNOWLEDGEMENTS

Fiona Hazard and Vanessa Radnidge at Hachette kicked off this whole book thing – thanks for sliding into my DMs. And thank you to my agent Catherine Drayton for helping make the book happen.

Huge editorial thanks are owed to Fiona Hazard and Rebecca Allen at Hachette, and freelance editors Meaghan Amor and Deonie Fiford. You've all made me a better writer – thank you.

I'm full of love for my beta readers: Kimberly Luffman, Keren Port, Rae-ann Sinclair and Sarah Brazel. I was not prepared for your commitment and generosity. Your feedback and responses to the manuscript improved it immeasurably. Any success is yours too.

Thanks are owed to Mum and her hypochondriasis, without which I probably wouldn't have had a colonoscopy. Your decision to organise one for me, and also to not give me away twenty-eight years earlier, means I'm here in this place at this time. I wouldn't have it any other way.

Thank you to my sister, Kim, dad, Ian, and friends who helped me throughout cancer and medical school. I should also use this opportunity to apologise for ignoring you so much once I got to medical school, and then again once I was working as a doctor. I should probably apologise in advance too – there are still many years of training left.

I will always be indebted to my treatment team. I am especially grateful to my surgeon for being awesome – despite his crazy schedule, he fact-checked some of my recollections of treatment. I admire him so much, he's the best of the best.

To the passionate and compassionate teachers, classmates and colleagues (both junior and senior) – you were hope. Special thanks to my primary tutors in first- and second-year medicine – you are exceptional educators and people.

Thanks to Claudine Ryan and Sophie Scott at the ABC for giving me an opportunity to begin to publish articles as a med student, and to Clarissa Sebag-Montefiore for editorial help with those.

My story is Sana's story too. She has been with me the whole time, and I'm better off because of her. Illness bonded us initially, but hope came in and sealed the deal. Sana had significant editorial input on my book proposal and manuscript. Her feedback was excellent – partly because she's a skilled journalist and partly because she lived it all with me. Hugs and kisses, forever.

Originally a zoologist and science communicator, Ben Bravery worked for the Australian and Chinese governments before being diagnosed with stage 3 colorectal cancer at age twenty-eight. After undergoing eighteen months of cancer treatment, Ben decided on a career change. He became a doctor in 2018 and is now undertaking speciality training in psychiatry. Ben volunteers, advocates, writes and speaks about colorectal cancer, living with cancer, cancer in young adults, medicine and medical education, and is committed to advocating for change in Australia's healthcare system.

Ben lives in Sydney with his wife and son.

If you would like to find out more about Hachette Australia, our authors, upcoming events and new releases, you can visit our website or our social media channels:

hachette.com.au

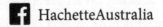 HachetteAustralia

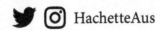 HachetteAus